AWS Administration Cookbook

Harness the full capability of AWS

Lucas Chan
Rowan Udell

BIRMINGHAM - MUMBAI

AWS Administration Cookbook

Copyright © 2017 Packt Publishing

All rights reserved. No part of this book may be reproduced, stored in a retrieval system, or transmitted in any form or by any means, without the prior written permission of the publisher, except in the case of brief quotations embedded in critical articles or reviews.

Every effort has been made in the preparation of this book to ensure the accuracy of the information presented. However, the information contained in this book is sold without warranty, either express or implied. Neither the authors, nor Packt Publishing, and its dealers and distributors will be held liable for any damages caused or alleged to be caused directly or indirectly by this book.

Packt Publishing has endeavored to provide trademark information about all of the companies and products mentioned in this book by the appropriate use of capitals. However, Packt Publishing cannot guarantee the accuracy of this information.

First published: April 2017

Production reference: 1140417

Published by Packt Publishing Ltd.
Livery Place
35 Livery Street
Birmingham
B3 2PB, UK.

ISBN 978-1-78712-763-0

www.packtpub.com

Credits

Authors

Lucas Chan
Rowan Udell

Reviewer

Michael Kelly

Commissioning Editor

Kartikey Pandey

Acquisition Editor

Meeta Rajani

Content Development Editor

Sweeny Dias

Technical Editor

Khushbu Sutar

Copy Editors

Safis Editing
Madhusudan Uchil

Project Coordinator

Virginia Dias

Proofreader

Safis Editing

Indexer

Tejal Daruwale Soni

Graphics

Kirk D'Penha

Production Coordinator

Nilesh Mohite

About the Authors

Lucas Chan has been working in tech since 1995 in a variety of development, systems admin, and DevOps roles. He is currently a senior consultant and engineer at Versent and technical director at Stax. He's been running production workloads on AWS for over 10 years. He's also a member of the APAC AWS warriors program and holds all five of the available AWS certifications.

I'd like to thank Rowan Udell and everyone at Packt Publishing for giving me the opportunity to write my first book! Dr. Michael Kelly, for graciously offering his spare time to review and critique our work. My mum, dad and sister, for putting up with my absence and occasional crankiness for the past few months. Hannah, for simply being an all-around amazing human. Damian Wilson, who gave me my first tech job way back in 1995: I wouldn't be where I am today without the opportunities he gave me. Thor Essman and James Coxon, who created the amazing company that we both work for and whose support knows no bounds. Trang, for keeping me sane and occasionally dragging me to the beach when I needed a break from writing. Lastly, a shout out to those who suffer from vestibular migraines—may you walk with a steady foot, see the world with clarity and hear with grace and harmony.

Rowan Udell has been working in development and operations for 15 years. He has held a variety of positions, such as SRE, frontend developer, backend developer, consultant, technical lead, and team leader. His travels have seen him work in start-ups and enterprises in the finance, education, and web industries in Australia and Canada. He currently works as a senior consultant with Versent, an AWS Advanced Partner in Sydney. He specializes in serverless applications and architectures on AWS, and contributes actively in the Serverless Framework community. He regularly blogs at `http://blog.rowanudell.com`.

Firstly I'd like to thank my partner, Marie-Pier, for making this book possible for me—having two small children does not make writing a book easy! Thanks to my family for all their encouragement over the years. To all my colleagues and peers at Versent, thank you for setting the bar so high and making a great company to work for. Much thanks to our colleague Dr. Michael Kelly for reviewing the book, and the team at Packt for their support. Finally, thanks to Lucas for the great work, and picking up my slack.

About the Reviewer

Michael Kelly is a DevOps engineer and consultant in the financial services industry at Versent in Sydney. In his past, Michael worked as a developer and DevOps engineer at start-ups, developing Infrastructure as Code solutions. Michael is AWS certified and holds a PhD in computer science. In his downtime, Michael also blogs about cloud solutions at `https://blog.ashiny.cloud`.

I'd like to thank Rowan and Lucas for letting me be a part of this. It has really come together to be an excellent book—congratulations. To Anna and my family, thank you for always being there whenever I have needed you. To everyone at Versent, I am very proud to be in the company of such skilled craftsmen and women who put quality into everything they do. Thank you.

www.PacktPub.com

For support files and downloads related to your book, please visit www.PacktPub.com.

Did you know that Packt offers eBook versions of every book published, with PDF and ePub files available? You can upgrade to the eBook version at www.PacktPub.com and as a print book customer, you are entitled to a discount on the eBook copy. Get in touch with us at service@packtpub.com for more details.

At www.PacktPub.com, you can also read a collection of free technical articles, sign up for a range of free newsletters and receive exclusive discounts and offers on Packt books and eBooks.

https://www.packtpub.com/mapt

Get the most in-demand software skills with Mapt. Mapt gives you full access to all Packt books and video courses, as well as industry-leading tools to help you plan your personal development and advance your career.

Why subscribe?

- Fully searchable across every book published by Packt
- Copy and paste, print, and bookmark content
- On demand and accessible via a web browser

Customer Feedback

Thanks for purchasing this Packt book. At Packt, quality is at the heart of our editorial process. To help us improve, please leave us an honest review on this book's Amazon page at https://www.amazon.com/dp/178712763X.

If you'd like to join our team of regular reviewers, you can e-mail us at customerreviews@packtpub.com. We award our regular reviewers with free eBooks and videos in exchange for their valuable feedback. Help us be relentless in improving our products!

Table of Contents

Preface

The AWS platform is growing at a rapid rate, and it's being increasingly adopted across all industries and sectors. As the saying goes, friends don't let friends build data centers. No matter how you look at it, the model of pay-as-you-go compute, network, and storage is here to stay. It's also becoming increasingly hard to argue against *standing on the shoulders of giants*, especially when you look the rate with which features and enhancements are added to the AWS platform compared to what you'd typically get out of other cloud providers or a so-called *private* cloud.

We work with a lot of technical professionals who are highly knowledgeable in their domain, but often completely new to the AWS platform. Alternatively, they might be familiar with AWS but new to automation and infrastructure code practices.

We wanted to write a book for these people.

This book is intended to kick-start your AWS journey by providing recipes, patterns, and best practices across the areas we are often asked to help with on our consulting engagements. All the recipes and recommendations contained in this book are based on our personal experiences and observations from our time helping customers on the AWS platform.

CloudFormation is the AWS-native method for automating the (repeatable and reliable) deployment of AWS resources, and we use it extensively throughout this book. The recipes that follow will help you get well acquainted with CloudFormation, and you'll soon be on your way to customizing and building your own templates. With so much power at your fingertips, there's a lot of potential for finding yourself in a rabbit hole. This book aims to steer you in the right direction and help you adopt the platform in a sustainable and maintainable way.

What this book covers

Chapter 1, *AWS Fundamentals*, is an overview of Infrastructure as Code, CloudFormation, and the AWS CLI tools.

Chapter 2, *Managing AWS Accounts*, covers everything you need to know to manage your accounts and get started with AWS organizations.

Chapter 3, *Storage and Content Delivery*, shows you how to back up your data and serve file objects to your users.

Chapter 4, *Using AWS Compute*, dives deep into how to run VMs (EC2 instances) on AWS, how to auto scale them, and how to create and manage load balancers.

Chapter 5, *Management Tools*, provides an overview of how to audit your account and monitor your infrastructure.

Chapter 6, *Database Services*, shows you how to create, manage, and scale databases on the AWS platform.

Chapter 7, *Networking*, introduces private networks, routing, and DNS.

Chapter 8, *Security and Identity*, offers advice and practical solutions for managing identities and role-based access.

Chapter 9, *Estimating Costs*, provides an overview of how to estimate your spend on the AWS platform as well as how to reduce your costs by purchasing reserved instance capacity.

What you need for this book

The recipes in this book show you how to deploy a wide variety of resources on AWS, so you'll need at least one AWS account with full administrative access. You'll also need a text editor to edit YAML/JSON CloudFormation templates, and the AWS CLI tools, which are supported on common operating systems (macOS/Linux/Windows).

Who this book is for

This book is for anyone with a technical background who is interested in using AWS, either for moving existing workloads or deploying completely new applications. Those who want to learn CloudFormation will also find this book useful.

Sections

In this book, you will find several headings that appear frequently (*Getting ready*, *How to do it...*, *How it works...*, *There's more...*, and *See also*).

To give clear instructions on how to complete a recipe, we use these sections as follows:

Getting ready

This section tells you what to expect in the recipe, and describes how to set up any software or any preliminary settings required for the recipe.

How to do it...

This section contains the steps required to follow the recipe.

How it works...

This section usually consists of a detailed explanation of what happened in the previous section.

There's more...

This section consists of additional information about the recipe in order to make the reader more knowledgeable about the recipe.

See also

This section provides helpful links to other useful information for the recipe.

Conventions

In this book, you will find a number of text styles that distinguish between different kinds of information. Here are some examples of these styles and an explanation of their meaning.

Code words in text, database table names, folder names, filenames, file extensions, pathnames, dummy URLs, user input, and Twitter handles are shown as follows: "You should now have an active session under `PowerUserRole` in the application account."

A block of code is set as follows:

```
Parameters:
  EC2KeyName:
    Type: String
    Description: EC2 Key Pair to launch with
```

When we wish to draw your attention to a particular part of a code block, the relevant lines or items are set in bold:

```
Parameters:
  EC2KeyName:
    Type: String
    Description: EC2 Key Pair to launch with
```

Any command-line input or output is written as follows:

```
aws ec2 describe-availability-zones --output json
```

New terms and **important words** are shown in bold. Words that you see on the screen, for example, in menus or dialog boxes, appear in the text like this: "Clicking the **Next** button moves you to the next screen."

Warnings or important notes appear in a box like this.

Tips and tricks appear like this.

Reader feedback

Feedback from our readers is always welcome. Let us know what you think about this book—what you liked or disliked. Reader feedback is important for us as it helps us develop titles that you will really get the most out of.

To send us general feedback, simply e-mail `feedback@packtpub.com`, and mention the book's title in the subject of your message.

If there is a topic that you have expertise in and you are interested in either writing or contributing to a book, see our author guide at `www.packtpub.com/authors`.

Customer support

Now that you are the proud owner of a Packt book, we have a number of things to help you to get the most from your purchase.

Downloading the example code

You can download the example code files for this book from your account at `http://www.packtpub.com`. If you purchased this book elsewhere, you can visit `http://www.packtpub.com/support` and register to have the files e-mailed directly to you.

You can download the code files by following these steps:

1. Log in or register to our website using your e-mail address and password.
2. Hover the mouse pointer on the **SUPPORT** tab at the top.
3. Click on **Code Downloads & Errata**.
4. Enter the name of the book in the **Search** box.
5. Select the book for which you're looking to download the code files.
6. Choose from the drop-down menu where you purchased this book from.
7. Click on **Code Download**.

You can also download the code files by clicking on the **Code Files** button on the book's webpage at the Packt Publishing website. This page can be accessed by entering the book's name in the **Search** box. Please note that you need to be logged in to your Packt account. Once the file is downloaded, please make sure that you unzip or extract the folder using the latest version of:

- WinRAR / 7-Zip for Windows
- Zipeg / iZip / UnRarX for Mac
- 7-Zip / PeaZip for Linux

The code bundle for the book is also hosted on GitHub at `https://github.com/PacktPublishing/AWS-Administration-Cookbook`. We also have other code bundles from our rich catalog of books and videos available at `https://github.com/PacktPublishing/`. Check them out!

Errata

Although we have taken every care to ensure the accuracy of our content, mistakes do happen. If you find a mistake in one of our books—maybe a mistake in the text or the code—we would be grateful if you could report this to us. By doing so, you can save other readers from frustration and help us improve subsequent versions of this book. If you find any errata, please report them by visiting http://www.packtpub.com/submit-errata, selecting your book, clicking on the **Errata Submission Form** link, and entering the details of your errata. Once your errata are verified, your submission will be accepted and the errata will be uploaded to our website or added to any list of existing errata under the **Errata** section of that title.

To view the previously submitted errata, go to https://www.packtpub.com/books/content/support and enter the name of the book in the search field. The required information will appear under the Errata section.

Piracy

Piracy of copyrighted material on the Internet is an ongoing problem across all media. At Packt, we take the protection of our copyright and licenses very seriously. If you come across any illegal copies of our works in any form on the Internet, please provide us with the location address or website name immediately so that we can pursue a remedy.

Please contact us at copyright@packtpub.com with a link to the suspected pirated material.

We appreciate your help in protecting our authors and our ability to bring you valuable content.

Questions

If you have a problem with any aspect of this book, you can contact us at questions@packtpub.com, and we will do our best to address the problem.

1

AWS Fundamentals

In this chapter, we will cover:

- Infrastructure as Code
- AWS CloudFormation
- The AWS command-line tool

Introduction

Amazon Web Services (AWS) is a public cloud provider. It provides infrastructure and platform services at a pay-per-use rate. This means you get on-demand access to resources that you used to have to buy outright. You can get access to enterprise-grade services while only paying for what you need, usually down to the hour.

AWS prides itself on providing the primitives to developers so that they can build and scale the solutions that they require.

Creating an account

In order to follow along with the recipes, you will need an AWS account. Create an account at https://aws.amazon.com/ by clicking on the **Sign Up** button and entering your details.

 Even though we will be taking advantage of the *free tier* wherever possible, you will need a valid credit card to complete the signup process. Go to https://aws.amazon.com/free/ for more information. Note that the free tier only applies for the first year of your account's lifetime.

Regions and Availability Zones

A fundamental concept of AWS is that its services and the solutions built on top of them are *architected for failure*. This means that a failure of the underlying resources is a scenario actively planned for, rather than avoided until it cannot be ignored.

Due to this, all the services and resources available are divided up in to geographically diverse **Regions**. Using specific regions means you can provide services to your users that are optimized for speed and performance.

Within a region, there are always multiple **Availability Zones** (a.k.a. **AZ**). Each AZ represents a geographically distinct—but still close—physical data center. AZs have their own facilities and power source, so an event that might take a single AZ offline is unlikely to affect the other AZs in the region.

The smaller regions have at least two AZs, and the largest has five.

At the time of writing, the following regions are active:

Code	Name	Availability Zones
us-east-1	N. Virginia	5
us-east-2	Ohio	3
us-west-1	N. California	3
us-west-2	Oregon	3
ca-central-1	Canada	2
eu-west-1	Ireland	3
eu-west-2	London	2
eu-central-1	Frankfurt	2
ap-northeast-1	Tokyo	3
ap-northeast-2	Seoul	2
ap-southeast-1	Singapore	2
ap-southeast-2	Sydney	3
ap-south-1	Mumbai	2
sa-east-1	Sao Paulo	3

The AWS web console

The web-based console is the first thing you will see after creating your AWS account, and you will often refer to it when viewing and confirming your configuration.

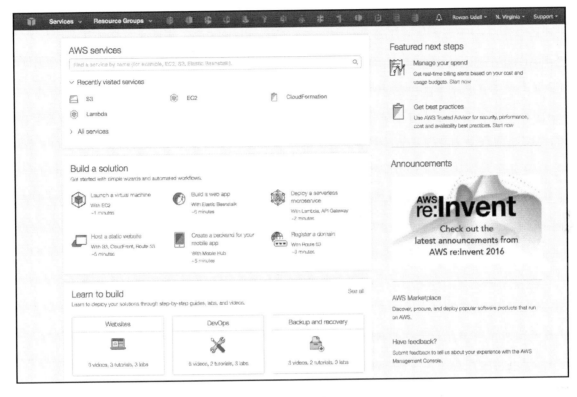

The AWS web console

The console provides an overview of all the services available as well as associated billing and cost information. Each service has its own section, and the information displayed depends on the service being viewed. As new features and services are released, the console will change and improve. Don't be surprised if you log in and things have changed from one day to the next.

Keep in mind that the console always shows your resources *by region*. If you cannot see a resource that you created, make sure you have the right region selected.

Choose the region closest to your physical location for the fastest response times. Note that not all regions have the same services available. The larger, older regions generally have the most services available. Some of the newer or smaller regions (that might be closest to you) might not have all services enabled yet. While services are continually being released to regions, you may have to use another region if you simply must use a newer service.

The `us-east-1` (a.k.a. North Virginia) region is special given its status as the first region. All services are available there, and new services are *always* released there.

As you get more advanced with your use of AWS, you will spend less time in the console and more time controlling your services programmatically via the AWS CLI tool and CloudFormation, which we will go into in more detail in the next few topics.

CloudFormation templates

Where possible, we have based the recipes around a CloudFormation template. CloudFormation is the *Infrastructure as Code* service from AWS.

Where CloudFormation was not applicable, we have used the AWS CLI to make the process repeatable and automatable.

Since the recipes are based on CloudFormation templates, you can easily combine different templates to achieve your desired outcomes. By editing the templates or joining them, you can create more useful and customized configurations with minimal effort.

Infrastructure as Code

Infrastructure as Code (IaC) is the practice of managing infrastructure though code definitions.

On an **Infrastructure-as-a-Service (IaaS)** platform such as AWS, IaC is needed to get the most utility and value. IaC differs primarily from traditional *interactive* methods of managing infrastructure because it is machine processable. This enables a number of benefits:

- Improved visibility of resources

- Higher levels of consistency between deployments and environments
- Easier troubleshooting of issues
- The ability to scale more with less effort
- Better control over costs

On a less tangible level, all of these factors contribute to other improvements for your developers: you can now leverage tried-and-tested software development practices for your infrastructure and enable DevOps practices in your teams.

Visibility

As your infrastructure is represented in machine-readable files, you can treat it like you do your application code. You can take the best-practice approaches to software development and apply them to your infrastructure. This means you can store it in version control (for example, Git and SVN) just like you do your code, along with the benefits that it brings:

- All changes to infrastructure are recorded in commit history
- You can review changes before accepting/merging them
- You can easily compare different configurations
- You can pick and use specific point-in-time configurations

Consistency

Consistent configuration across your environments (for example, dev, test, and prod) means that you can more confidently deploy your infrastructure. When you know what configuration is in use, you can easily test changes in other environments due to a common baseline.

IaC is not the same as *just writing scripts* for your infrastructure. Most tools and services will leverage higher-order languages and DSLs to allow you to focus on your higher-level requirements. It enables you to use advanced software development techniques, such as static analysis, automated testing, and optimization.

Troubleshooting

IaC makes replicating and troubleshooting issues easier: since you can duplicate your environments, you can accurately reproduce your production environment for testing purposes.

In the past, test environments rarely had exactly the same infrastructure due to the prohibitive cost of hardware. Now that it can be created and destroyed on demand, you are able to duplicate your environments only when they are needed. You only need to pay for the time that they are running for, usually down to the hour. Once you have finished testing, simply turn your environments off and stop paying for them.

Even better than troubleshooting is fixing issues before they cause errors. As you refine your IaC in multiple environments, you will gain confidence that is difficult to obtain without it. By the time you deploy your infrastructure in to production, you have done it multiple times already.

Scale

Configuring infrastructure by hand can be a tedious and error-prone process. By automating it, you remove the potential variability of a manual implementation: computers are good at boring, repetitive tasks, so use them for it!

Once automated, the labor cost of provisioning more resources is effectively zero—you have already done the work. Whether you need to spin up one server or a thousand, it requires no additional work.

From a practical perspective, resources in AWS are effectively unconstrained. If you are willing to pay for it, AWS will let you use it.

Costs

AWS have a vested (commercial) interest in making it as easy as possible for you to provision infrastructure. The benefit to you as the customer is that you can create *and destroy* these resources on demand.

Obviously, destroying infrastructure on-demand in a traditional, physical hardware environment is simply not possible. You would be hard-pressed to find a data center that will allow you to stop paying for servers and space simply because you are not currently using them.

Another use case where on-demand infrastructure can make large cost savings is your development environment. It only makes sense to have a development environment while you have developers to use it. When your developers go home at the end of the day, you can switch off your development environments so that you no longer pay for them. Before your developers come in in the morning, simply schedule their environments to be created.

DevOps

DevOps and IaC go hand in hand. The practice of storing your infrastructure (traditionally the concern of Operations) as code (traditionally the concern of Development) encourages a sharing of responsibilities that facilitates collaboration.

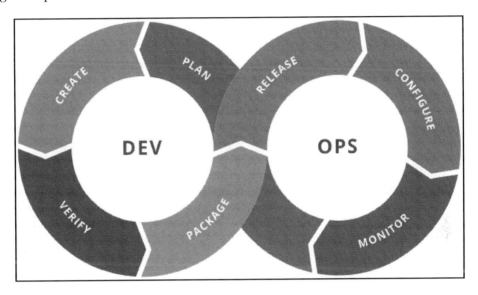

Image courtesy: Wikipedia

By automating the **PACKAGE, RELEASE,** and **CONFIGURE** activities in the software development life cycle (as pictured), you increase the speed of your releases while also increasing confidence.

Cloud-based IaC encourages *architecture for failure*: as your resources are virtualized, you must plan for the chance of physical (host) hardware failure, however unlikely.

Being able to recreate your entire environment in minutes is the ultimate recovery solution.

Unlike physical hardware, you can easily simulate and test failure in your software architecture by deleting key components—they are all virtual anyway!

Server configuration

Server-side examples of IaC are configuration-management tools such as Ansible, Chef, and Puppet.

While important, these configuration-management tools are not specific to AWS, so we will not be covering them in detail here. There are a myriad of books and courses devoted to this topic if you need to know more.

IaC on AWS

CloudFormation is the IaC service from AWS.

Templates written in a specific format and language define the AWS resources that should be provisioned. CloudFormation is declarative and cannot only provision resources, but also update them.

We will go into CloudFormation in greater detail in the next topic.

CloudFormation

We'll use CloudFormation extensively throughout this book, so it's important that you have an understanding of what it is and how it fits in to the AWS ecosystem. There should easily be enough information here to get you started, but where necessary, we'll refer you to AWS' own documentation.

What is CloudFormation?

The **CloudFormation** service allows you to provision and manage a collection of AWS resources in an automated and repeatable fashion. In AWS terminology, these collections are referred to as **stacks**. Note however that a stack can be as large or as small as you like. It might consist of a single S3 bucket, or it might contain everything needed to host your three-tier web app.

In this chapter, we'll show you how to define the resources to be included in your CloudFormation stack. We'll talk a bit more about the composition of these stacks and why and when it's preferable to divvy up resources between a number of stacks. Finally, we'll share a few of the tips and tricks we've learned over years of building countless CloudFormation stacks.

Be warned!
Pretty much everyone incurs at least one or two flesh wounds along their journey with CloudFormation. It is all very much worth it, though.

Why is CloudFormation important?

By now, the benefits of automation should be starting to become apparent to you. But don't fall in to the trap of thinking CloudFormation will be useful only for large collections of resources. Even performing the simplest task of, say, creating an S3 bucket can get very repetitive if you need to do it in every region.

We work with a lot of customers who have very tight controls and governance around their infrastructure, and especially in the network layer (think VPCs, NACLs, and security groups). Being able to express one's cloud footprint in YAML (or JSON), store it in a source code repository, and funnel it through a high-visibility pipeline gives these customers confidence that their infrastructure changes are peer-reviewed and will work as expected in production. Discipline and commitment to IaC SDLC practices are of course a big factor in this, but CloudFormation helps bring us out of the era of following 20-page run-sheets for manual changes, navigating untracked or unexplained configuration drift, and unexpected downtime caused by fat fingers.

The layer cake

Now is a good time to start thinking about your AWS deployments in terms of layers. Your layers will sit atop one another, and you will have well-defined relationships between them.

Here's a bottom-up example of how your layer cake might look:

- VPC with CloudTrail
- Subnets, routes, and NACLs
- NAT gateways, VPN or bastion hosts, and associated security groups
- App stack 1: security groups, S3 buckets
- App stack 1: cross-zone RDS and read replica
- App stack 1: app and web server auto scaling groups and ELBs
- App stack 1: CloudFront and WAF config

In this example, you may have many occurrences of the app stack layers inside your VPC, assuming you have enough IP addresses in your subnets! This is often the case with VPCs living inside development environments. So immediately, you have the benefit of multi-tenancy capability with application isolation.

One advantage of this approach is that while you are developing your CloudFormation template, if you mess up the configuration of your app server, you don't have to wind back all the work CFN did on your behalf. You can just turf that particular layer (and the layers that depend on it) and restart from there. This is not the case if you have everything contained in a single template.

We commonly work with customers for whom ownership and management of each layer in the cake reflects the structure of the technology divisions within a company. The traditional infrastructure, network, and cyber security folk are often really interested in creating a safe place for digital teams to deploy their apps, so they like to heavily govern the foundational layers of the cake. **Conway's Law**, coined by Melvin Conway, starts to come in to play here:

> *"Any organization that designs a system will inevitably produce a design whose structure is a copy of the organization's communication structure."*

Finally, even if you are a single-person infrastructure coder working in a small team, you will benefit from this approach. For example, you'll find that it dramatically reduces your exposure to things such as AWS limits, timeouts, and circular dependencies.

CloudFormation templates

This is where we start to get our hands dirty. CloudFormation template files are the codified representation of your stack, expressed in either YAML or JSON. When you wish to create a CloudFormation stack, you push this template file to CloudFormation, through its API, web console, command line tools, or some other method (such as the SDK).

Templates can be replayed over and over again by CloudFormation, creating many instances of your stack.

YAML versus JSON

Up until recently, JSON was your only option. We'll actually encourage you to adopt YAML, and we'll be using it for all of the examples shown in this book. Some of the reasons are as follows:

- It's just nicer to look at. It's less syntax heavy, and should you choose to go down the path of generating your CloudFormation templates, pretty much every language has a YAML library of some kind.
- The size of your templates will be much smaller. This is more practical from a developer's point of view, but it also means you're less likely to run into the CloudFormation size limit on template files (50 KB).
- The string-substitution features are easier to use and interpret.
- Your EC2 `UserData` (the script that runs when your EC2 instance boots) will be much easier to implement and maintain.

A closer look at CloudFormation templates

CloudFormation templates consist of a number of parts, but these are the four we're going to concentrate on:

- Parameters
- Resources
- Outputs
- Mappings

Here's a short YAML example:

```
AWSTemplateFormatVersion: '2010-09-09'
Parameters:
  EC2KeyName:
    Type: String
    Description: EC2 Key Pair to launch with
Mappings:
  RegionMap:
    us-east-1:
      AMIID: ami-9be6f38c
    ap-southeast-2:
      AMIID: ami-28cff44b
Resources:
  ExampleEC2Instance:
    Type: AWS::EC2::Instance
    Properties:
```

```
        InstanceType: t2.nano
        UserData:
          Fn::Base64:
            Fn::Sub': |
              #!/bin/bash -ex
              /opt/aws/bin/cfn-signal '${ExampleWaitHandle}'
        ImageId:
          Fn::FindInMap: [ RegionMap, Ref: 'AWS::Region', AMIID ]
        KeyName:
          Ref: EC2KeyName
    ExampleWaitHandle:
      Type: AWS::CloudFormation::WaitConditionHandle
      Properties:
    ExampleWaitCondition:
      Type: AWS::CloudFormation::WaitCondition
      DependsOn: ExampleEC2Instance
      Properties:
        Handle:
          Ref: ExampleWaitHandle
        Timeout: 600
Outputs:
  ExampleOutput:
    Value:
      Fn::GetAtt: ExampleWaitCondition.Data
      Description: The data signaled with the WaitCondition
```

Parameters

CloudFormation parameters are the input values you define when creating or updating your stack, similar to how you provide parameters to any command-line tools you might use. They allow you to customize your stack without making changes to your template. Common examples of what parameters might be used for are as follows:

- **EC2 AMI ID**: You may wish to redeploy your stack with a new AMI that has the latest security patches installed.
- **Subnet IDs**: You could have a list of subnets that an auto scaling group should deploy servers in. These subnet IDs will be different between your dev, test, and production environments.
- **Endpoint targets and credentials**: These include things such as API hostnames, usernames, and passwords.

You'll find that there are a number of parameter types. In brief, they are:

- String
- Number
- List
- CommaDelimitedList

In addition to these, AWS provides some AWS-specific parameter types. These can be particularly handy when you are executing your template via the CloudFormation web console. For example, a parameter type of `AWS::EC2::AvailabilityZone::Name` will cause the web console to display a drop-down list of valid Availability Zones for this parameter. In the `ap-southeast-2` region, the list would look like this:

- `ap-southeast-2a`
- `ap-southeast-2b`
- `ap-southeast-2c`

The list of AWS-specific parameter types is steadily growing and is large enough that we can't list them here. We'll use many of them throughout this book, however, and they can easily be found in the AWS CloudFormation documentation.

When creating or updating a stack, you will need to provide values for all the parameters you've defined in your template. Where it makes sense, you can define default values for a parameter. For example, you might have a parameter called `debug` that tells your application to run in debug mode. You typically don't want this mode enabled by default, so you can set the default value for this parameter to `false`, `disabled`, or something else your application understands. Of course, this value can be overridden when creating or updating your stack.

You can and should provide a short, meaningful description for each parameter. These are displayed in the web console next to each parameter field. When used properly, they provide hints and context to whoever is trying to run your CloudFormation template.

At this point, we need to introduce the inbuilt `Ref` function. When you need to reference a parameter value, you use this function to do so:

```
KeyName:
   Ref: EC2KeyName
```

While `Ref` isn't the only inbuilt function you'll need to know, it's almost certainly going to be the one you'll use the most. We'll talk more about inbuilt functions later in this chapter.

Resources

Resources are your actual pieces of AWS infrastructure. These are your EC2 instances, S3 buckets, ELBs, and so on. Almost any resource type you can create by pointing and clicking in the AWS web console can also be created using CloudFormation.

 It's not practical to list all the AWS resource types in this chapter, although you will get familiar with the most common types as you work your way through the recipes in this book. AWS keeps a definitive list of resources types here
http://docs.aws.amazon.com/AWSCloudFormation/latest/UserGuide
/aws-template-resource-type-ref.html.

There are a few important things to keep in mind about CloudFormation resources:

- New or bleeding-edge AWS resources are often not immediately supported. CloudFormation support typically lags a few weeks (sometimes months) behind the release of new AWS features. This used to be quite frustrating for anyone to whom infrastructure automation is key. Fast-forward to today, and this situation is somewhat mitigated by the ability to use custom resources. These are discussed further on in this chapter.

- Resources have a default return value. You can use `Ref` to fetch these return values for use elsewhere in your template. For example, the `AWS::EC2::VPC` resource type has a default return value that is the ID of the VPC. They look something like this: `vpc-11aa111a`.

- Resources often contain additional return values. These additional values are fetched using the inbuilt `Fn::GetAtt` function. Continuing from the previous example, the `AWS::EC2::VPC` resource type also returns the following:
  - `CidrBlock`
  - `DefaultNetworkAcl`
  - `DefaultSecurityGroup`
  - `Ipv6CidrBlocks`

Outputs

Just like AWS resources, CloudFormation stacks can also have return values, called **outputs**. These values are entirely user defined. If you don't specify any outputs, then nothing is returned when your stack is completed.

Outputs can come in handy when you are using a CI/CD tool to create your CloudFormation stacks. For example, you might like to output the public hostname of an ELB so your CI/CD tool can turn it into a clickable link within the job output.

You'll also use them when your are linking together pieces of your layer cake. You may want to reference an S3 bucket or security group created in another stack. This is much easier to do with the new cross-stack references feature, which we'll discuss later in this chapter. You can expect to see the `Ref` and `Fn::GetAtt` functions a lot in the output section of any CloudFormation template.

Mappings

The mappings section is used to define a set of key/value pairs. If you require any kind of AWS region portability, perhaps for DR or availability purposes or simply to get your application closer to your end user, you'll almost certainly need to specify some mappings in your template. This is particularly necessary if you are referencing anything in your template that is region specific.

The canonical example would be to specify a map of EC2 AMI IDs in your template. This is because AMIs are a region-specific resource, so a reference to a valid **Amazon Machine Image (AMI)** ID in one region will be invalid in another.

Mappings look like this:

```
Mappings:
  RegionMap:
    us-east-1:
      AMIID: ami-9be6f38c
    ap-southeast-2:
      AMIID: ami-28cff44b
```

Dependencies and ordering

When executing your template, CloudFormation will automatically work out which resources depend on each other and order their creation accordingly. Additionally, resource creation is parallelized as much as possible so that your stack execution finishes in the timeliest manner possible. Things occasionally become unstuck, however.

Let's take an example where an app server depends on a DB server. In order to connect to the database, the app server needs to know its IP address or hostname. This situation would actually require you to create the DB server first so that you can use `Ref` to fetch its IP and provide it to your app server. CloudFormation has no way of knowing about the coupling between these two resources, so it will go ahead and create them in any order it pleases (or in parallel if possible).

To fix this situation, we use the `DependsOn` attribute to tell CloudFormation that our app server depends on our DB server. In fact, `DependsOn` can actually take a list of strings if a resource happens to depend on multiple resources before it can be created. So if our app server were to also depend on, say, a Memcached server, then we use `DependsOn` to declare both dependencies.

If necessary, you can take this further. Let's say that after your DB server boots, it will automatically start the database, set up a schema, and import a large amount of data. It may be necessary to wait for this process to complete before we create an app server that attempts to connect to a DB expecting a complete schema and data set. In this scenario, we want a way to signal to CloudFormation that the DB server has completed its initialization so it can go ahead and create resources that depend on it. This is where `WaitCondition` and `WaitConditionHandle` come in.

Firstly, you create an `AWS::CloudFormation::WaitConditionHandle` type, which you can later reference via `Ref`.

Next, you create an `AWS::CloudFormation::WaitCondition` type. In our case, we want the wait period to start as soon as the DB server is created, so we specify that this `WaitCondition` resource `DependsOn` our DB server.

After the DB server has finished importing data and is ready to accept connections, it calls the callback URL provided by the `WaitConditionHandle` resource to signal to CloudFormation that it can stop waiting and start executing the rest of the CloudFormation stack. The URL is supplied to the DB server via `UserData`, again using `Ref`. Typically, `curl`, `wget` or some equivalent is used to call the URL.

A `WaitCondition` resource can have a `Timeout` period too. This is a value specified in seconds. In our example, we might supply a value of `900` because we know that it should never take more than 15 minutes to boot our DB and import the data.

Here's an example of what `DependsOn`, `WaitConditionHandle`, and `WaitCondition` look like combined:

```
ExampleWaitHandle:
  Type: AWS::CloudFormation::WaitConditionHandle
```

```
      Properties:
ExampleWaitCondition:
   Type: AWS::CloudFormation::WaitCondition
   DependsOn: ExampleEC2Instance
   Properties:
      Handle:
         Ref: ExampleWaitHandle
      Timeout: 600
```

Functions

CloudFormation provides some inbuilt functions to make composing your templates a lot easier. We've already looked at `Ref` and `Fn::GetAtt`. Let's look at some others you are likely to encounter.

Fn::Join

Use `Fn::Join` to concatenate a list of strings using a specified delimiter, like this, for example:

```
"Fn::Join": [ ".", [ 1, 2, 3, 4 ] ]
```

This would yield the following value:

```
"1.2.3.4"
```

Fn::Sub

Use `Fn::Sub` to perform string substitution. Consider this:

```
DSN: "Fn::Sub"
   - mysql://${db_user}:${db_pass}@${db_host}:3306/wordpress
   - { db_user: lchan, db_pass: ch33s3, db_host: localhost }
```

This would yield the following value:

```
mysql://lchan:ch33s3@localhost:3306/wordpress
```

When you combine these functions with `Ref` and `Fn::GetAtt`, you can start doing some really powerful stuff, as we'll be seeing in the recipes throughout this book.

Other available inbuilt functions include:

- `Fn::Base64`
- `Fn::FindInMap`
- `Fn::GetAZs`
- `Fn::ImportValue`
- `Fn::Select`

 Documentation on all of these functions is available here `http://docs.aw s.amazon.com/AWSCloudFormation/latest/UserGuide/intrinsic-func tion-reference.html`.

Conditionals

It's reasonably common to provision a similar but distinct set of resources based on which environment your stack is running in. In your development environment, for example, you may not wish to create an entire fleet of database servers (HA master and read slaves), instead opting for just a single database server. You can achieve this by using conditionals:

- `Fn::And`
- `Fn::Equals`
- `Fn::If`
- `Fn::Not`
- `Fn::Or`

Permissions and service roles

One important thing to remember about CloudFormation is that it's more or less just making API calls on your behalf. This means that CloudFormation will assume the very same permissions or role you use to execute your template. If you don't have permission to create a new hosted zone in Route 53, for example, any template you try to run that contains a new Route 53-hosted zone will fail.

On the flip side, this has created a somewhat tricky situation where anyone developing CloudFormation typically has a very elevated level of privileges, and these privileges are somewhat unnecessarily granted to CloudFormation each time a template is executed.

If my CloudFormation template contains only one resource, which is a Route 53-hosted zone, it doesn't make sense for that template to be executed with full admin privileges to my AWS account. It makes much more sense to give CloudFormation a very slim set of permissions to execute the template with, thus limiting the blast radius if a bad template were to be executed (that is, a bad copy-and-paste operation resulting in deleted resources).

Thankfully, service roles have recently been introduced, and you can now define an IAM role and tell CloudFormation to use this role when your stack is being executed, giving you a much safer space to play in.

Custom resources

As discussed previously in this chapter, it's common for there to be a lengthy wait between the release of a new AWS feature and your ability to use that feature in CloudFormation.

Before custom resources, this led AWS developers down the path of doing over 95 percent of their automation in CloudFormation and then running some CLI commands to fill in the gaps. It was often difficult to tell exactly which resources belonged to which stack, and knowing exactly when your stack had finished execution became a guessing game.

Fast forward to today, and the emerging pattern is to use a custom resource to delegate to a AWS **Lambda** function. Lambda can fill in the gaps by making API calls on your behalf, and it becomes much easier to track the heritage and completion of these resources.

With any luck, you won't need to use this feature for a while. In the meantime, the AWS custom resource documentation is quite comprehensive. If you are trying to use CloudFormation to create a resource that you can't find in the AWS docs, then it's likely that it's not supported in CloudFormation yet and using custom resources is your answer. For more information, refer to http://docs.aws.amazon.com/AWSCloudFormation/latest/UserGuide/template-custom-resources.html.

Cross-stack references

When using the layered cake approach, it's very common to want to use outputs from one stack as inputs in another stack. For example, you may create a VPC in one stack and require its VPC ID when creating resources in another.

For a long time, one needed to provide some glue around stack creation to pass output between stacks. AWS recently introduced cross-stack references, which provide a more native way of doing this.

You can now *export* one or more outputs from your stack. This makes those outputs available to other stacks. Note that the name of this value needs to be unique, so it's probably a good idea to include the CloudFormation stack name in the name you're exporting to achieve this.

Once a value is exported, it becomes available to be imported in another stack using the `Fn::ImportValue` function—very handy!

Make sure, however, that during the time an exported value is being referenced, you are not able to delete or modify it. Additionally, you won't be able to delete the stack containing the exported value. Once something is referencing an exported value, it's there to stay until there are no stacks referencing it at all.

Updating resources

One of the principles of IaC is that all changes should be represented as code for review and testing. This is especially important where CloudFormation is concerned.

After creating a stack for you, the CloudFormation service is effectively hands off. If you make a change to any of the resources created by CloudFormation (in the web console, command line, or by some other method), you're effectively causing configuration drift. CloudFormation no longer knows the exact state of the resources in your stack.

The correct approach is to make these changes in your CloudFormation template and perform an update operation on your stack. This ensures that CloudFormation always knows the state of your stack and allows you to maintain confidence that your infrastructure code is a complete and accurate representation of your running environments.

Change sets

When performing a stack update, it can be unclear exactly what changes are going to be made to your stack. Depending on which resource you are changing, you may find that it will need to be deleted and recreated in order to implement your change. This, of course, is completely undesired behavior if the resource in question contains data you'd like to keep. Keep in mind that RDS databases can be a particular pain point.

To mitigate this situation, CloudFormation allows you to create and review a *change set* prior to executing the update. The change set shows you which operations CloudFormation intends to perform on your resources. If the change set looks good, you can choose to proceed. If you don't like what you see, you can delete the change set and choose another course of action—perhaps choosing to create and switch to an entirely new stack to avoid a service outage.

Other things to know

There are a few other things you should keep in the back of your mind as you start to build out your own CloudFormation stacks. Let's take a look.

Name collisions

Often, if you omit the name attribute from a resource, CloudFormation will generate a name for you. This can result in weird-looking resource names, but it will increase the *replayability* of your template. Using AWS::S3::Bucket as an example, if you specify the BucketName parameter but don't ensure its uniqueness, CloudFormation will fail to execute your template the second time around because the bucket will already exist. Omitting BucketName fixes this. Alternatively, you may opt to generate your own unique name each time the template is run. There's probably no right or wrong approach here, so just do what works for you.

Rollback

When creating a CloudFormation stack, you are given the option of disabling rollback. Before you go ahead and set this to true, keep in mind that this setting persists beyond stack creation. We've ended up in precarious situations where updating an existing stack has failed (for some reason) but rollback has been disabled. This is a fun situation for no one.

Limits

The limits most likely to concern you are as follows:

- The maximum size allowed for your CloudFormation template is 50 KB. This is quite generous, and if you hit this limit, you almost certainly need to think about breaking up your template into a series of smaller ones. If you absolutely need to exceed the 50 KB limit, then the most common approach is to first upload your template to S3 and then provide an S3 URL to CloudFormation to execute.

- The maximum number of parameters you can specify is *60*. If you need more than this then again, consider whether or not you need to add more layers to your cake. Otherwise, lists or mappings might get you out of trouble here.
- Outputs are also limited to *60*. If you've hit this limit, it's probably time to resort to a series of smaller templates.
- Resources are limited to *200*. The same rules apply here as before.
- By default, you're limited to a total of *200* CloudFormation stacks. You can have this limit increased simply by contacting AWS.

Circular dependencies

Something to keep in the back of your mind is that you may run in to a circular dependency scenario, where multiple resources depend on each other for creation. A common example is where two security groups reference each other in order to allow access between themselves.

A workaround for this particular scenario is to use the `AWS::EC2::SecurityGroupEgress` and `AWS::EC2::SecurityGroupIngress` types instead of the ingress and egress rule types for `AWS::EC2::SecurityGroup`.

DSLs and generators

DSLs and generators can be a point of hot debate among infrastructure coders. Some love them, some hate them. Some of the reasons why people love them include the following:

- They allow CloudFormation to be written in a language that is more native to them or their team.
- They allow the use some advanced programming constructs. Iteration is a particularly well-cited example.
- Until YAML was supported by CloudFormation, using a DSL usually resulted in code that was easier to read and far less verbose.

Some of the reasons people dislike them are:

- DSLs have a history of becoming abandonware or significantly lagging behind CloudFormation, although there are a couple of well-supported DSLs out there
- Developers are potentially required to learn a new language and navigate another new set of documentation, on top of learning CloudFormation and navigating the AWS documentation
- Google and Stack Overflow become a little less useful because one needs to translate questions and answers

Beyond what is written here, this topic won't come up again in this book. We can't give specific advice as to which road you should take because it's almost always a highly personal and situational choice. However, a sensible approach, especially while coming to grips with AWS and CloudFormation, would be to stick with YAML (or JSON) until you get to the point where you think a DSL or generator might be useful.

Credentials

Under no circumstances do you want to have credentials hardcoded in your templates or committed to your source code repository. Doing this doesn't just increase the chance your credentials will be stolen, it also reduces the portability of your templates. If your credentials are hardcoded and you need to change them, that obviously requires you to edit your CloudFormation template.

Instead, you should add credentials as parameters in your template. Be sure to use the NoEcho parameter when you do this so that CloudFormation masks the value anywhere the parameters are displayed.

Stack policies

If there are resources in your stack you'd like to protect from accidental deletion or modification, applying a stack policy will help you achieve this. By default, all resources are able to be deleted or modified. When you apply a stack policy, all resources are protected unless you explicitly allow them to be deleted or modified in the policy. Note that stack policies do not apply during stack creation—they only take effect when you attempt to update a stack.

The command-line interface tool

The AWS **command-line interface** (**CLI**) tool is an important piece of the AWS administrator's toolkit.

The CLI tool is often one of the quickest and easiest ways to interact with the API. As a text-based tool, it scales much easier than using the web console. Unlike the console, it can be automated, for example, via scripts. The AWS **application programming interface** (**API**) represents all the functionality available to you as an AWS administrator. It is also easier to keep a track of through your command-line history. Like all good CLI tools, simple individual commands can be chained (or *piped*) together to perform complex tasks.

The CLI tool is open source software, maintained on GitHub `https://git hub.com/aws/aws-cli`. For more detailed documentation, refer to the AWS CLI homepage `https://aws.amazon.com/cli`.

Installation

The CLI tool requires Python 2.6.5 or greater.

The easiest way to install it is to use the Python package manager, `pip`:

```
pip install awscli
```

This will make the command `aws` available on your system.

Upgrade

AWS frequently releases new services and functionality. In order to use the new features, you will need to upgrade the CLI tool.

To upgrade, run the following `pip` command periodically:

```
pip install --upgrade awscli
```

Configuration

Authentication between the CLI tool and the AWS API is done via two pieces of information:

- Access key ID
- Secret access key

 As the name suggests, you should keep your secret access key a secret! Be careful where you store or send it.

Once you have created a user, you can configure the tool to use it for authentication purposes.

While you can configure the CLI tool with access keys directly, this should be avoided. Instead, you should use profiles to store your credentials. Using profiles gives you a more consistent and manageable centralized location to secure your secret keys.

Default profile

Without any additional configuration or options, your CLI tool commands will use the default profile.

To set up the default profile, you can use the following command:

```
aws configure
```

This will prompt you for an access key ID, secret access key, region, and output format.

Named profiles

In addition to the default profile, you can configure other, named profiles. This is useful for switching between users with different levels of access (for example, read-only and administrator) or even between users in different accounts.

```
aws configure --profile <profile-name>
```

Once you have responded to the prompts, you can reference the named profile by passing the `--profile <profile-name>` option with your command.

Environment variables

You can also configure the CLI via the use of environment variables:

```
export AWS_PROFILE=<profile-name>
```

While you should prefer to use profiles over setting your access ID and secret keys directly, sometimes you may have to do it. If you *must* set your keys directly, do so via environment variables so that you do not need to pass your keys around or hardcode them:

```
export AWS_ACCESS_KEY_ID=<access-key-id>
export AWS_SECRET_ACCESS_KEY=<secret-access-key>
```

Instance roles

When running the CLI tool on an EC2 instance, you can leverage the instance's IAM role to make calls. This means you do not need to configure credentials or set environment variables (manually).

Behind the scenes, the instance will retrieve and set its own AWS environment variables that allow API calls. You do need to ensure the instance has appropriate permissions.

 The AWS CLI tool comes preinstalled on AWS Linux-based instances.

Usage

All CLI tool commands are service based. Using service commands and subcommands, you can make calls directly to the AWS API.

Commands

Each command represents an AWS service. While most services have one command associated with them, some services have multiple commands (for example, S3 has `s3` and `s3api`).

 Run `aws help` to see all the commands/services that are available—they will probably have changed by the time this book prints!

Subcommands

Each command has a selection of subcommands to perform service-specific actions.

Run `aws <command> help` to see all subcommands.

Options

Subcommands take options, which start with `--`.

See all options and their purpose with `aws <command> <subcommand> help`.

While most are optional (hence the name), those that are *not* surrounded by square brackets (`[]`) are required. You will get an error message (with appropriate details) if you do not include them.

The built-in documentation is the best place to start looking for answers. There are usually examples after all of the options have been described. Otherwise, there are plenty of examples available online.

Some options are available to all or most commands, so they are particularly useful to know.

Output

The CLI tool can be configured to output in JSON, table, or text format. To control the output type, use the `--output` option.

To set a default output type for all your commands, set the `output` parameter for your profile.

JSON

JavaScript Object Notation (JSON) (http://json.org/), a standard, machine- and human-readable information interchange format. Here's what the AZs in the us-east-1 (North Virginia) region look like represented as JSON:

```
aws ec2 describe-availability-zones --output json
{
"AvailabilityZones": [
        {
"State": "available",
"RegionName": "us-east-1",
"Messages": [],
"ZoneName": "us-east-1a"
        },
        {
"State": "available",
"RegionName": "us-east-1",
"Messages": [],
"ZoneName": "us-east-1c"
        },
        {
"State": "available",
"RegionName": "us-east-1",
"Messages": [],
"ZoneName": "us-east-1d"
        },
        {
"State": "available",
"RegionName": "us-east-1",
"Messages": [],
"ZoneName": "us-east-1e"
        }
    ]
}
```

Table

The table format displays a text/ASCII table of results. This can be useful for generating printable reports:

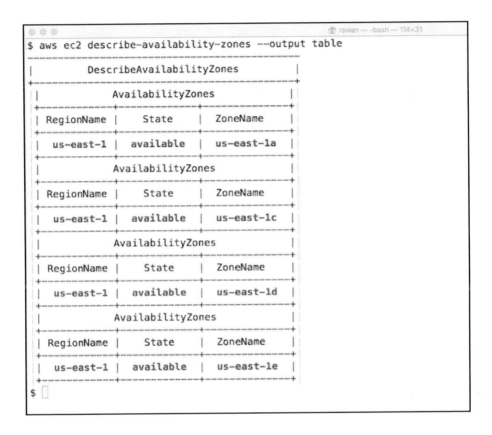

Text

The text output format only displays the resulting key/value response. No additional formatting or display characters are added.

```
$ aws ec2 describe-availability-zones --output text
AVAILABILITYZONES      us-east-1      available      us-east-1a
AVAILABILITYZONES      us-east-1      available      us-east-1c
AVAILABILITYZONES      us-east-1      available      us-east-1d
AVAILABILITYZONES      us-east-1      available      us-east-1e
$
```

Querying

The CLI tool supports transforming the response from the API with the `--query` option. This option takes a JMESPath query as a parameter and returns the query result.

 JMESPath is a query language for JSON. For more information, visit `http://jmespath.org/`.

As the query is processed as part of the command, it takes place on the server, not the client. By offloading work to the server, you can reduce the size of the resulting payload and improve response times.

JMESPath can be used to transform the response that you receive:

```
$ aws ec2 describe-availability-zones \
  --output json \
  --query 'AvailabilityZones[].ZoneName'
  [
  "us-east-1a",
  "us-east-1c",
  "us-east-1d",
  "us-east-1e"
  ]
```

It can also be used to filter the data that is received:

```
$ aws ec2 describe-availability-zones
  --output json
  --query "AvailabilityZones[?ZoneName == 'us-east-1a'].State"
  [
  "available"
  ]
```

Generate CLI skeleton

When performing complex tasks with the CLI tool, it may be easier to pass a JSON object of options. This kind of interaction may signify that you should use one of the AWS **software development kits (SDKs)**.

Input

To generate a sample JSON object that will be accepted, run the command with the --generate-cli-skeleton option:

```
$ aws ec2 describe-availability-zones --generate-cli-skeleton
{
"DryRun": true,
"ZoneNames": [
""
    ],
"Filters": [
        {
"Name": "",
"Values": [
""
            ]
        }
    ]
}
```

You can then copy, edit, and use this object to define your command options without passing lots of individual options. It works best for commands with arrays of options or a variable number of options.

Output

You can also get a preview of the output of a command by calling the command with the --generate-cli-skeleton output option. This can speed up the process of combining CLI commands as you can see a response without actually calling the API:

```
$ aws ec2 describe-availability-zones --generate-cli-skeleton output
{
"AvailabilityZones": [
        {
"ZoneName": "ZoneName",
"State": "State",
"RegionName": "RegionName",
"Messages": [
            {
"Message": "Message"
            }
        ]
    }
]
}
```

Pagination

Results returned by the CLI tool are limited to 1,000 resources by default.

This is not normally an issue, but at a certain scale, you may run into pagination issues. A common example is files in an S3 bucket.

 If you are absolutely sure you should be seeing a particular resource in a response but cannot, check your pagination. The resource may be included in the matching resources, just not in the part of the response that was returned to you.

The following options allow you to control the number and starting point of the results returned to you from the API:

- `--page-size`: This limits how many resources *will be displayed to you*, but does not actually limit the number returned. The default number of items (that is, 1,000) will still be processed and returned to you.
- `--max-items`: This sets an upper limit on how many items will actually be returned in the response. You may receive fewer items, but you will not receive more than this number.
- `--starting-token`: This changes where the response starts. Use this to display subsequent results, beyond the first page.

```
aws s3 ls --bucket bucket-name --max-items 100 --starting-token None___100
```

Autocomplete

You can enable tab-completion of commands, subcommands, and options by configuring the completer included with the CLI tool.

On OS X, Linux, and Windows systems with a bash shell, you can load the completer with the following command:

```
complete -C 'which aws_completer'aws
```

By default, the `aws_completer` program is installed in `/usr/local/bin`. If your tool is installed to a non-standard location, you will need to find it and change the `which aws_completer` command to the relevant path.

Related tools

The following program work nicely with the AWS CLI tool, and may come in handy.

jq

jq is a lightweight tool for processing and transforming JSON. It follows the *Unix philosophy* of doing one thing and doing it well. It can be found at `https://stedolan.github.io/jq/`.

 While jq and JMESPath are similar, jq is a lot easier to get started with. It also supports transforming JSON into plaintext; JMESPath queries will always return more JSON.

You can pipe JSON results from the CLI tool to it, and easily transform the results for use elsewhere. This example uses jq's property name selectors to convert JSON output to text:

```
$ aws ec2 describe-availability-zones --output json | jq
'.AvailabilityZones[].ZoneName'
"us-east-1a"
"us-east-1c"
"us-east-1d"
"us-east-1e"
```

2

Managing AWS Accounts

In this chapter, we will cover the following topics:

- Setting up a master account
- Creating a member account
- Inviting an account
- Managing your accounts
- Adding a service control policy

Introduction

We work with a lot of companies who maintain a large, ever-growing number of AWS accounts. Keeping a handle on all these accounts has typically been quite difficult to do—even for the most seasoned AWS users.

With the release of AWS Organizations, you now have the ability to centrally manage your AWS accounts, to arrange them into logical groupings and hierarchies, and to apply controls to them in ways which haven't previously been possible on the AWS platform.

Setting up a master account

All accounts that use AWS Organizations for billing and control purposes must have a *master account*. This account controls membership to the organization, and pays the bills of all the members (someone's got to do it).

How to do it...

To set up a master account, perform the following steps:

1. Go to the **My Organization** section of the account you want to become the master. You must be logged in with your root credentials (that is, those you created the account with):

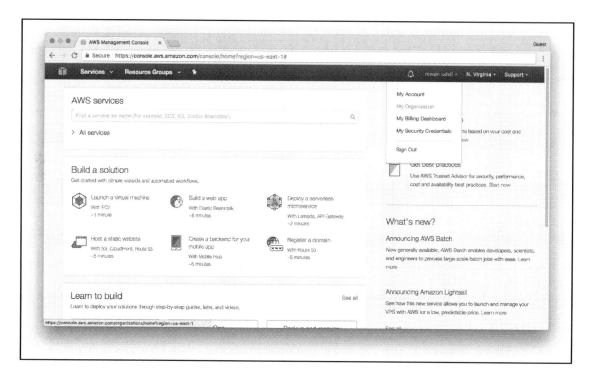

2. In the **AWS Organizations** section of the AWS console, click on **Create organization**, as shown in the following screenshot:

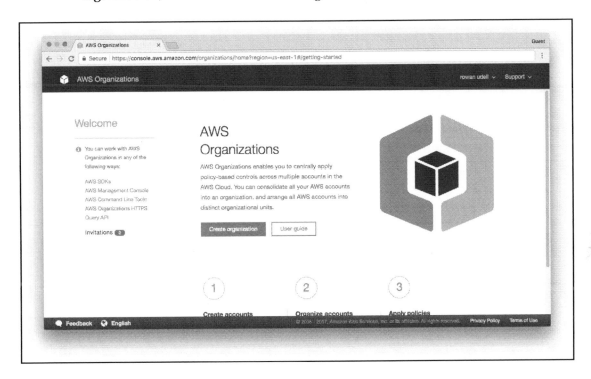

3. Unless you have a specific requirement, choose **ENABLE ALL FEATURES** to get the full benefit of organizations, as shown in the following screenshot:

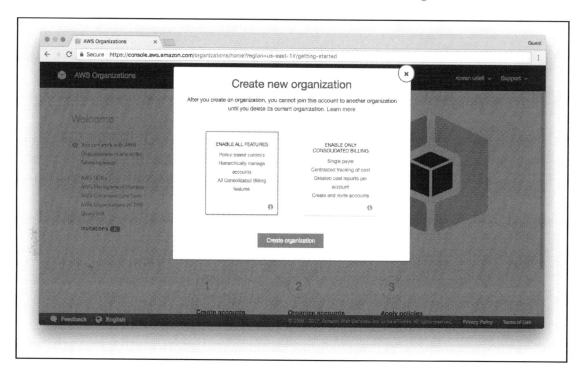

4. Now that your account has been converted, you can return to the **AWS Organizations** page to see a list of all your accounts:

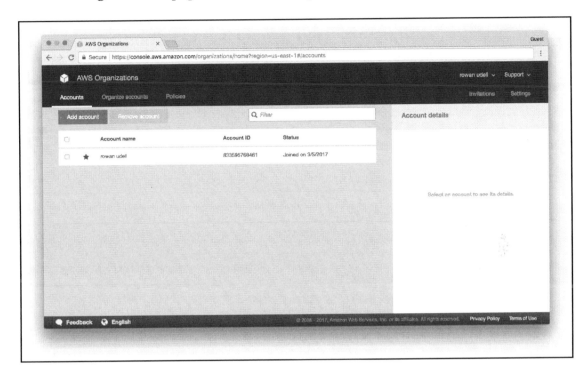

How it works...

While this is a very simple recipe, it's the first thing you must do before you can use any of the useful features of AWS Organizations.

Here you can see a high-level diagram of the relationships between master accounts, members, and **organizational units (OUs)**:

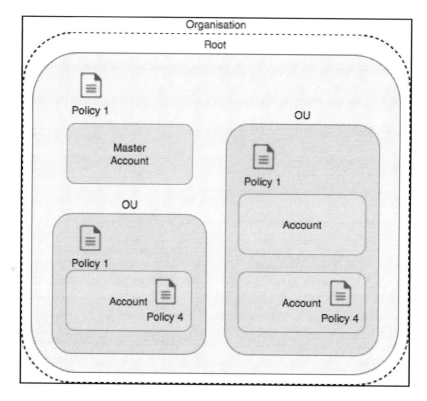

We deliberately enable all the features of organizations. The consolidated billing option is available for backward compatibility—before organizations, consolidated billing was your only option to link accounts.

  Do not use your master account for day-to-day tasks. Since it is so important, it doesn't make sense to risk using it and/or having access keys for it. If your master account was to become compromised somehow, it would impact all of your member accounts. Just don't do it.

The master account will always have a star next to its name.

There's more...

All of the organizations functionality is exposed via the API. This means you can use the AWS SDKs or the CLI tool to do the same things you would in the web console.

Multi-factor authentication

As mentioned in the consolidated billing confirmation e-mail, it is advisable to configure **multi-factor authentication (MFA)** on your console. To do this, log in as your root user (that is, the credentials you used when first creating your account), go to the **Identity and Access Management (IAM)** console, and follow the **Activate MFA on your root account** prompts.

Using the CLI

You can easily create your master account with the CLI tool. The following command will turn your account into a master account, with all organizations features enabled:

```
aws organizations create-organization
```

See also

- The *Inviting an account* recipe
- The *Creating a member account* recipe

Creating a member account

Once your organization is up and running, the most common use you will have for it is automating the account creation process. Accounts created inside an organization are referred to as **member accounts**.

All charges incurred by a member account will be billed to the master account.

Getting ready

Obviously, you will need an organization to perform this recipe. See the other recipes in this chapter to get started.

How to do it...

1. Run the CLI tool command to create a new account, with appropriate values:

```
aws organizations create-account \
  --email <member-account-owners@email.com> \
  --account-name <member-account-name> \
  --query 'CreateAccountStatus.Id'
```

2. This command will return a `create account status` request ID value that you can use to check the status:

```
aws organizations describe-create-account-status \
  --create-account-request-id <your-create-account-status-id>
```

How it works...

The command to create a member account in your organization is extremely simple.

The e-mail address used cannot be associated with any other AWS accounts.

The account creating process takes some time, so it is done *asynchronously*. This means that you won't receive an immediate status to your `create-account` command. Instead, the command in this recipe will return a request ID.

This ID is then passed to another account to check the status of the creation. When the status is CREATED, you can start to use the new account.

There's more...

While this functionality is definitely useful, the AWS Organizations service is relatively new. This means there are a few *features* you should be aware of.

Accessing the member account

Once you've created your member account, it's time to put it to work!

An IAM role will be present in the new account, with a default name of `OrganizationAccountAccessRole`. This is so you can assume the role (from your master account) and administer the member account. While this name is as good as any, it can be configured by passing the `--role-name` argument when creating the account.

In order to assume the role, you need to know its **Amazon Resource Name (ARN)**. Working out the ARN is a multi-step process:

1. List your member accounts by running the following command in your master account:

   ```
   aws organizations list-accounts
   ```

2. Find the account you created (by its name) and note the ID value in the record. Using that ID, generate the role's ARN by following this pattern:

   ```
   arn:aws:iam::<your-member-account-
   id>:role/OrganizationAccountAccessRole
   ```

3. If you have changed the created role's name, update the last part of the ARN accordingly.

See the recipes in `Chapter 8`, *Security and Identity* for information on how to best manage multiple accounts.

Service control policies

The **service control policies (SCPs)** are another major feature of AWS Organizations. You can apply them at multiple levels/resources, including accounts (both member accounts and invited accounts). Check the other recipes in this chapter for more details.

Root credentials

Some activities still require the root credentials of the account. An example activity would be closing (or deleting) an account (see the next section for more details).

In order to do this, you will need to do the password recovery process for the e-mail that was associated with the account when the `create-account` request was sent.

Deleting accounts

At the time of writing, *there is no way to delete an account created in your organization via the API*. We can only imagine that being able to programmatically delete a member account created in an organization will be a *highly requested* feature, and will be addressed soon. You can still go into the member account and close it using the root credentials, but these don't exist by default.

 While you can technically delete your *organization* via the API, you cannot do it if you have created any member accounts in your organization (because you can't delete them, your organization will never be empty). This should improve in the near future, but is still worth being aware of now.

See also

- The *Setting up a master account* recipe
- The *Adding a service control policy* recipe
- The *Cross-account user roles* recipe in `Chapter 8`, *Security and Identity*

Inviting an account

While it makes sense to create new accounts in your organization, what do you do with all the other accounts you have now?

You can invite existing accounts to your organization, which means you can treat them just like a member account from an administrative point of view. This greatly simplifies the administrative overhead of your accounts, as there isn't a separate process for *old* and *new* accounts.

As this is generally performed once for each existing account, we will use the console.

 All the AWS organizations functionality is available via the SDKs and AWS CLI tool. If you need to automate this process, you can.

Getting ready

You must have enabled AWS Organizations for one of your accounts (your master account), and have another account that has not been made part of an organization yet (that you will invite).

How to do it...

1. From the AWS console of the master account, click on your username, and select **My Organization** from the drop-down menu:

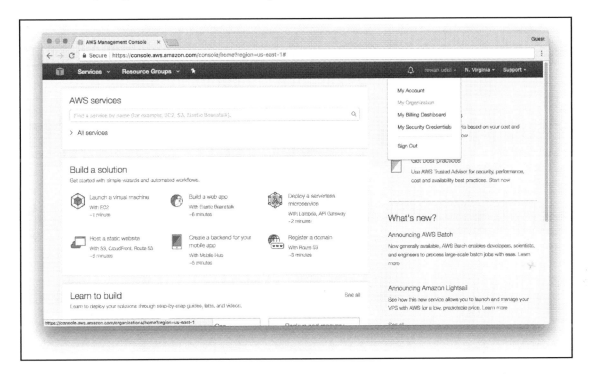

2. You will be taken to the **AWS Organizations** console, where you will see your current account:

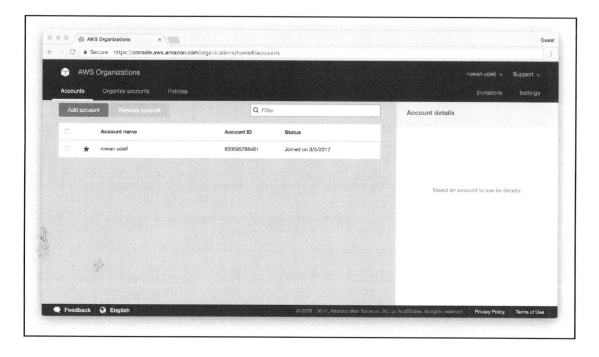

3. Click on the **Invitations** tab in the top-right of the console:

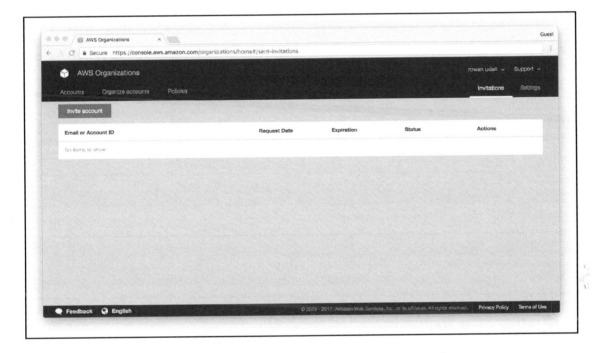

4. Click on the **Invite account** button. Specify the account ID (or main e-mail address) of the account to invite:

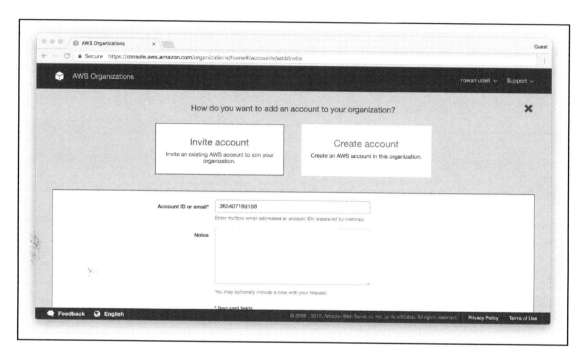

5. Once you click **Invite**, you will be taken to a list of invitations where you can view the status:

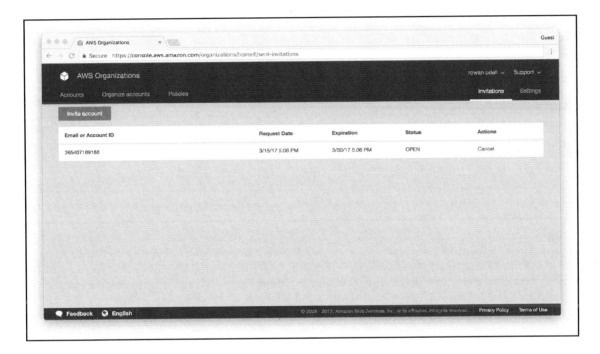

6. At this stage, the target/invited account will receive an e-mail notifying them of the invite:

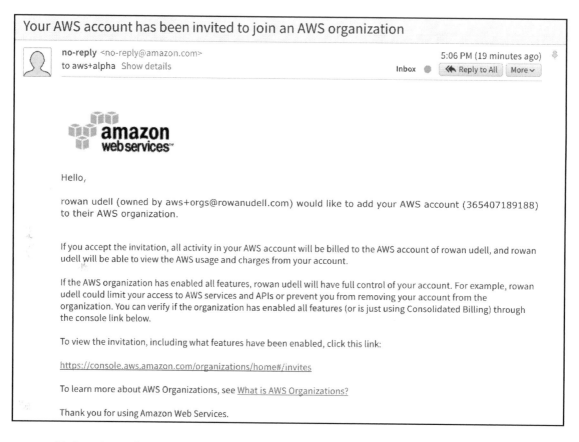

7. Log in to the invited account and go to the **My Organization** link under the user menu:

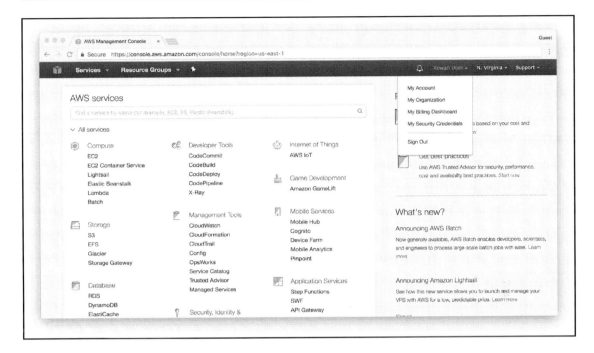

8. In the **AWS Organizations** console, you can see the pending invite on the left:

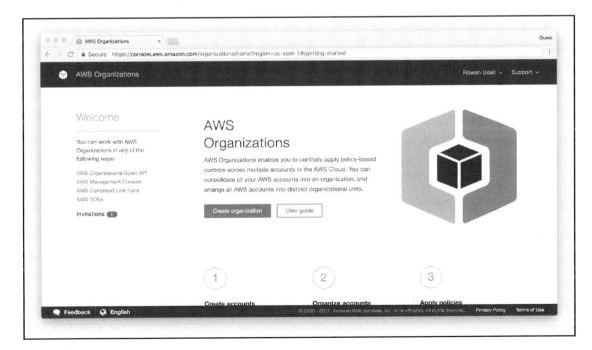

9. Clicking on the invite, you can see its details:

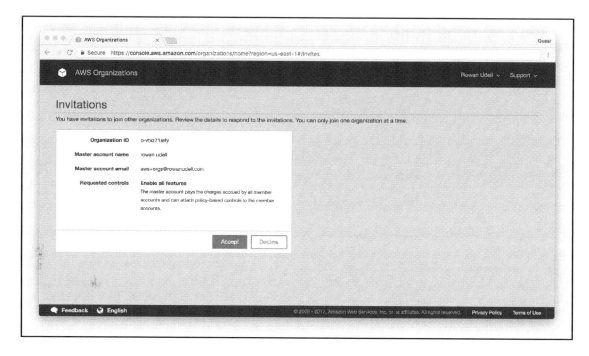

10. When the invite includes all features, you will be asked to confirm your acceptance:

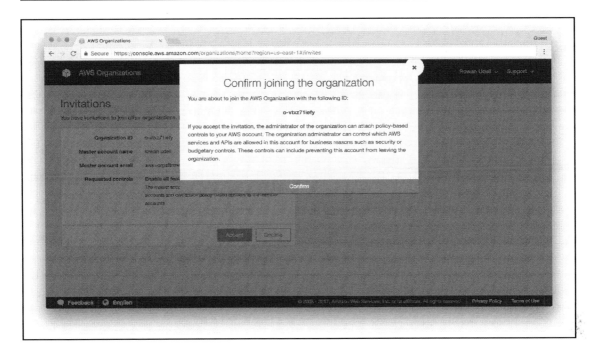

11. Once confirmed, you can now see the details of the organization you have joined:

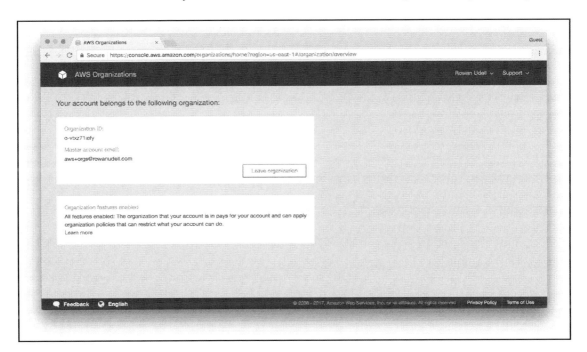

12. At this stage, the master account will be notified of the accepted invite:

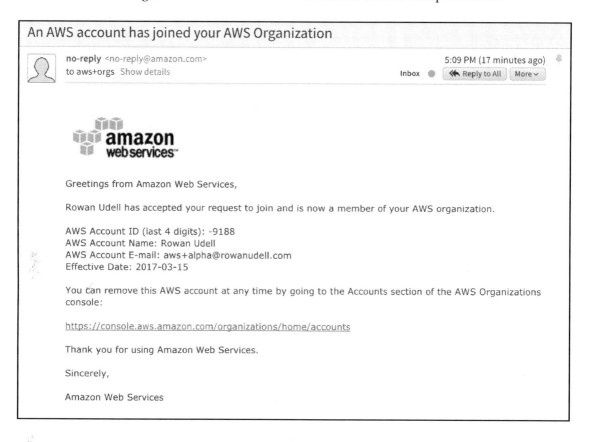

13. Back in the master account, you can now see the new account alongside the master:

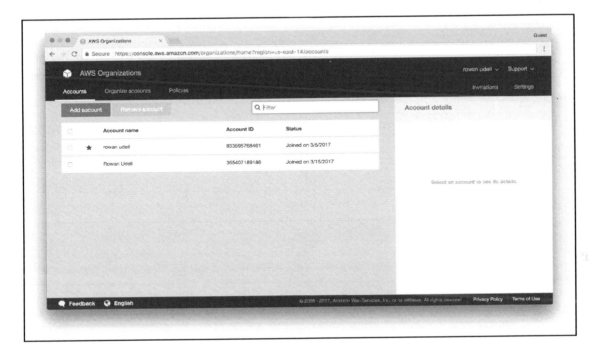

How it works...

While there are many steps involved, the process of inviting an existing account is a relatively simple *handshake* process. This means that both sides must actively initiate/accept the invite, in order for it to succeed—an invite cannot be forced.

After specifying the target account's account ID (or e-mail address), the e-mail address associated will be notified.

As part of the handshake process, the invited account must explicitly accept the invite.

 It is important to note that the default invite type (and what we have used in the recipe) is to use the full feature set for AWS Organizations. As noted in the console, this means that the invited account *could be prevented from leaving the organization* if the relevant policies are configured.

After confirmation, both parties will receive an e-mail detailing the membership. From this point forward, the bill for the invited account will be paid by the master account.

There's more...

Invited accounts are treated differently to accounts created via the organizations functionality.

Removing accounts

Unlike *member accounts* (which are created via the AWS Organizations API), invited accounts can be removed from an organization.

Consolidated billing

As an alternative to the *full feature* invite, it is possible to specify just *consolidated billing* mode for an organization. In this mode, no OUs or policies will be available, only the billing relationship will be shared between the accounts (that is, the master account will pay the bill of the member accounts).

 Any pre-existing accounts that were configured to use consolidated billing will have been *automatically* migrated to AWS Organizations *in consolidated billing mode.*

See also

- The *Creating a member account* recipe

Managing your accounts

There are a number of ways to group and arrange your AWS accounts. How you do this is completely up to you, but here are a few examples to consider:

- **Business unit (BU) or location**: You may wish to allow each BU to work in isolation on their own products or services, on their own schedule, without impacting other parts of the business
- **Cost center**: Grouping according to cost may help you track spend versus allocated budget

- **Environment type**: It may make sense to group your development, test, and production environments together in a way which helps you manage the controls across each environment
- **Workload type or data classification**: Your company may want to isolate workload types from each other, or ensure that particular controls are applied to all accounts containing a particular kind of data

In the following fictitious example, we have isolated the **Sitwell Enterprises Account** from the rest of the organization by placing it in an OU called **Sudden Valley**. Perhaps they operate in a different geographical location and have different regulatory requirements around controls and access.

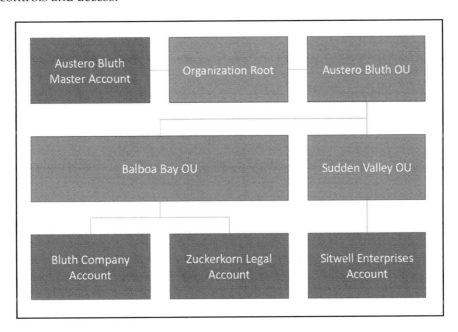

Organization hierarchy

Note that while it's also technically possible for us to put the master account inside an OU, we avoid doing this to make it obvious that:

- It's the master account and has control over the entire organization
- The rules we set, using SCPs for the member accounts in our organization, do not apply to the master account (because they can't)

Learn more about SCPs in the *Adding a service control policy* recipe in this chapter.

Getting ready

Before we can proceed, you should have already done the following:

- Set up a master AWS account
- Created an organization
- Created member accounts in your organization, or manually added member accounts (by invitation) to your organization

How to do it...

We'll now cover the one-line commands you'll need to perform the common tasks required to manage your OU. These commands can only be performed in your master account.

Getting the root ID for your organization

You can run this command to get the ID of the root for your organization. The root is created automatically for you when you create your organization in your master account. The ID returned to you will look something like this: r-bmdw.

```
aws organizations list-roots
```

Creating an OU

To create an OU, perform the following steps:

1. Determine where you'd like this OU to live. If it lives directly underneath the root, then your root ID will be the parent. Alternatively, if this OU is going to be a child of another OU, use the ID of the OU instead. Obviously, if this is the first OU you're creating, the root will be the parent.

2. Use the CLI to create your OU like so:

```
aws organizations create-organizational-unit \
  --parent-id <root-id or parent-ou-id> \
  --name <desired-ou-name>
```

Getting the ID of an OU

If you need to fetch the ID of an OU, you can use the CLI to do so; note that you'll need to know the parent of the OU. Here is how you'd get a list of all the OUs and their IDs in a root or OU:

```
aws organizations list-organizational-units-for-parent \
    --parent-id <root-id or parent-ou-id>
```

Adding an account to an OU

To add an account to an OU, perform the following steps:

1. When an account is initially added to your organization, it will be a child of the organization root. To add it to the OU you just created, you need to move it using the following CLI command:

```
aws organizations move-account \
    --account-id <twelve-digit-account-id> \
    --source-parent-id <root-id> \
    --destination-parent-id <new-parent-ou-id>
```

2. If you wish to move an account from one OU to another, simply use the same command but use the existing parent OU ID instead of the root ID.

Removing an account from an OU

To remove an account from an OU, perform the following steps:

1. If you wish to remove an account from an OU, you have two options. You can move it to another OU, or you can move it back to the root. If you decide you want to delete an OU, you'll need to make sure no accounts exist inside it first (we'll show you how to do this next).

2. Run the following command to move an account back to the root:

```
aws organizations move-account \
    --account-id <twelve-digit-account-id> \
    --source-parent-id <existing-parent-ou-id> \
    --destination-parent-id <root-id>
```

Deleting an OU

To delete an OU, you'll first need to make sure it's empty by removing its child accounts (as mentioned previously). You can then go ahead and delete the OU like so:

```
aws organizations delete-organizational-unit \
  --organizational-unit-id <ou-id>
```

How it works...

If done right, grouping your accounts together using OUs will help you simplify the way you manage and administer them. Try to use only *just enough* OUs to get the job done. The idea is to use OUs to make your life easier, not harder.

There's more...

- The **organizational control policies (OCPs)** can be attached to your root, OU, or AWS accounts. At this time, only one kind of OCP is supported: SCP.
- Accounts can only belong to one OU or root.
- Similarly, OUs can only belong to one OU or root.
- It's best to avoid deploying resources in the master account because this account can't be controlled with SCPs. The master account should be treated as a management account for audit, control, and billing purposes only.

See also

- The *Adding a service control policy* recipe

Adding a service control policy

Before we begin, we should talk through what SCPs are and how they apply to your organization.

An SCP consists of a policy document which defines (by way of filtering) the services and actions which are able to be used and performed within an OU or in an AWS account. If you've previously configured an IAM policy, then you will have more than enough background knowledge to get started with SCPs. Apart from a couple of minor exceptions, they look exactly the same.

SCPs can be applied at different levels throughout an organization. These are the levels, starting from the bottom and going up:

- **AWS account level**: An SCP applied to an AWS account takes effect on only that account. It's important to note that the SCP is very separate from the IAM policies which live inside the account. For example, an SCP might allow full access to S3 for an AWS account but the IAM policies inside the account may deny it (for certain roles and/or users).
- **OU level**: An SCP applied at the OU level will apply to all the AWS accounts which live inside the OU as well as any child OUs (remember that an OU can by a member of an OU).
- **Root level**: If an SCP is applied at this level, it will apply to all AWS accounts inside the organization.

Things can start to get really interesting when you have an SCP applied at multiple levels. The *intersection* of the polices at the root, OU, account, and IAM levels is evaluated and will determine whether or not an API call is allowed to be made. For example, someone belonging to an IAM role which has full administrator access to an account still won't be able to call any EC2 APIs if any of the SCPs above it (account, OU, root) deny EC2 access.

In the following example, we have a top-level OU, Austero Bluth, with an SCP which allows access to all AWS resources for all OUs and accounts underneath it:

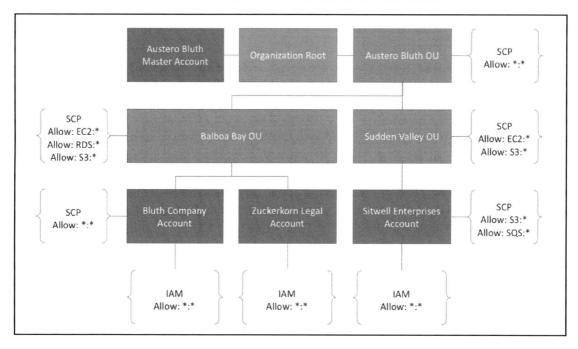

Organization hierarchy and policies

Austero Bluth has two child OUs; let's focus on Sudden Valley. It has an SCP which allows only EC2 and S3. By using a whitelisting approach, anything except these two services will be denied. Remembering that SCPs act like a filter, any OU or AWS accounts living underneath the Sudden Valley OU will, at most, have access to EC2 and S3.

The **Sitwell Enterprises Account** also has an SCP attached to it. This particular SCP allows S3 and SQS. Note that the SQS statement will have no effect here because the Sitwell account is inside an OU which does not allow SQS. Also note that this account has no access to EC2 despite the **Sudden Valley OU** allowing it; this is because EC2 wasn't explicitly allowed in the SCP attached to the account.

At the IAM level, we have a role in the Sitwell AWS account which allows full administrator privileges. But, because the intersection of the SCPs governing this account will only allow S3, anyone using this role will be denied access if they attempt to use EC2 or SQS, for example.

Let's also take a look at the **Bluth Company Account**. The SCP which is attached to it allows full AWS access; however, it lives inside an OU (Balboa Bay) which only allows EC2, RDS, and S3. There is an IAM role inside this account which also allows full admin access but, again, administrators in this account will be limited to EC2, RDS, and S3.

Getting ready

We're going to step through creating an SCP and adding it to an OU.

You're going to need the ID of the OU in question; you can fetch it from the organizations web console or use the CLI. It will look something like this: `ou-bmdw-omzypry7`.

We'll be preparing a policy document as well. In this example, we're going to add an SCP to the Sudden Valley OU to allow access to EC2 and S3. Here's what our SCP looks like:

```
{
    "Version":"2012-10-17",
    "Statement":[
        {
            "Effect":"Allow",
            "Action":["EC2:*","S3:*"],
            "Resource":"*"
        }
    ]
}
```

How to do it...

1. Open a new file in your text editor, add your JSON policy document, and save it.
2. Run the `create-policy` CLI command like so. We're getting a little tricky with the `tr` command here: we're using it to remove the carriage returns from the policy document, so pay close attention to the syntax in the example provided. Unfortunately, the organizations CLI doesn't allow us to provide the path to the policy document directly:

```
aws organizations create-policy \
    --content "$(tr -d '\n' < my-policy-file.json)" \
    --description "A policy description goes here" \
    --name "My policy" \
    --type SERVICE_CONTROL_POLICY
```

3. If the preceding CLI command works successfully, some JSON will be returned to you containing the ID of the policy we just added. It will look something like this: `p-o9too04s7`.

4. You can now go ahead and attach this policy to the OU. Use the following CLI command to do this:

```
aws organizations attach-policy \
   --target-id <ou-or-aws-account-id> \
   --policy-id <policy-id>
```

5. Unfortunately, the preceding command does not output anything if it ran successfully. You can double-check your handiwork in the AWS web console or use the following CLI command to verify that it worked:

```
aws organizations list-targets-for-policy \
   --policy-id <policy-id>
```

How it works...

Again, the policies you add will act as a filter at each level of your organizational structure. With this in mind, it might be a good time to point out that testing your policies on a single account before applying them organization-wide will save you a lot of heartache. Making sweeping changes to an SCP living at the top of your organization may create an unforeseen situation at the AWS account level at the bottom of the chain. A local admin in an AWS account is not able to override SCPs.

There's more...

- At the time of publishing, you are only able to have a single root inside an organization (it's created automatically for you when you create an organization).
- For obvious reasons, the master account is not affected by any SCPs which are attached to it. You may also notice that it's technically possible to place the master account in an OU; again, it will be unaffected by any SCPs which have been attached to that OU.
- Since the master account is unaffected by SCPs, it's a good idea to leave it as empty as possible and to not create any resources in it. Use child AWS accounts instead so you can apply fine-grained controls to them.
- SCPs are required on each OU and account but shouldn't be considered the only form of access control for your AWS accounts. Apply IAM where appropriate.

- When creating our policy, we have to specify a `--type` parameter. At the time of publishing, AWS only supports one variant of OCP: `SERVICE_CONTROL_POLICY`.

- As much as possible, follow the principle of least privilege. You want to give your AWS accounts access to only the services they need. This helps you mitigate damage caused by misclicks, programming errors, or compromised accounts.

- In the long run, you may find it advantageous to not assign controls at the root level. Instead, you may be better off adding *all* accounts to an OU and applying your controls to the OU instead.

- Your policies can take a whitelisting or blacklisting approach. In this recipe, we've used a whitelist approach, but you may instead prefer to allow your OUs and accounts to use all services except the ones you explicitly disallow. You should choose one of these approaches and stick with it, as mixing the two will cause you lots of confusion down the road.

- Unlike IAM policies, you can't specify conditions in SCP documents and `Resource` *must* be `*`.

See also

- The *Federating with your AWS account* recipe in `Chapter 8`, *Security and Identity* for some discussion around IAM roles

3

Storage and Content Delivery

In this chapter, we will cover the following recipes:

- Hosting a static website
- Caching a website
- Working with network storage
- Backing up data for compliance

Introduction

Each of these recipes is backed by a CloudFormation template that makes them quick and easy to reproduce and modify.

Storage

Storage is an integral part of any organization's cloud usage. When used correctly, servers are short-lived and replaceable. This means that having a durable, available storage service is critical to persisting and sharing state.

Here is a high-level summary of the storage services AWS offers:

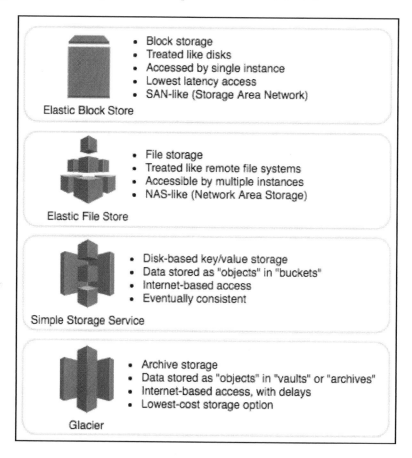

- Block storage
- Treated like disks
- Accessed by single instance
- Lowest latency access
- SAN-like (Storage Area Network)

Elastic Block Store

- File storage
- Treated like remote file systems
- Accessible by multiple instances
- NAS-like (Network Area Storage)

Elastic File Store

- Disk-based key/value storage
- Data stored as "objects" in "buckets"
- Internet-based access
- Eventually consistent

Simple Storage Service

- Archive storage
- Data stored as "objects" in "vaults" or "archives"
- Internet-based access, with delays
- Lowest-cost storage option

Glacier

Storage services from AWS

Elastic Block Store

Elastic Block Store (EBS) provides block-device storage as volumes to EC2 instances. It behaves similarly to a **storage area network** (SAN) and offers the lowest-latency access of the various storage services offered. EBS volumes can only be accessed by one instance at a time. The size of a volume must be specified when they are provisioned, and cannot be changed after.

Volumes are hosted on redundant hardware in a specific AZ, but they do not offer redundancy across AZs.

Some recommended use cases for EBS are:

- Instance boot volumes
- Intensive data processing
- Transactional writes

We will cover EBS in more detail in the `Chapter 4`, *Using AWS Compute*, as its primary use is as the underlying storage for EC2 instances.

Elastic File System

Elastic File System (EFS) provides a file-storage service that can be accessed simultaneously by many instances, similar to **Network Attached Storage** (**NAS**). While not as fast as EBS, it still provides low-latency access. As it may be accessed by multiple clients at a time, it can reach much higher levels of throughput than EBS. EFS filesystems also in size scale dynamically and so do not need to be preallocated or modified during use. Filesystems are stored redundantly across AZs.

Some recommended use cases for EFS are:

- Home directories
- Serving shared web content
- Content management

> EFS performance scales according to the filesystem size. As the filesystem size is not preallocated, the only way to increase your performance is to add more data to it.

Simple Storage Service

Simple Storage Service (**S3**) provides a web-based service for hosting files. Files are referred to as **objects** and grouped in **buckets**. Objects are effectively a key-value pair, similar to a document database. Keys are used like file paths, with / used as a separator and grouping character. Buckets can be easily accessed like a website via an automatically generated domain name.

Due to being associated with a domain name, bucket names must be *globally* unique.

Some recommended usecases for S3 are:

- Static website assets
- Sharing large files
- Short-term (a.k.a. *warm*) backups

Glacier

Glacier is a companion service to S3, but is the **cold** storage option. Cold storage is a service where you are not able to directly access your data; you must lodge a request for data to be restored (to S3), and you are notified when it is ready. A physical example of cold storage might be backup tapes that are stored in a secure location. Similar to S3, files are referred to as *objects*. Files are grouped together and stored in **archives**. Archives can be created and deleted, but never modified. Archives are grouped together in to **vaults**, which allow you to control access.

The shortest restoration time is 1-5 minutes (with limitations). Standard restoration times take 3-5 hours, with some other options available.

Some recommended usecases for Glacier are:

- Long-term (a.k.a. *cold*) backups
- Compliance backups

Content delivery

Content delivery is aimed at quickly and efficiently distributing your content to users. The best practice way to do this is to leverage a **Content Delivery Network (CDN)**. Amazon's CDN service is **Amazon CloudFront**.

While AWS currently has 14 regions, it has an additional 68 edge locations that can be used as part of CloudFront. This gives you a massive global network of resources you can use to improve your users' experience of your application.

CloudFront works closely with S3 to serve static assets. In addition to this, it can be configured to cache dynamic content. This gives you an easy way to improve the performance of applications that are not even aware of CloudFront.

CloudFront websites are referred to as **distributions** which speaks to their CDN role.

 Distributions can also be used to provide a common frontend for multiple, disparate, sources of content.

Hosting a static website

It's really easy to host a static website on AWS. It turns out it's also dirt cheap, fast, reliable, and massively scalable too.

You do this by storing your content in an S3 bucket and configuring that bucket to behave like a website.

It's important to note that we're talking about static content only. This method doesn't work for websites requiring server-side processing or some other backend functionality. WordPress, for example, requires PHP which means you need a fully functional web server to run it. S3 won't interpret PHP pages for you, it will just serve files straight to the browser.

So, why would you want to host a static website in S3? Common scenarios we see are:

- Simply, your website is completely static and you don't change it very often.
- Your company is launching a new product or service. You're expecting very large numbers of customers to visit a mini-site within a short time period; likely more traffic than your existing web hosting environment can handle.
- You need somewhere to host a failover or *down for maintenance* style page which is separate from your existing web hosting environment.

HTTPS is not supported by S3 when it is used to serve static content.

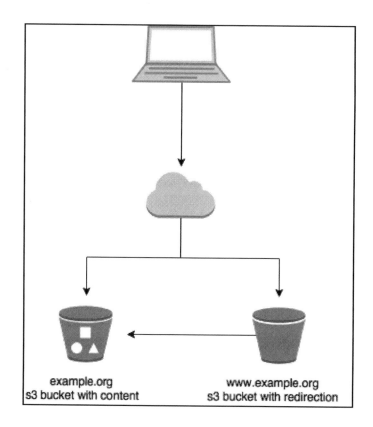

How to do it...

This recipe provides you with the CloudFormation necessary to create:

- An S3 bucket for hosting your content
- A Route 53 hosted zone and necessary DNS records
- A redirection from www to root/apex for your domain

After running this CloudFormation you will of course need to upload your content to the buckets which CloudFormation created for you.

Creating S3 buckets and hosting content

In this example, we're actually going to create two S3 buckets for our site
`http://www.example.org/`. They correspond to the hostnames:

- `www.example.org`
- `example.org`

 It might be a good time to remind you that S3 bucket names are globally unique. You'll also need to substitute `example.org` for a domain which you own.

1. We're going to put all our content in our `example.org` bucket and tell S3 that requests to `www.example.org` should be redirected to the other bucket. Here's what the relevant parts of the CloudFormation would look like for creating these buckets (note that we'll be expanding on this example as we proceed through this recipe):

```
Resources:
  ApexBucket:
    Type: AWS::S3::Bucket
    Properties:
      BucketName: !Ref DomainName
  WWWBucket:
    Type: AWS::S3::Bucket
    Properties:
      BucketName: !Sub
        - www.${Domain}
        - Domain: !Ref DomainName
```

2. We won't be hardcoding our domain name into the bucket names. Instead we're going to supply our domain as a parameter to the CloudFormation template in order to maximize its reusability, then reference it via `!Ref DomainName`. To keep this recipe as simple as possible we're going to set up a single page website. In the real world, your website will of course consist of multiple files but the process you need to follow is exactly the same.

3. Configuring the index document:
   - The **index** document is the file which S3 will serve by default when someone types your domain name into the address bar in their browser. This precludes the user from having to type the full path to a file, that is, example.org/index.html.
   - Typically, your index document will be called index.html. We'll provide a code snippet for this file towards the end of this chapter.

4. Configuring the error document:
   - The **error** document is the file S3 will serve if something goes wrong (missing files, forbidden access, bad requests, and so on). To keep things consistent we're going to call ours error.html. Again, we'll provide a code snippet for this later in the chapter.

5. Enabling website hosting on your bucket:
   - As mentioned previously, we're going to need to tell S3 that it should serve static website content from our example.org bucket. Often users will perform this configuration through the S3 web console. We're going to do it in CloudFormation however. The CLI also offers a nice one-liner for doing this. You're not going to need to run this command, we're just adding it here for reference:

```
aws s3 website s3://example.org/
    --index-document index.html --error-document error.html
```

6. Setting up redirection from the www hostname:
   - When performing this task manually one has little option but to fire up the web console and configure the www.example.org bucket to redirect to the example.org bucket. There's no handy one-line CLI command for this one. Fortunately, it's easy in CloudFormation as you'll soon see in the upcoming CloudFormation snippet.

7. Configuring permissions:
   - The last bucket setup task is to configure permissions. By default S3 buckets are private and only the bucket owner can see its contents. This is not much use to us in this scenario because we need *everyone* to be able to see our bucket contents. This is a public website after all.

8. If we were configuring our bucket manually we would apply a bucket policy which looks something like this:

```
{
    "Version":"2012-10-17",
    "Statement": [{
        "Sid": "Allow Public Access to everything in our bucket",
        "Effect": "Allow",
        "Principal": "*",
        "Action": "s3:GetObject",
        "Resource": "arn:aws:s3:::example.org/*"
    }
  ]
}
```

9. Fortunately, in CloudFormation the task is much simpler. Building on the previous example, the Resources section of our CloudFormation template now looks like this:

```
ApexBucket:
  Type: AWS::S3::Bucket
  Properties:
    BucketName:
      Ref: DomainName
    AccessControl: PublicRead
    WebsiteConfiguration:
      IndexDocument: index.html
      ErrorDocument: error.html
WWWBucket:
  Type: AWS::S3::Bucket
  Properties:
    BucketName:
      Fn::Join: [ ., [ www, Ref: DomainName ] ]
    AccessControl: BucketOwnerFullControl
    WebsiteConfiguration:
      RedirectAllRequestsTo:
        HostName:
          Ref: ApexBucket
```

Creating a hosted zone

In order to start adding DNS records we first need to add a hosted zone to Route 53. As you can see in the following code, this is reasonably simple to do. The `Name` we are going to supply will be provided as a parameter to our CloudFormation template:

```
DNSHostedZone:
  Type: "AWS::Route53::HostedZone"
  Properties:
    Name:
      Ref: DomainName
```

Creating DNS records

1. Now that we have a hosted zone we can go ahead and create DNS records for it. For this we use the AWS resource type `AWS::Route53::RecordSetGroup`.

2. We're going to create an A record for our domain's `root/apex` entry and we'll make it an alias. This alias will be configured to point to the AWS endpoint for S3-hosted websites in the particular region we choose to run this CloudFormation in.

3. In order to archive region portability in our template, we'll use a *mapping* to provide all the endpoints. The values in this map are published by AWS in their API endpoints documentation. You won't need to look these up, however, because our code sample provides the most up-to-date endpoints (as of the time of writing this). The endpoints tend not to change, but the list obviously grows when AWS adds more regions.

4. The mapping will look like this:

```
us-east-1:
  S3HostedZoneID: Z3AQBSTGFYJSTF
  S3AliasTarget: s3-website-us-east-1.amazonaws.com
us-east-2:
  S3HostedZoneID: Z2O1EMRO9K5GLX
  S3AliasTarget: s3-website.us-east-2.amazonaws.com
```

We'll also need a `CNAME` for `www` which will point at our `WWWBucket` so that redirection can take place. The final resource for our DNS records will look like this:

```
DNSRecords:
  Type: "AWS::Route53::RecordSetGroup"
  Properties:
    HostedZoneId:
```

```
          Ref: DNSHostedZone
      RecordSets:
        - Name:
            Ref: DomainName
          Type: A
          AliasTarget:
            HostedZoneId:
              Fn::FindInMap: [ RegionMap, Ref: "AWS::Region",
                S3HostedZoneID ]
            DNSName:
              Fn::FindInMap: [ RegionMap, Ref: "AWS::Region",
                S3AliasTarget ]
        - Name:
            Fn::Join: [ ., [ www, Ref: DomainName ] ]
          Type: CNAME
          TTL: 300
          ResourceRecords:
            - Fn::GetAtt: WWWBucket.DomainName
```

5. We're ready for launch. It's time to create our CloudFormation stack. You can do so using the following CLI command:

```
aws cloudformation create-stack \
  --stack-name static-website-1 \
  --template-body file://03-hosting-a-static-website.yaml \
  --parameters \
  ParameterKey=DomainName,ParameterValue=<your-domain-name>
```

Uploading website content

It's now time to upload some content to our S3 buckets. Here are the snippets we promised you earlier. There's nothing fancy here. Once you've got these examples working, you can try replacing them with your real website content:

- `index.html`

```html
<html>
  <head>
    <title>Welcome to exmaple.org</title>
  </head>
  <body>
    <h1>example.org</h1>
    <p>Hello World!</p>
  </body>
</html>
```

- `error.html`

```html
<html>
  <head>
    <title>Error</title>
  </head>
  <body>
    <h1>example.org</h1>
    <p>Something went wrong!</p>
  </body>
</html>
```

How it works...

That's it! As soon as S3 has an `index.html` file to serve up, you will be hosting a single-page website on S3. Go ahead and test it out. The supplied CloudFormation example will output a URL you can use to see your new website. After you've verified it's working, you can go ahead and upload your real static website and enjoy fast, cheap, and server-free hosting.

There's more...

Let's look at some additional things to consider.

Delegating your domain to AWS

While we've created a hosted zone and some DNS records in Route 53, no one can actually see them yet. In order to send your website visitors to your new S3 static website, you'll need to delegate your domain to Route 53. This is left to you as an exercise; however, there are some important things to remember:

- The DNS servers to delegate your domain to can be found in the NS record for your hosted zone.
- If your domain is already live and production-like, you'll need to make sure all your DNS records for your zone are recreated in Route 53, including things such as MX records, which are critical for the continuity of your e-mail service.
- Before delegating to AWS, you may consider reducing the TTL values on your DNS records. This will be useful if for some reason you need to re-delegate or make changes to them. Once your DNS setup is stable, you can increase TTLs.

Cross-origin resource sharing

It's worth discussing **cross-origin resource sharing (CORS)** here because the more static web content hosting you do in S3, the higher your chances are of needing to know about this, particularly where web fonts are concerned.

Some browsers implement a *same origin* policy restriction. This prevents the browser from loading certain kinds of assets from hostnames that are different from the page being displayed to the user. Web fonts fall under this restriction and are an often-cited example because when they don't load correctly, your website will usually look a lot different to how you intended. The solution to this is to add a CORS configuration to your bucket to allow its content to be loaded by the particular origin or hostname that requested it.

We'll leave the CORS configuration out of our full example, but if you need to add one to your bucket, here's how you can do it. Update your `AllowedOrigins` property to look similar to the following CloudFormation and you should be all set:

```
ApexBucket:
  Type: AWS::S3::Bucket
  Properties:
    BucketName: !Ref DomainName
    AccessControl: PublicRead
    WebsiteConfiguration:
      IndexDocument: index.html
      ErrorDocument: error.html
    CorsConfiguration:
      CorsRules:
```

```
        - AllowedOrigins:
            - example.net
            - www.example.net
            - example.com
            - www.example.com
        AllowedMethods:
            - GET
        MaxAge: 3000
        AllowedHeaders:
            - Content-*
            - Host
```

Caching a website

In this recipe, we'll show you how to use AWS CloudFront to cache your website.

The primary reasons you'll want to consider doing this are as follows:

- Copies of your content will be geographically located closer to your end users, thus improving their experience and delivering content to them faster.
- The burden for serving content will be removed from your fleet of servers. This could potentially result in a large cost saving if you're able to turn off some servers or reduce your bandwidth bill.
- You may need to be shielded from large and unexpected spikes in traffic.
- While not the focus of this chapter, CloudFront gives you the ability to implement **Web Application Firewall (WAF)** as an added layer of protection from the bad guys.

 Unlike most AWS services, which are region specific, CloudFront is a *global* service.

Getting ready

First of all, you're going to need a publicly accessible website. This could be a static website hosted in S3, or it could be a dynamically generated website hosted in EC2. In fact, your website doesn't even need to be hosted in AWS in order to use CloudFront. As long as your website is publicly accessible, you should be good to go.

You'll also need to have the ability to modify the DNS records for your website. Instead of pointing to your web server (or S3 bucket), we'll eventually point them to CloudFront.

About dynamic content

If your website consists of mostly dynamic content, you can still benefit from implementing CloudFront.

First of all, CloudFront will maintain a pool of persistent connections with your origin servers. This lessens the time it takes for files to be served to your users because the number of three-way handshakes they'll need to perform is reduced.

Second, CloudFront implements some additional optimizations around TCP connections for high performance. More data is able to initially be transferred over the wire because CloudFront uses a wider initial TCP window.

Finally, implementing a CDN such as CloudFront *does* give you the opportunity to review your caching strategy and how you use cache-control headers. If your home page is dynamically generated, you'll get some benefit straight away by serving it via CloudFront, but the benefits will be much greater if you were to let CloudFront cache it for a few minutes. Again, cost, end user, and backend performance are all things you should take into consideration.

Configuring CloudFront distributions

Distributions can be configured with a fairly wide array of options. Our recipe is going to be quite simple so that you can get up and running as quickly as possible. But we will talk through some of the more common configuration options:

- **Origins**: A distribution needs to have at least one origin. An origin, as the name indicates, is where your website content originates from your public-facing website. The properties you'll most likely be concerned with are:
    - **Origin Domain Name**: This is the hostname of your public-facing website. The CloudFormation template we supply accepts this hostname as a parameter.
    - **Origin Path**: It's possible to configure the distribution to fetch content from a directory or subfolder at the origin, for example, `/content/images` if you were using CloudFront to cache images only. In our case, we are caching our entire website, so we don't specify an **Origin Path** at all.

- **Origin ID**: This is particularly important when you are using nondefault cache behavior settings and therefore have configured multiple origins. You need to assign a unique ID to the origins so that the cache behaviors know which origin to target. There'll be more discussion on cache behaviors later.
- **HTTP Port, HTTPS Port**: If your origin is listening on nonstandard ports for HTTP or HTTPS, you would use these parameters to define those ports.
- **Origin Protocol Policy**: You are able to configure the distribution to talk to your origin via:
  - **HTTP Only**
  - **HTTPS Only**
  - **Match Viewer**

  The **Match Viewer** option forwards requests to the origin based on which protocol the user requested with in their browser. Again, we are keeping things quite simple in this recipe, so we'll be opting for **HTTP Only**.

- **Logging**: Keep in mind that because less traffic will be hitting your origin, fewer access logs will also be captured. It makes sense to have CloudFront keep these logs for us in an S3 bucket. This is included in the CloudFormation provided with this recipe:
  - **Cache behaviors**: In this recipe, we'll configure a single (default) cache behavior, which will forward all requests to our origin.
  - **CloudFront**: It allows you to get quite fine grained with the behaviors you configure. You might, for example, want to apply a rule to all the `.js` and `.css` files on your origin. Perhaps you want to forward query strings to the origin for these file types. Similarly, you might want to ignore the TTL the origin is trying to set for image files, instead telling CloudFront to cache for a minimum of 24 hours.
- **Aliases**: These are additional hostnames you want the distribution to serve traffic for. For example, if your **Origin Domain Name** is configured to `loadbalancer.example.org`, then you probably want aliases that look something like this:
  - `example.org`
  - `www.example.org`

The CloudFormation template provided with this recipe expects one or more aliases to be provided in the form of a comma-delimited list of strings.

- **Allowed HTTP Methods**: By default, CloudFront will only forward **GET** and **HEAD** requests to your origin. This recipe doesn't change those defaults, so we don't declare this parameter in the provided template. If your origin is serving dynamically generated content, then you will likely want to declare this parameter and set its values to **GET, HEAD, OPTIONS, PUT, POST, PATCH,** and **DELETE**.

- TTLs (minimum/maximum/default): You can optionally define how long you'd like objects to stay in CloudFront's caches before expiring and being refetched from the origin. Again, we've opted to stick to CloudFront's default values to keep this recipe simple, so we've omitted this parameter from our template. The defaults are as follows:
    - **Minimum TTL**: 0 seconds
    - **Default TTL**: 1 day
    - **Maximum TTL**: 1 year

- **Price Class**: By default, CloudFront will serve your content from all of its edge locations, giving you the maximum performance possible. We're going to deploy our distribution using the lowest possible price class, **Price Class** *100*. This corresponds to edge locations in the United States, Canada, and Europe. Users from Australia would not benefit too much from this **Price Class**, but you're also paying less for it. **Price Class** *200* adds Asian regions, and **Price Class** *All* adds South America and Australia.

 A comprehensive list and detailed explanation on which values can be specified when creating a CloudFront distribution can be found here at `ht tp://docs.aws.amazon.com/AmazonCloudFront/latest/DeveloperGuid e/distribution-web-values-specify.html`.

How to do it...

The first (and only) thing we need to do is configure a CloudFront distribution as shown in the following diagram:

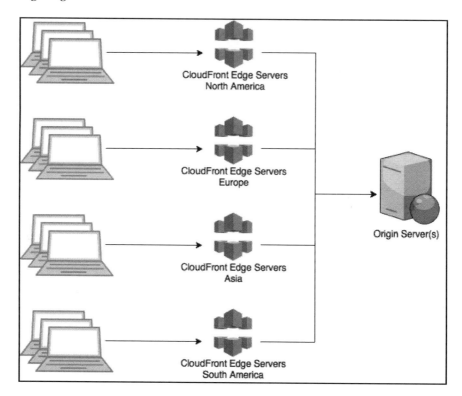

1. Create a new CloudFormation template and add the following code:

```
AWSTemplateFormatVersion: '2010-09-09'
Parameters:
  OriginDomainName:
    Description: The hostname of your origin
      (i.e. www.example.org.s3-website-ap-southeast-2.amazonaws.com)
    Type: String
  Aliases:
    Description: Comma delimited list of aliases
      (i.e. example.org,www.example.org)
    Type: CommaDelimitedList
Resources:
  DistributionALogBucket:
    Type: AWS::S3::Bucket
```

```
    DistributionA:
      Type: AWS::CloudFront::Distribution
      Properties:
        DistributionConfig:
          Origins:
          - DomainName:
              Ref: OriginDomainName
            Id: OriginA
            CustomOriginConfig:
              OriginProtocolPolicy: http-only
          Enabled: true
          Logging:
            IncludeCookies: false
            Bucket:
              Fn::GetAtt: DistributionALogBucket.DomainName
            Prefix: cf-distribution-a
          Aliases:
            Ref: Aliases
          DefaultCacheBehavior:
            TargetOriginId: OriginA
            ForwardedValues:
              QueryString: false
            ViewerProtocolPolicy: allow-all
          PriceClass: PriceClass_100
  Outputs:
    DistributionDomainName:
      Description: The domain name of the CloudFront Distribution
      Value:
        Fn::GetAtt: DistributionA.DomainName
    LogBucket:
      Description: Bucket where CloudFront logs will be stored
      Value:
        Ref: DistributionALogBucket
```

2. Using the template we created above, go ahead and create your CloudFront distribution. Expect to wait around 20-25 minutes for this stack to finish creating. It takes a while for your distribution configuration to be pushed out to all the AWS CloudFront locations:

```
aws cloudformation create-stack \
  --stack-name cloudfont-cache-1 \
  --template-body file://03-caching-a-website.yaml \
  --parameters \
  ParameterKey=OriginDomainName,ParameterValue=<your-domain-name> \
  ParameterKey=Aliases,ParameterValue='<alias-1>\,<alias-2>'
```

Working with network storage

In this recipe, we will use the Amazon EFS to provide network-based storage to instances.

Some of the benefits of using EFS compared to other AWS services are as follows:

- Guaranteed write order between distributed clients
- Automatic resizing—no need to preallocate and no need to downsize
- You only pay for the space you use (per GB)—no transfer or extra costs

Getting ready

This example works with the default VPC and subnets, present in all AWS accounts when they are created. Even if you have changed you network configuration, all you need is a working VPC with two or more subnets in different AZs for this recipe.

How to do it...

1. Open your favorite text editor, and start a new CloudFormation template by defining the AWSTemplateFormatVersion and Description:

   ```
   AWSTemplateFormatVersion: "2010-09-09"
   Description: Create an EFS file system and endpoints.
   ```

2. Create a top-level Parameters section, and define the required parameters, VpcId and SubnetIds, inside it:

   ```
   VpcId:
     Description: VPC ID that contains the subnets that will
       access the file system
     Type: AWS::EC2::VPC::Id
   SubnetIds:
     Description: Subnet IDs allowed to access the EFS file system
     Type: List<AWS::EC2::Subnet::Id>
   ```

3. Create a top-level Resources property, which will contain all the resources defined.

4. Under the `Resources` property, add the `EFS` filesystem resource:

```
FileSystem:
  Type: AWS::EFS::FileSystem
  Properties:
    FileSystemTags:
      - Key: Name
        Value:
          Fn::Sub: "${AWS::StackName} EFS File System"
    PerformanceMode: generalPurpose
```

5. Add mount target resources for connecting to the filesystem you just created:

```
MountTargetA:
  Type: AWS::EFS::MountTarget
  Properties:
    FileSystemId:
      Ref: FileSystem
    SecurityGroups:
      - Fn::GetAtt: MountTargetSecurityGroup.GroupId
    SubnetId:
      Fn::Select: [ 0, Ref: SubnetIds ]
MountTargetB:
  Type: AWS::EFS::MountTarget
  Properties:
    FileSystemId:
      Ref: FileSystem
    SecurityGroups:
      - Fn::GetAtt: MountTargetSecurityGroup.GroupId
    SubnetId:
      Fn::Select: [ 1, Ref: SubnetIds ]
```

6. Create a security group to control access to the mount targets:

```
MountTargetSecurityGroup:
  Type: AWS::EC2::SecurityGroup
  Properties:
    GroupDescription: EFS endpoint security group
    Tags:
      - Key: Name
        Value: MountTargetSecurityGroup
    VpcId:
      Ref: VpcId
```

7. Create a security group to access the mount target security group you created in the previous step:

```
MountTargetAccessSecurityGroup:
  Type: AWS::EC2::SecurityGroup
  Properties:
    GroupDescription: EFS endpoint access security group
  Tags:
    - Key: Name
      Value: MountTargetAccessSecurityGroup
  VpcId:
    Ref: VpcId
```

8. Define the ingress and egress rules for the mount target security group:

```
MountTargetIngress:
  Type: AWS::EC2::SecurityGroupIngress
  Properties:
    FromPort: 2049
    GroupId:
      Fn::GetAtt: MountTargetSecurityGroup.GroupId
    IpProtocol: tcp
    SourceSecurityGroupId:
      Fn::GetAtt: MountTargetAccessSecurityGroup.GroupId
    ToPort: 2049
MountTargetEgress:
  Type: AWS::EC2::SecurityGroupEgress
  Properties:
    DestinationSecurityGroupId:
      Fn::GetAtt: MountTargetAccessSecurityGroup.GroupId
    FromPort: 2049
    GroupId:
      Fn::GetAtt: MountTargetSecurityGroup.GroupId
    IpProtocol: tcp
    ToPort: 2049
```

9. Define the ingress and egress rules for the mount target access security group:

```
MountTargetAccessIngress:
  Type: AWS::EC2::SecurityGroupIngress
  Properties:
    FromPort: 22
    GroupId:
      Fn::GetAtt: MountTargetAccessSecurityGroup.GroupId
    IpProtocol: tcp
    CidrIp: 0.0.0.0/0
    ToPort: 22
MountTargetAccessEgress:
  Type: AWS::EC2::SecurityGroupEgress
  Properties:
    DestinationSecurityGroupId:
      Fn::GetAtt: MountTargetSecurityGroup.GroupId
    FromPort: 2049
    GroupId:
      Fn::GetAtt: MountTargetAccessSecurityGroup.GroupId
    IpProtocol: tcp
    ToPort: 2049
```

10. Save your template with the name `03-working-with-network-storage.yaml`.

11. Launch the CloudFormation stack with the following AWS CLI command, substituting your own VPC ID and subnet IDs:

```
aws cloudformation create-stack \
  --stack-name wwns1 \
  --template-body file://03-working-with-network-storage.yaml \
  --parameters \
  ParameterKey=VpcId,ParameterValue=<your-vpc-id> \
  ParameterKey=SubnetIds,ParameterValue="<subnet-id-1>\, \
    <subnet-id-2>"
```

How it works...

Here is what the created resources will look like at the end of the recipe:

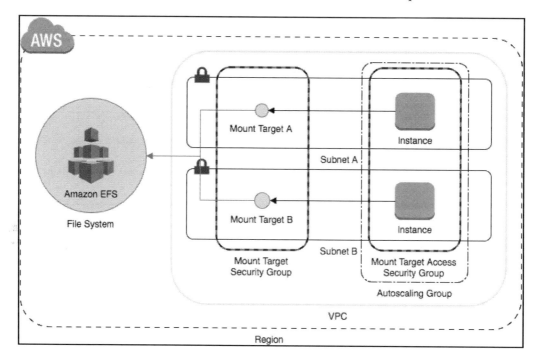

Working with network storage

We start by creating the standard CloudFormation template properties in step 1.

In step 2, you define the template's parameters that will be used when configuring the resources.

Steps 3 and 4 are where the EFS resources are specified. They consist of an EFS filesystem and mount targets in each of the AZs that will access it.

We then create the security groups in steps 5 and 6: one for the mount targets and one for the instances that are allowed to connect to the mount targets.

As these two security groups contain two-way (or circular) references to each other, we must define the rules between them in separate resources in steps 7 and 8.

In step 9, you save the template with a specific filename so that it can be referenced in the command to launch the stack in step 10.

There's more...

To confirm that your EFS filesystem, mount targets, and security groups are working, you can also provision some client instances to connect to them. Add the following resources and parameters to the template you have already created:

1. Add the following parameters to your top-level `Parameters` section to configure your instances:

```
MountPoint:
  Description: The path on disk to mount the EFS file system
  Type: String
  Default: /mnt/efs
KeyName:
  Description: The SSH key pair allowed to connect to the client
    instance
  Type: AWS::EC2::KeyPair::KeyName
```

2. Add an `AutoScalingGroup` under the `Resources` section; regardless of which AZ your servers are provisioned to, they will have access to the `EFS` filesystem via the local mount point:

```
AutoScalingGroup:
  Type: AWS::AutoScaling::AutoScalingGroup
  DependsOn: MountTargetA
  Properties:
    MinSize: 2
    MaxSize: 2
    LaunchConfigurationName:
      Ref: LaunchConfiguration
    Tags:
      - Key: Name
        Value:
          Fn::Sub: "${AWS::StackName} EFS Client"
        PropagateAtLaunch: true
    VPCZoneIdentifier:
      Ref: SubnetIds
```

3. Still in the `Resources` section, add a launch configuration:

```
LaunchConfiguration:
  Type: AWS::AutoScaling::LaunchConfiguration
  DependsOn: FileSystem
  Properties:
    ImageId: ami-1e299d7e
    SecurityGroups:
```

```
    - Ref: MountTargetAccessSecurityGroup
InstanceType: t2.micro
KeyName:
  Ref: KeyName
UserData:
  Fn::Base64:
  Fn::Sub: |
    #!/bin/bash -xe
    mkdir -p ${MountPoint}
    echo 'Waiting for mount target DNS to propagate'
    sleep 90
    echo '${FileSystem}.efs.${AWS::Region}.amazonaws.com:/
    ${MountPoint} nfs4
    nfsvers=4.1,rsize=1048576,wsize=1048576,hard,timeo=600,
    retrans=2 0 0' >>
    /etc/fstab
    mount -a\nchown ec2-user: ${MountPoint}\n"
```

4. Launch the CloudFormation stack with the following AWS CLI command, substituting your own parameter values:

```
aws cloudformation create-stack \
  --stack-name wwns1 \
  --template-body file://03-working-with-network-storage.yaml \
  --parameters \
  ParameterKey=VpcId,ParameterValue=<vpc-id> \
  ParameterKey=SubnetIds,ParameterValue='<subnet-id-1>\, \
    <subnet-id-1>' \
  ParameterKey=MountPoint,ParameterValue=<local-path-to-mount-efs> \
  ParameterKey=KeyName,ParameterValue=<existing-key-pair-name>
```

Once the new stack is ready, you will be able to SSH to your instances and verify that they have mounted the EFS filesystem.

Backing up data for compliance

We work with a lot of companies (especially in the finance industry) that have strict rules around the minimum time data needs to be kept for. This can become quite onerous and expensive if you need to keep customer records for a minimum of 7 years, for example.

Using S3, Glacier, and life cycle rules, we can create a flexible long-term backup solution while also automating the archiving and purging of backups and reducing costs.

We are also going to utilize *versioning* in order to mitigate the damaged caused by a file being accidentally deleted or overwritten in our backup bucket.

How to do it...

1. First, we need to define a few parameters:

   - ExpirationInDays: This is the maximum amount of time we want to have our files kept in backup for. We've set a default for this value of 2,555 days (7 years).

   - TransitionToInfrequentAccessInDays: After a backup has been copied to S3, we want to move it to the *infrequently accessed* class to reduce our costs. This doesn't affect the durability of the backup, but it does have a small impact on its availability. We'll set this to 30 days.

   - TransitionToGlacierInDays: After the backup has been kept in the infrequently accessed class for a while, we want to move it to Glacier. This again helps us reduce our costs at the expense of retrieval times. If we need to fetch a backup from Glacier, the wait time will be approximately 3-5 hours. We'll set the default for this to 60 days.

   - PreviousVersionsExpirationInDays: Given that we will have versioning enabled on our bucket, we want to make sure old versions of files aren't kept forever—we're using this feature only to mitigate accidents. We'll set this value to 60 days, which gives us more than enough time to identify and recover from an accidental deletion or overwrite.

   - PreviousVersionsToInfrequentAccessInDays: Just like our other backup files, we want to move our old versions to the infrequently accessed class after a period of time in order to minimize costs. We'll set this to 30 days:

   ```
   AWSTemplateFormatVersion: '2010-09-09'
   Parameters:
     ExpirationInDays:
       Description: The maximum amount of time to keep files
         for
       Type: Number
       Default: 2555
     TransitionToInfrequentAccessInDays:
       Description: How many days until files are moved to
         the Infrequent Access class
       Type: Number
       Default: 30
     TransitionToGlacierInDays:
       Description: How many days until files are moved
         to Glacier
       Type: Number
   ```

```
         Default: 60
      PreviousVersionsExpirationInDays:
         Description: The maximum amount of time to keep previous
            versions of files for
         Type: Number
         Default: 60
      PreviousVersionsToInfrequentAccessInDays:
         Description: How many days until previous versions
            of files are moved to the Infrequent Access class
         Type: Number
         Default: 30
```

2. Next, we'll need to create the S3 bucket to store our backups in. Note that we're omitting the `name` property for this bucket in order to avoid bucket name conflicts and maximize region portability. We're also enabling versioning and adding our life cycle rules from our previous `Parameters`:

```
Resources:
   BackupBucket:
      Type: AWS::S3::Bucket
      Properties:
         VersioningConfiguration:
            Status: Enabled
         LifecycleConfiguration:
            Rules:
               - Status: Enabled
                 ExpirationInDays:
                    Ref: ExpirationInDays
                 Transitions:
                    - StorageClass: STANDARD_IA
                      TransitionInDays:
                         Ref: TransitionToInfrequentAccessInDays
                    - StorageClass: GLACIER
                      TransitionInDays:
                         Ref: TransitionToGlacierInDays
                 NoncurrentVersionExpirationInDays:
                    Ref: PreviousVersionsExpirationInDays
                 NoncurrentVersionTransitions:
                    - StorageClass: STANDARD_IA
                      TransitionInDays:
                         Ref: PreviousVersionsToInfrequentAccessInDays
```

3. Finally, let's add an output so we know which bucket to store our backups in:

```
Outputs:
   BackupBucket:
      Description: Bucket where backups are stored
```

```
Value:
    Ref: BackupBucket
```

How it works...

Go ahead and launch this CloudFormation stack. If you're happy with the default values for the parameters, you don't need to provide them with the CLI command:

```
aws cloudformation create-stack \
  --stack-name backup-s3-glacier-1 \
  --template-body file://03-backing-up-data-for-compliance.yaml
```

Once the stack has been created, you'll be all set to start copying backups to the S3 bucket and to start worrying less about your backups' life cycle and management. If you decide that the expiry or transition times need to change after you've created the bucket, you can do this by simply updating the parameters for the stack.

4
Using AWS Compute

In this chapter, we will cover:

- Creating a key pair
- Launching an instance
- Attaching storage
- Securely accessing private instances
- Auto scaling an application server
- Creating machine images
- Creating security groups
- Creating a load balancer

Introduction

Elastic Cloud Compute (EC2) is by far the most utilized and complex service in the AWS catalogue. More than *just virtual machines*, EC2 provides a framework of sub-services to help you secure and manage your instances elastically.

Creating a key pair

A key pair is used to access your instances via SSH. This is the quickest and easiest way to access your instances.

Getting ready

To perform this recipe, you must have your AWS CLI tool configured correctly.

How to do it...

1. Create the key pair, and save it to disk:

```
aws ec2 create-key-pair \
  --key-name MyEC2KeyPair \
  --query 'KeyMaterial' \
  --output text > ec2keypair.pem
```

2. Change the permissions on the created file:

```
chmod 600 ec2keypair.pem
```

How it works...

This call requests a new private key from EC2. The response is then parsed using a JMESPath query, and the private key (in the `KeyMaterial` property) is saved to a new key file with the `.pem` extension.

Finally, we change the permissions on the key file so that it cannot be read by other users—this is required before SSH will allow you to use it.

Launching an instance

There will be scenarios—usually when testing and developing your infrastructure code—when you need quick access to an instance. Creating it via the AWS CLI is the quickest and most consistent way to create one-off instances.

There are other recipes in the book that will require a running instance. This recipe will get you started.

Getting ready

For this recipe, you must have an existing key pair.

In this recipe, we are launching an instance of AWS Linux using an AMI ID in the us-east-1 region. If you are working in a different region, you will need to update your image-id parameter.

You must have configured your AWS CLI tool with working credentials.

How to do it...

Run the following AWS CLI command, using your own key-pair name:

```
aws ec2 run-instances \
  --image-id ami-9be6f38c \
  --instance-type t2.micro \
  --key-name <your-key-pair-name>
```

How it works...

While you can create an instance via the AWS web console, it involves many distracting options. When developing and testing, the CLI tool is the best way to provision instances.

While the key-name argument is optional, you will not be able to connect to your instance unless you have pre-configured some other way of logging in.

 The t2.micro instance type used in this recipe is included in the AWS free tier. You can run one micro instance per month for free during the first 12 months of your usage. See https://aws.amazon.com/free for more information.

As no VPC or security groups are specified, the instance will be launched in your account's default VPC and security group. The default security group allows access from anywhere, on all ports, and so is not suitable for long-lived instances. You can modify an instance's security groups after it is launched, without stopping it.

There's more...

If you have created your own AMI, then you can change the `image-id` argument to quickly launch your specific AMI.

You may also want to take note of the `InstanceId` value in the response from the API, as you may need it for future commands.

See also

- The *Creating a key pair* recipe
- The *Creating machine images* recipe

Attaching storage

Ideally, you will have defined all your storage requirements up-front as code using a service such as CloudFormation. However, sometimes that is not possible due to application restrictions or changing requirements.

You can easily add additional storage to your instances while they are running by attaching a new volume.

Getting ready

For this recipe, you will need the following:

- A running instance's ID. It will start with `i-` followed by alphanumeric characters.
- The AZ the instance is running in. This looks like the region name with a letter after it; for example, `us-east-1a`.

In this recipe, we are using an AWS Linux instance. If you are using a different operating system, the steps to mount the volume will be different. We will be running an instance in the AZ `us-east-1a`.

You must have configured your AWS CLI tool with working credentials.

How to do it...

1. Create a volume:

```
aws ec2 create-volume --availability-zone us-east-1a
```

 Take note of the returned `VolumeId` in the response. It will start with `vol-` followed by alphanumeric characters.

2. Attach the volume to the instance, using the volume ID noted in the last step and the instance ID you started with:

```
aws ec2 attach-volume \
  --volume-id <your-volume-id> \
  --instance-id <your-instance-id> \
  --device /dev/sdf
```

3. On the instance itself, mount the volume device:

```
mount /dev/xvdf /mnt/volume
```

How it works...

In this recipe, we start by creating a volume. Volumes are created from snapshots. If you do not specify a snapshot ID it uses a blank snapshot, and you get a blank volume.

While volumes are hosted redundantly, they are only hosted in a single AZ, so must be provisioned in the same AZ the instance is running in.

The `create-volume` command returns a response that includes the newly created volume's `VolumeId`. We then use this ID in the next step.

 It can sometimes take a few seconds for a volume to become available. If you are scripting these commands, use the `aws ec2 wait` command to wait for the volume to become available.

In step 3, we attach a volume to the instance. When attaching to an instance, you must specify the name of the device that it will be presented to the operating system as. Unfortunately, this does not guarantee what the device will appear as. In the case of AWS Linux, `/dev/sdf` becomes `/dev/xvdf`.

 Device naming is kernel-specific, so if you are using something other than AWS Linux, the device name may be different. See `http://docs.aws.amazon.com/AWSEC2/latest/UserGuide/device_naming .html` for full details.

See also

- The *Launching an instance* recipe
- The *Working with network storage* recipe in `Chapter 3`, *Storage and Content Delivery*

Securely accessing private instances

Any instance or resource living in a private subnet in your VPC will be inaccessible from the Internet. This makes good sense from a security perspective because it gives your instances a higher level of protection.

Of course, if they can't be accessed from the Internet, then they're not going to be easy to administer.

One common pattern is to use a VPN server as a single, highly controlled, entry point to your private network. This is what we're going to show you in this recipe, as pictured in the following diagram:

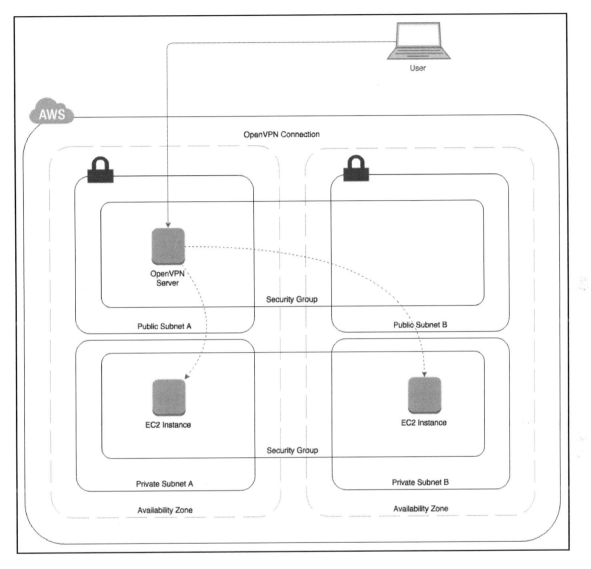

Accessing private instances securely

Getting ready

We're going to use OpenVPN for this example. They provide a free (for up to two users) AMI in the AWS marketplace, which has OpenVPN already installed and configured. You'll need to accept the terms and conditions for using this AMI. You can do so by visiting the AMI's marketplace page at `https://aws.amazon.com/marketplace/pp/B00MI40CAE/`.

You need to decide on a password, which will be your *temporary* admin password. We'll feed this password into a CloudFormation template and then change it after we create our stack.

> You can use the default VPC for this example.

How to do it...

1. Create a new CloudFormation template and add the following Mappings. This is a list of all the latest OpenVPN AMIs in each region. We're adding these to maximize region portability for our template—you can omit the regions you have no intention of using:

```
Mappings:
  AWSRegion2AMI: # Latest OpenVPN AMI at time of publishing: 2.1.4
    us-east-1:
      AMI: ami-bc3566ab
    us-east-2:
      AMI: ami-10306a75
    us-west-2:
      AMI: ami-d3e743b3
    us-west-1:
      AMI: ami-4a02492a
    eu-west-1:
      AMI: ami-f53d7386
    eu-central-1:
      AMI: ami-ad1fe6c2
    ap-southeast-1:
      AMI: ami-a859ffcb
    ap-northeast-1:
      AMI: ami-e9da7c88
    ap-southeast-2:
      AMI: ami-89477aea
    sa-east-1:
      AMI: ami-0c069b60
```

2. We now need to define some `Parameters`. Firstly we'll need to know which VPC and subnet to deploy our VPN instance to. Note that you need to specify a *public* subnet here, otherwise you won't be able to access your OpenVPN server:

```
VpcId:
  Type: AWS::EC2::VPC::Id
  Description: VPC where load balancer and instance will launch
SubnetId:
  Type: List<AWS::EC2::Subnet::Id>
  Description: Subnet where OpenVPN server will launch
    (pick at least 1)
```

3. We also need to define `InstanceType` and `KeyName`. These are the EC2 instance class and SSH key pair to use to launch our OpenVPN server:

```
InstanceType:
  Type: String
  Description: OpenVPN server instance type
  Default: m3.medium
KeyName:
  Type: AWS::EC2::KeyPair::KeyName
  Description: EC2 KeyPair for SSH access
```

4. We need a parameter for `AdminPassword`. This is the temporary password which will be given to the `openvpn` user (administrator) when the server starts up:

```
AdminPassword:
  Type: String
  Description: Password for 'openvpn' user
  Default: openvpn
  NoEcho: true
```

5. The last parameter is the CIDR block, which we wish to allow to connect to our VPN server. You may wish to lock this down to the public IP range of your corporate network, for example:

```
AllowAccessFromCIDR:
  Type: String
  Description: IP range/address to allow VPN connections from
  Default: "0.0.0.0/0"
```

6. The first `Resource` we need to define is the security group our OpenVPN server will live in. You'll also use this security group to allow access to other resources in your network. Add it to your template as follows:

```
VPNSecurityGroup:
  Type: AWS::EC2::SecurityGroup
  Properties:
    GroupDescription: Inbound access to OpenVPN server
    VpcId: !Ref VpcId
    SecurityGroupIngress:
    - CidrIp: !Ref AllowAccessFromCIDR
      FromPort: 443
      IpProtocol: tcp
      ToPort: 443
    - CidrIp: !Ref AllowAccessFromCIDR
      FromPort: 22
      IpProtocol: tcp
      ToPort: 22
    - CidrIp: !Ref AllowAccessFromCIDR
      FromPort: 1194
      IpProtocol: udp
      ToPort: 1194
```

7. We can now define the actual OpenVPN instance itself. You'll notice that we are explicitly configuring the network interface. This is required, because we want to declare that this instance must get a public IP address (otherwise you won't be able to access it). In the `UserData`, we declare some variables that the OpenVPN software will pick up when it starts so that it can configure itself:

```
OpenVPNInstance:
  Type: AWS::EC2::Instance
  Properties:
    ImageId: !FindInMap [ AWSRegion2AMI, !Ref "AWS::Region", AMI ]
    InstanceType: !Ref InstanceType
    KeyName: !Ref KeyName
    NetworkInterfaces:
      - AssociatePublicIpAddress: true
        DeviceIndex: "0"
        GroupSet:
          - !Ref VPNSecurityGroup
        SubnetId: !Select [ 0, Ref: SubnetId ]
    Tags:
      - Key: Name
        Value: example-openvpn-server
    UserData:
      Fn::Base64: !Sub
        - |
```

```
public_hostname=openvpn
admin_user=openvpn
admin_pw=${admin_pw}
reroute_gw=1
reroute_dns=1
- admin_pw: !Ref AdminPassword
```

8. Finally, we add some helpful `Outputs`:

```
Outputs:
  OpenVPNAdministration:
    Value:
      Fn::Join:
        - ""
        - - https://
          - !GetAtt OpenVPNInstance.PublicIp
          - /admin/
    Description: Admin URL for OpenVPN server
  OpenVPNClientLogin:
    Value:
      Fn::Join:
        - ""
        - - https://
          - !GetAtt OpenVPNInstance.PublicIp
          - /
    Description: Client login URL for OpenVPN server
  OpenVPNServerIPAddress:
    Value: !GetAtt OpenVPNInstance.PublicIp
    Description: IP address for OpenVPN server
```

9. Go ahead and launch this stack in the CloudFormation web console, or via the CLI, with the following command:

```
aws cloudformation create-stack \
  --template-body file://04-securely-access-private-instances.yaml \
  --stack-name example-vpn \
  --parameters \
  ParameterKey=KeyName,ParameterValue=<key-pair-name> \
  ParameterKey=VpcId,ParameterValue=<your-vpc-id> \
  ParameterKey=SubnetId,ParameterValue=<your-public-subnet-id>
```

Configuration

1. Once your stack is created, you'll want to change the password for the `openvpn` user (administrator). Go to the admin control panel and do this now: `https://<ip-or-hostname-of-vpn-server>/admin`. If your VPN server is operating as expected you'll be greeted with a status page after logging in, as pictured in the following screenshot:

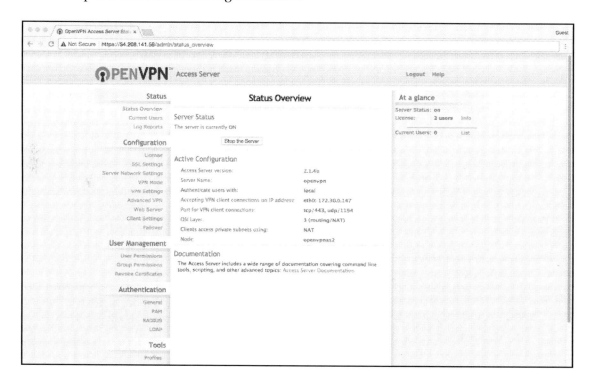

While you're there, you should create a non-administrator user account. This will be the account you'll use to connect to the VPN. Add this account on the **User Permissions** page as pictured in the following screenshot:

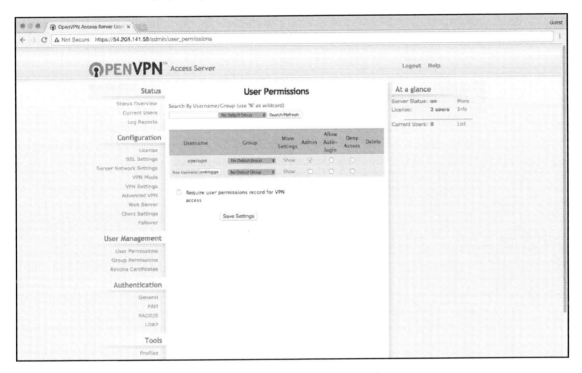

2. Under **Server Network Settings**, in the **Hostname or IP address** field, enter the hostname or IP address of the server. This step is important, and when you download your OpenVPN config file from the server (next step), it will make your life much easier if it has the correct hostname or IP address in it. The next screenshot shows what you can expect to see on the **Server Network Settings** page:

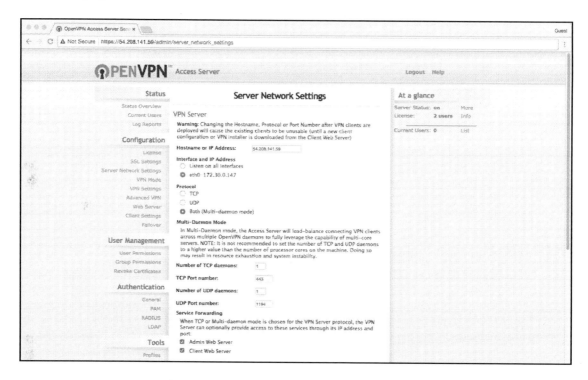

How it works...

You should now be able to connect to your VPN server. Go to the user login page and log in with the credentials you gave to the previously mentioned non-administrator user:

```
https://<ip-or-hostname-of-vpn-server>/
```

After logging in, you will have the option to download the OpenVPN client with configuration which is specific to your account. Alternatively, if you already have a VPN client installed, you can just download the configuration on its own.

There's more...

There are a couple of important points you'll need to keep in mind now that you are up and running with an OpenVPN server:

- If you need to SSH to the instance, you must connect with the username `openvpnas`
- To access your other instances, you'll need to allow connections from the VPN security group created in this recipe

Auto scaling an application server

Auto scaling is a fundamental component of compute in the cloud. It provides not only the ability to scale up and down in response to application load, but also redundancy, by ensuring that capacity is always available. Even in the unlikely event of an AZ outage, the auto scaling group will ensure that instances are available to run your application.

Auto scaling also allows you to pay for only the EC2 capacity you need, because underutilized servers can be automatically de-provisioned.

Getting ready

You must supply two or more subnet IDs for this recipe to work.

The following example uses an AWS Linux AMI in the `us-east-1` region. Update the parameters as required if you are working in a different region.

How to do it...

1. Start by defining the template version and description:

```
AWSTemplateFormatVersion: "2010-09-09"
Description: Create an Auto Scaling Group
```

2. Add a `Parameters` section with the required parameters that will be used later in the template:

```
Parameters:
  SubnetIds:
```

```
Description: Subnet IDs where instances can be launched
Type: List<AWS::EC2::Subnet::Id>
```

3. Still under the `Parameters` section, add the optional instance configuration parameters:

```
AmiId:
  Description: The application server's AMI ID
  Type: AWS::EC2::Image::Id
  Default: ami-9be6f38c # AWS Linux in us-east-1
InstanceType:
  Description: The type of instance to launch
  Type: String
  Default: t2.micro
```

4. Still under the `Parameters` section, add the optional auto scaling group-configuration parameters:

```
MinSize:
  Description: Minimum number of instances in the group
  Type: Number
  Default: 1
MaxSize:
  Description: Maximum number of instances in the group
  Type: Number
  Default: 4

ThresholdCPUHigh:
  Description: Launch new instances when CPU utilization
    is over this threshold
  Type: Number
  Default: 60

ThresholdCPULow:
  Description: Remove instances when CPU utilization
    is under this threshold
  Type: Number
  Default: 40

ThresholdMinutes:
  Description: Launch new instances when over the CPU
    threshold for this many minutes
  Type: Number
  Default: 5
```

5. Add a `Resources` section, and define the auto scaling group resource:

```
Resources:
  AutoScalingGroup:
    Type: AWS::AutoScaling::AutoScalingGroup
    Properties:
      MinSize: !Ref MinSize
      MaxSize: !Ref MaxSize
      LaunchConfigurationName: !Ref LaunchConfiguration
      Tags:
        - Key: Name
          Value: !Sub "${AWS::StackName} server"
          PropagateAtLaunch: true
      VPCZoneIdentifier: !Ref SubnetIds
```

6. Still under the `Resources` section, define the launch configuration used by the auto scaling group:

```
LaunchConfiguration:
  Type: AWS::AutoScaling::LaunchConfiguration
  Properties:
    ImageId: !Ref AmiId
    InstanceType: !Ref InstanceType
    UserData:
      Fn::Base64: !Sub |
        #!/bin/bash -xe
        # This will be run on startup, launch your application here
```

7. Next, define two scaling policy resources—one to scale up and the other to scale down:

```
ScaleUpPolicy:
  Type: AWS::AutoScaling::ScalingPolicy
  Properties:
    AdjustmentType: ChangeInCapacity
    AutoScalingGroupName: !Ref AutoScalingGroup
    Cooldown: 60
    ScalingAdjustment: 1

ScaleDownPolicy:
  Type: AWS::AutoScaling::ScalingPolicy
  Properties:
    AdjustmentType: ChangeInCapacity
    AutoScalingGroupName: !Ref AutoScalingGroup
    Cooldown: 60
    ScalingAdjustment: -1
```

8. Define an alarm that will alert when the CPU goes *over* the `ThresholdCPUHigh` parameter:

```
CPUHighAlarm:
  Type: AWS::CloudWatch::Alarm
  Properties:
    ActionsEnabled: true
    AlarmActions:
      - !Ref ScaleUpPolicy
    AlarmDescription: Scale up on CPU load
    ComparisonOperator: GreaterThanThreshold
    Dimensions:
      - Name: AutoScalingGroupName
        Value: !Ref AutoScalingGroup
    EvaluationPeriods: !Ref ThresholdMinutes
    MetricName: CPUUtilization
    Namespace: AWS/EC2
    Period: 60
    Statistic: Average
    Threshold: !Ref ThresholdCPUHigh
```

9. Finally, define an alarm that will alert when the CPU goes *under* the `ThresholdCPULow` parameter:

```
CPULowAlarm:
  Type: AWS::CloudWatch::Alarm
  Properties:
    ActionsEnabled: true
    AlarmActions:
      - !Ref ScaleDownPolicy
    AlarmDescription: Scale down on CPU load
    ComparisonOperator: LessThanThreshold
    Dimensions:
      - Name: AutoScalingGroupName
        Value: !Ref AutoScalingGroup
    EvaluationPeriods: !Ref ThresholdMinutes
    MetricName: CPUUtilization
    Namespace: AWS/EC2
    Period: 60
    Statistic: Average
    Threshold: !Ref ThresholdCPULow
```

10. Save the template with the filename `04-auto-scaling-an-application-server.yaml`.

11. Launch the template with the following AWS CLI command, supplying your subnet IDs:

```
aws cloudformation create-stack \
  --stack-name asg \
  --template-body file://04-auto-scaling-an-application-server.yaml \
  --parameters \
  ParameterKey=SubnetIds,ParameterValue='<subnet-id-1>\, \
    <subnet-id-2>'
```

How it works...

This example defines an auto scaling group and the dependent resources. These include the following:

- A launch configuration to use when launching new instances
- Two scaling policies, one to scale the number of instances up, and an inverse policy to scale back down
- An alarm to alert when the CPU crosses a certain threshold, for a certain number of minutes

The auto scaling group and launch-configuration resource objects in this example use mostly default values. You will need to specify your own `SecurityGroups` and a `KeyName` parameter in the `LaunchConfiguration` resource configuration if you want to be able to connect to the instances (for example, via SSH).

AWS will automatically take care of spreading your instances evenly over the subnets you have configured, so make sure they are in different AZs! When scaling down, the oldest instances will be removed before the newer ones.

Scaling policies

The scaling policies detail how many instances to create or delete when they are triggered. It also defines a `Cooldown` value, which helps prevent *flapping* servers—when servers are created and deleted before they have finished starting and are useful.

> While the scaling policies in this example use equal values, you might want to change that so your application can scale *up* quickly, and scale *down* slowly for the best user experience.

Alarms

The `CPUHighAlarm` parameter will alert when the average CPU utilization goes over the value set in the `ThresholdCPUHigh` parameter. This alert will be sent to the `ScaleUpPolicy` resource provisioning more instances, which will bring the average CPU utilization down across the whole auto scaling group. As the name suggests, the `CPULowAlarm` parameter does the reverse when the average CPU utilization goes under the `ThresholdCPULow` parameter.

This means that new instances will be launched until the CPU utilization across the auto scaling group stabilizes somewhere between 40-60% (based on the default parameter values), or the `MaxSize` of instances is reached.

 It is very important to leave a gap between the high and low alarms thresholds. If they are too close together, the alarms will not stabilize and you will see instances created and destroyed almost continually.

The minimum charge for an instance is *one hour*, so creating and destroying them multiple times in one hour may result in higher than expected charges.

Creating machine images

Creating or *baking* your own **Amazon Machine Images** (**AMIs**) is a key part of systems administration in AWS. Having a pre-baked image helps you provision your servers faster, easier, and more consistently than configuring it by hand.

Packer is the de facto standard tool that helps you make your own AMIs. By automating the launch, configuration, and clean-up of your instances, it makes sure you get a repeatable image every time.

In this recipe, we will create an image with the Apache web server pre-installed and configured. While this is a simple example, it is also a very common use-case.

By baking-in your web server, you can scale up your web serving layer to dynamically match the demands on your websites. Having the software already installed and configured means you get the fastest and most reliable start-up possible.

Getting ready

For this recipe, you must have the Packer tool available on your system. Download and install Packer from the project's website `https://www.packer.io/downloads.html`.

How to do it...

1. Create a new Packer template file, and start by defining an `amazon-ebs` builder in the `builders` section:

```
"builders": [
  {
    "type": "amazon-ebs",
    "instance_type": "t2.micro",
    "region": "us-east-1",
    "source_ami": "ami-9be6f38c",
    "ssh_username": "ec2-user",
    "ami_name": "aws-linux-apache {{timestamp}}"
  }
],
```

 The entire template file must be a valid JSON object. Remember to enclose the sections in curly braces: { ... }.

2. Create a `provisioners` section, and include the following snippet to install and activate Apache:

```
"provisioners": [
  {
    "type": "shell",
    "inline": [
      "sudo yum install -y httpd",
      "sudo chkconfig httpd on"
    ]
  }
]
```

3. Save the file with a specific name, such as `04-creating-machine-images.json`.

4. Validate the configuration file you've created with the following `packer validate` command:

```
packer validate 04-creating-machine-images.json
```

5. When valid, build the AMI with the following command:

```
packer build 04-creating-machine-images.json
```

6. Wait until the process is complete. While it is running, you will see an output similar to the following:

```
awsac — packer • packer build src/04-creating-machine-images.json — 114×31
$ packer build src/04-creating-machine-images.json
amazon-ebs output will be in this color.

==> amazon-ebs: Prevalidating AMI Name...
    amazon-ebs: Found Image ID: ami-9be6f38c
==> amazon-ebs: Creating temporary keypair: packer_587a9f63-1bcc-7e85-b9c9-eeec160cc172
==> amazon-ebs: Creating temporary security group for this instance...
==> amazon-ebs: Authorizing access to port 22 the temporary security group...
==> amazon-ebs: Launching a source AWS instance...
    amazon-ebs: Instance ID: i-0c249b526d0cabe9b
==> amazon-ebs: Waiting for instance (i-0c249b526d0cabe9b) to become ready...
==> amazon-ebs: Waiting for SSH to become available...
==> amazon-ebs: Connected to SSH!
==> amazon-ebs: Provisioning with shell script: /var/folders/vt/1kw7w5ns6h16vt8j_tk08pzm0000gn/T/packer-shell21831
1435
    amazon-ebs: Loaded plugins: priorities, update-motd, upgrade-helper
    amazon-ebs: Resolving Dependencies
    amazon-ebs: --> Running transaction check
    amazon-ebs: ---> Package httpd.x86_64 0:2.2.31-1.8.amzn1 will be installed
```

7. Take note of the AMI ID returned by Packer so that you can use it when launching instances in the future:

```
●●●                            ▓ awsac — -bash — 114×31
   amazon-ebs: Verifying   : httpd-tools-2.2.31-1.8.amzn1.x86_64            1/5
   amazon-ebs: Verifying   : apr-1.5.1-1.12.amzn1.x86_64                    2/5
   amazon-ebs: Verifying   : httpd-2.2.31-1.8.amzn1.x86_64                  3/5
   amazon-ebs: Verifying   : apr-util-ldap-1.4.1-4.17.amzn1.x86_64          4/5
   amazon-ebs: Verifying   : apr-util-1.4.1-4.17.amzn1.x86_64               5/5
   amazon-ebs:
   amazon-ebs: Installed:
   amazon-ebs: httpd.x86_64 0:2.2.31-1.8.amzn1
   amazon-ebs:
   amazon-ebs: Dependency Installed:
   amazon-ebs: apr.x86_64 0:1.5.1-1.12.amzn1          apr-util.x86_64 0:1.4.1-4.17.amzn1
   amazon-ebs: apr-util-ldap.x86_64 0:1.4.1-4.17.amzn1 httpd-tools.x86_64 0:2.2.31-1.8.amzn1
   amazon-ebs:
   amazon-ebs: Complete!
==> amazon-ebs: Stopping the source instance...
==> amazon-ebs: Waiting for the instance to stop...
==> amazon-ebs: Creating the AMI: aws-linux-apache 1484431202
   amazon-ebs: AMI: ami-fb816ded
==> amazon-ebs: Waiting for AMI to become ready...
==> amazon-ebs: Terminating the source AWS instance...
==> amazon-ebs: Cleaning up any extra volumes...
==> amazon-ebs: No volumes to clean up, skipping
==> amazon-ebs: Deleting temporary security group...
==> amazon-ebs: Deleting temporary keypair...
Build 'amazon-ebs' finished.

==> Builds finished. The artifacts of successful builds are:
--> amazon-ebs: AMIs were created:

us-east-1: ami-fb816ded
$ ▯
```

How it works...

While this is a very simple recipe, there is a lot going on behind the scenes. This is why we recommend you use Packer to create your machine images.

Template

In the `builders` section of the template, we define our build details.

We are using the most common type of AMI builder: `amazon-ebs`. There are other types of AWS builders, for instance, storage-backed instance types.

Next, we define the type of instance to use when baking.

> Make sure that you can often decrease the time it takes to bake your instance by using a larger instance size. Remember that the minimum price paid for an instance is one hour of billable time.

The `source_ami` property in this recipe is an AWS Linux AMI ID in the `region` we have specified. The `ssh_username` allows you to set the username used to connect and run `provisioners` on the instance. This will be determined by your operating system, which in our case is `ec2-user`.

Finally, the `ami_name` field includes the built-in Packer variable `{{timestamp}}`. This ensures the AMI you create will always have a unique name.

Validate the template

The `packer validate` command is a quick way to ensure your template is free of syntax errors before you launch any instances.

Build the AMI

Once you have created and validated your template, the `packer build` command does the following for you:

- Creates a one-time key pair for SSH access to the instance
- Creates a dedicated security group to control access to the instance
- Launches an instance
- Waits until SSH is ready to receive connections
- Runs the provisioner steps on the instance
- Stops the instance
- Generates an AMI from the stopped instance
- Terminates the instance

 Check the Packer documentation for more provisioners and functionality at `https://www.packer.io/docs/`.

There's more...

While Packer makes the administration of images much easier on AWS, there are still a few things to watch out for.

Debugging

Obviously, with so many steps being automated for you, there are many things that can potentially go wrong. Packer gives you a few different ways to debug issues with your builds.

One of the most useful arguments to use with Packer is the –debug flag. This will force you to manually confirm each step *before* it takes place. Doing this makes it easy to work out exactly which step in the command is failing, which in turn usually makes it obvious what needs to be changed.

Another useful thing to do is to raise the level of logging output during a Packer command. You can do this by setting the PACKER_LOG variable to true. The easiest way to do this is with PACKER_LOG=1 at the beginning of your Packer command line. This will mean you get a lot more information printed to the console (for example, SSH logs, AWS API calls, and so on) during the command. You may even want to run with this level of logging normally in your builds, for auditing purposes.

Orphaned resources

Packer does a great job of managing and cleaning up the resource it uses, but it can only do that while it is running.

If your Packer job aborts for any reason (most likely network issues) then there may be some resources left **orphaned**, or **unmanaged**. It is good practice to check for any Packer instances (they will have *Packer* in their name), and stop them if there are no active Packer jobs running.

You may also need to clean up any leftover key pairs and security groups, but this is less of an issue as there is no cost associated with them (unlike instances).

Deregistering AMIs

As it becomes easier to create AMIs, you may find you end up with more than you need!

AMIs are made up of EC2 snapshots, which are stored in S3. There is a cost associated with storing snapshots, so you will want to clean them up periodically. Given the size of most AMIs (usually a few GBs), it is unlikely to be one of your major costs.

An even greater cost is the administrative overhead of managing too many AMIs. As your images improve and fixes are applied (especially security fixes), you may want to prevent people from using them.

To remove an AMI, you must first *deregister* it, and then remove the underlying snapshots.

 Make sure you do not deregister AMIs that are currently in use. For example, an auto scaling group that references a deregistered AMI will fail to launch new instances!

You can easily deregister snapshots through the web console or using the AWS CLI tool.

Once an AMI is no longer registered, you can remove the associated snapshots. Packer automatically adds the AMI ID to the snapshots' description. By searching your snapshots for the deregistered AMI ID, you can find which ones need to be deleted.

You will not be able to delete snapshots if the AMI has not been deregistered, or if the deregistration is still taking place (it can take a few minutes).

Other platforms

It is also worth noting that Packer can build for more platforms that just AWS. You can also build images for VMWare, Docker, and many others.

This means you could build almost exactly the same machine image locally (for example, using Docker) as you do in AWS. This makes it much more convenient when setting up local development environments, for example.

Check the `builders` section of the Packer documentation for details.

Creating security groups

AWS describes security groups as *virtual firewalls*. While this analogy helps newcomers to the EC2 platform understand their purpose and function, it's probably more accurate to describe them as a *firewall-like* method of authorizing traffic. They don't offer all the functionality you'd find in a traditional firewall, but this simplification also makes them extremely powerful, particularly when combined with Infrastructure as Code and modern SDLC practices.

We're going to go through a basic scenario involving a web server and load balancer. We want the load balancer to respond to HTTP requests from everywhere, and we want to isolate the web server from everything except the load balancer.

Getting ready

Before we get started there's a small list of things you'll need to have ready:

- `AmiId` This is the ID of an AMI in your region. For this recipe, we'd recommend using an AWS Linux AMI because our instance will attempt to run some `yum` commands on startup.
- `VPCID`: This is the ID of the VPC you wish to launch the EC2 server into.
- `SubnetIDs`: These are the subnets which our EC2 instance can launch in.

How to do it...

1. Open up your text editor and create a new CloudFormation template. We're going to start by adding a few `Parameters` as follows:

```
AWSTemplateFormatVersion: '2010-09-09'
Parameters:
  AmiId:
    Type: AWS::EC2::AMI::Id
    Description: AMI ID to launch instances from
  VPCID:
    Type: AWS::EC2::VPC::Id
    Description: VPC where load balancer and instance will launch
  SubnetIDs:
    Type: List<AWS::EC2::Subnet::Id>
    Description: Subnets where load balancer and instance will launch
      (pick at least 2)
```

2. Let's take a look at a security group we'll apply to a public load balancer:

```
ExampleELBSecurityGroup:
  Type: AWS::EC2::SecurityGroup
  Properties:
    GroupDescription: Security Group for example ELB
    SecurityGroupIngress:
      - IpProtocol: tcp
        CidrIp: 0.0.0.0/0
        FromPort: 80
        ToPort: 80
```

Anything which resides in this security group will allow inbound TCP connections on port 80 from anywhere (0.0.0.0/0). Note that a security group can contain more than one rule; we'd almost certainly want to also allow HTTPS (443), but we've left it out to simplify this recipe.

3. Now let's look at a security group for a web server sitting behind our load balancer:

```
ExampleEC2InstanceSecurityGroup:
  Type: AWS::EC2::SecurityGroup
  Properties:
    GroupDescription: Security Group for example Instance
    SecurityGroupIngress:
      - IpProtocol: tcp
        SourceSecurityGroupName:
          Ref: ExampleELBSecurityGroup
        FromPort: 80
        ToPort: 80
```

Here you can see we are not specifying a source IP range. Instead, we're specifying a source security group, which we will accept connections from. In this case, we're saying that we want to allow anything from our ELB security group to connect to anything in our EC2 instance security group on port 80.

Since this is the only rule we're specifying, our web server will not accept connections from anywhere except our load balancer, to port 80 or otherwise. Our web server isn't wide open to the Internet, and it is even isolated from other instances in our VPC

> Remember that multiple instances can reside in a security group. In a scenario where you have multiple web servers attached to this load balancer it would be unnecessary, inefficient, and somewhat of an anti-pattern to create a new security group for each web server. Given that all web servers attached to this load balancer would be serving the same role or function, it makes sense to apply the same security group to them.

This is where the power of security groups really comes in. If an EC2 instance is serving multiple roles—let's say you have an outbound HTTP proxy server in your VPC which you also want to act as an SMTP relay—then you can simply apply multiple security groups to it.

4. Next, we need to add our load balancer. This is probably the most basic load balancer configuration you'll come across. The following code will give you a load balancer, a listener and a target group containing our EC2 instance.

```
ExampleLoadBalancer:
  Type: AWS::ElasticLoadBalancingV2::LoadBalancer
  Properties:
    Subnets:
      - Fn::Select: [ 0, Ref: SubnetIDs ]
      - Fn::Select: [ 1, Ref: SubnetIDs ]
    SecurityGroups:
      - Fn::GetAtt: ExampleELBSecurityGroup.GroupId
ExampleListener:
  Type: AWS::ElasticLoadBalancingV2::Listener
  Properties:
    LoadBalancerArn:
      Ref: ExampleLoadBalancer
    DefaultActions:
      - Type: forward
        TargetGroupArn:
          Ref: ExampleTargetGroup
    Port: 80
    Protocol: HTTP
ExampleTargetGroup:
  Type: AWS::ElasticLoadBalancingV2::TargetGroup
  Properties:
    Port: 80
    Protocol: HTTP
    VpcId:
      Ref: VPCID
    Targets:
      - Id:
          Ref: ExampleEC2Instance
```

5. The last resource we'll add to our template is an EC2 server. This server will install and start nginx when it boots.

```
ExampleEC2Instance:
  Type: AWS::EC2::Instance
  Properties:
    InstanceType: t2.nano
    UserData:
      Fn::Base64:
        Fn::Sub: |
          #!/bin/bash -ex
          yum install -y nginx
          service nginx start
```

```
                exit 0
ImageId:
  Ref: AmiId
SecurityGroupIds:
  - Fn::GetAtt: ExampleEC2InstanceSecurityGroup.GroupId
SubnetId:
  Fn::Select: [ 0, Ref: SubnetIDs ]
```

6. Lastly, we're going to add some Outputs to the template to make it a little more convenient to use our ELB and EC2 instance after the stack is created.

```
Outputs:
  ExampleEC2InstanceHostname:
    Value:
      Fn::GetAtt: [ ExampleEC2Instance, PublicDnsName ]
  ExampleELBURL:
    Value:
      Fn::Join:
        - ''
        - [ 'http://', { 'Fn::GetAtt': [ ExampleLoadBalancer,
            DNSName ] }, '/' ]
```

7. Go ahead and launch this template using the CloudFormation web console or the AWS CLI.

There's more...

You'll eventually run into circular dependency issues when configuring security groups using CloudFormation. Let's say you want all servers in our ExampleEC2InstanceSecurityGroup to be able to access each other on port 22 (SSH). In order to achieve this, you would need to add this rule as the separate resource type AWS::EC2::SecurityGroupIngress. This is because a security group can't refer to itself in CloudFormation when it is yet to be created. This is what the extra resource type looks like:

```
        ExampleEC2InstanceIngress:
          Type: AWS::EC2::SecurityGroupIngress
          Properties:
            IpProtocol: tcp
            SourceSecurityGroupName:
              Ref: ExampleEC2InstanceSecurityGroup
            GroupName:
              Ref: ExampleEC2InstanceSecurityGroup
            FromPort: 22
            ToPort: 22
```

Differences from traditional firewalls

- Security groups can't be used to explicitly block traffic. Only rules of a permissive kind can be added; deny style rules are not supported. Essentially, all inbound traffic is denied unless you explicitly allow it.
- Your rules also may not refer to source ports; only destination ports are supported.
- When security groups are created, they will contain a rule which allows all outbound connections. If you remove this rule, new outbound connections will be dropped. It's a common pattern to leave this rule in place and filter all your traffic using inbound rules only.
- If you do replace the default outbound rule, it's important to note that only new outbound connections will be filtered. Any outbound traffic being sent in response to an inbound connection will still be allowed. This is because security groups are *stateful*.
- Unlike security groups, network ACLs are not stateful and do support DENY rules. You can use them as a complementary layer of security inside your VPC, especially if you need to control traffic flow between subnets.

Creating a load balancer

AWS offers two kinds of load balancers:

- Classic load balancer
- Application load balancer

We're going to focus on the application load balancer. It's effectively an upgraded, second generation of the ELB service, and it offers a lot more functionality than the classic load balancer. HTTP/2 and WebSockets are supported natively, for example. The hourly rate also happens to be cheaper.

> Application load balancers do not support layer-4 load balancing. For this kind of functionality, you'll need to use a classic load balancer.

How to do it...

1. Open up your text editor and create a new CloudFormation template. We're going to require a VPC ID and some subnet IDs as `Parameters`. Add them to your template like this:

```
AWSTemplateFormatVersion: '2010-09-09'
Parameters:
  VPCID:
    Type: AWS::EC2::VPC::Id
    Description: VPC where load balancer and instance will launch
  SubnetIDs:
    Type: List<AWS::EC2::Subnet::Id>
    Description: Subnets where load balancer and instance will launch
      (pick at least 2)
```

2. Next we need to add some `Mappings` of ELB account IDs. These will make it easier for us to give the load balancer permission to write logs to an S3 bucket. Your mappings should look like this:

 You can find the complete list of ELB account IDs here `http://docs.aws.amazon.com/elasticloadbalancing/latest/classic/enable-access-logs.html#attach-bucket-policy`.

```
Mappings:
  ELBAccountMap:
    us-east-1:
  ELBAccountID: 127311923021
    ap-southeast-2:
  ELBAccountID: 783225319266
```

3. We can now start adding `Resources` to our template. First we're going to create an S3 bucket and bucket policy for storing our load balancer logs. In order to make this template portable, we'll omit a bucket name, but for convenience we'll include the bucket name in our outputs so that CloudFormation will echo the name back to us.

```
Resources:
  ExampleLogBucket:
    Type: AWS::S3::Bucket
  ExampleBucketPolicy:
    Type: AWS::S3::BucketPolicy
    Properties:
      Bucket:
```

```
      Ref: ExampleLogBucket
   PolicyDocument:
     Statement:
        -

        Action:
           - "s3:PutObject"
        Effect: "Allow"
        Resource:
          Fn::Join:
            - ""

            -

              - "arn:aws:s3:::"
              - Ref: ExampleLogBucket
              - "/*"
        Principal:
          AWS:
            Fn::FindInMap: [ ELBAccountMap, Ref: "AWS::Region",
            ELBAccountID ]
```

4. Next, we need to create a security group for our load balancer to reside in. This security group will allow inbound connections to port 80 (HTTP). To simplify this recipe, we'll leave out port 443 (HTTPS), but we'll briefly cover how to add this functionality later in this section. Since we're adding a public load balancer, we want to allow connections to it from everywhere (0.0.0.0/0). This is what our security group looks like:

```
ExampleELBSecurityGroup:
   Type: AWS::EC2::SecurityGroup
   Properties:
     GroupDescription: Security Group for example ELB
     SecurityGroupIngress:
        -

        IpProtocol: tcp
        CidrIp: 0.0.0.0/0
        FromPort: 80
        ToPort: 80
```

5. We now need to define a target group. Upon completion of this recipe, you can go ahead and register your instances in this group so that HTTP requests will be forwarded to it. Alternatively, you can attach the target group to an auto scaling group and AWS will take care of the instance registration and de-registration for you.

6. The target group is where we specify the health checks our load balancer should perform against the target instances. This health check is necessary to determine if a registered instance should receive traffic. The example provided with this recipe includes these health-check parameters with the values all set to their defaults. Go ahead and tweak these to suit your needs, or, optionally, remove them if the defaults work for you.

```
ExampleTargetGroup:
  Type: AWS::ElasticLoadBalancingV2::TargetGroup
  Properties:
    Port: 80
    Protocol: HTTP
    HealthCheckIntervalSeconds: 30
    HealthCheckProtocol: HTTP
    HealthCheckPort: 80
    HealthCheckPath: /
    HealthCheckTimeoutSeconds: 5
    HealthyThresholdCount: 5
    UnhealthyThresholdCount: 2
    Matcher:
      HttpCode: '200'
    VpcId:
      Ref: VPCID
```

7. We need to define at least one listener to be added to our load balancer. A listener will *listen* for incoming requests to the load balancer on the port and protocol we configure for it. Requests matching the port and protocol will be forwarded through to our target group.

   The configuration of our listener is going to be reasonably simple. We're listening for HTTP requests on port 80. We're also setting up a default action for this listener, which will forward our requests to the target group we've defined before. There is a limit of 10 listeners per load balancer.

 Currently, AWS only supports one action: forward.

```
ExampleListener:
  Type: AWS::ElasticLoadBalancingV2::Listener
  Properties:
    LoadBalancerArn:
      Ref: ExampleLoadBalancer
    DefaultActions:
```

```
        - Type: forward
          TargetGroupArn:
            Ref: ExampleTargetGroup
      Port: 80
      Protocol: HTTP
```

8. Finally, now that we have all `Resources` we need, we can go ahead and set up our load balancer. We'll need to define at least two subnets for it to live in—these are included as `Parameters` in our example template:

```
ExampleLoadBalancer:
  Type: AWS::ElasticLoadBalancingV2::LoadBalancer
  Properties:
    LoadBalancerAttributes:
      - Key: access_logs.s3.enabled
        Value: true
      - Key: access_logs.s3.bucket
        Value:
          Ref: ExampleLogBucket
      - Key: idle_timeout.timeout_seconds
        Value: 60
    Scheme: internet-facing
    Subnets:
      - Fn::Select: [ 0, Ref: SubnetIDs ]
      - Fn::Select: [ 1, Ref: SubnetIDs ]
    SecurityGroups:
      - Fn::GetAtt: ExampleELBSecurityGroup.GroupId
```

9. Lastly, we're going to add some `Outputs` to our template for convenience. We're particularly interested in the name of the S3 bucket we created and the URL of the load balancer.

```
Outputs:
  ExampleELBURL:
    Value:
      Fn::Join:
        - ''
        - [ 'http://', { 'Fn::GetAtt': [ ExampleLoadBalancer,
            DNSName ] }, '/' ]
  ExampleLogBucket:
    Value:
      Ref: ExampleLogBucket
```

How it works...

As you can see, we're applying a logging configuration which points to the S3 bucket we've created. We're configuring this load balancer to be Internet-facing, with an idle timeout of 60 seconds (the default).

All load balancers are Internet-facing by default, so it's not strictly necessary to define a Scheme in our example; however, it can be handy to include this anyway. This is especially the case if your CloudFormation template contains a mix of public and private load balancers.

 If you specify a logging configuration but the load balancer can't access the S3 bucket, your CloudFormation stack will fail to complete.

Private ELBs are not Internet-facing and are available only to resources which live inside your VPC.

That's it! You now have a working application load balancer configured to ship logs to an S3 bucket.

There's more...

Load balancers on AWS are highly configurable and there are many options available to you. Here are some of the more frequent ELB options you'll encounter:

HTTPS/SSL

If you wish to accept HTTPS requests, you'll need to configure an additional listener. It will look something like the following:

```
ExampleHTTPSListener:
  Type: AWS::ElasticLoadBalancingV2::Listener
  Properties:
    Certificates:
      - CertificateArn:
        arn:aws:acm:ap-southeast-2:123456789012:
        certificate/12345678-1234-1234-1234-123456789012
    LoadBalancerArn:
      Ref: ExampleLoadBalancer
    DefaultActions:
      - Type: forward
```

```
        TargetGroupArn:
            Ref: ExampleTargetGroup
    Port: 443
    Protocol: HTTPS
```

The listener will need to reference a valid **Amazon Resource Name** (**ARN**) for the certificate you wish to use. It's really easy to have AWS Certificate Manager create a certificate for you, but it does require validation of the domain name you're generating the certificate for. You can, of course, bring your own certificate if you wish. You'll need to import it in to AWS Certificate Manager before you can use it with your ELB (or CloudFront distribution).

Unless you have specific requirements around ciphers, a good starting approach is to not define an SSL Policy and let AWS choose what is currently *best of breed*.

Path-based routing

Once you are comfortable with ELB configuration, you can start to experiment with path-based routing. In a nutshell, it provides a way to inspect a request and proxy it to different targets based on the path requested.

One common scenario you might encounter is needing to route requests for /blog to a different set of servers running WordPress, instead of to your main server pool, which is running your Ruby on Rails application.

5
Management Tools

In this chapter, we will cover:

- Auditing your AWS account
- Recommendations with Trusted Advisor
- Creating e-mail alarms
- Publishing custom metrics in CloudWatch
- Creating monitoring dashboards
- Creating a budget
- Feeding log files into CloudWatch logs

Introduction

As with all administration, monitoring and alerting is a critical part of using AWS-based infrastructure. If anything, due to the ephemeral nature of cloud resources, keeping track and measuring your usage is even more important than when using on-premises systems.

Auditing your AWS account

We're now going to show you how to set up CloudTrail in your AWS account. Once CloudTrail has been enabled, it will start to record all of the API calls made in your account to the AWS service and then deliver them to you as log files in an S3 bucket.
When we talk about API calls we mean things like:

- Actions performed in the AWS console.
- Calls made to AWS APIs using the CLI or SDKs.
- Calls made on your behalf by AWS services. Think CloudFormation or the auto scaling service.

Each entry in the log will contain useful information, such as:

- The service that was called
- The action that was requested
- The parameters sent with the request
- The response that was returned by AWS
- The identity of the caller (including IP address)
- The date and time of the request

How to do it...

1. Create a new CloudFormation template file; we're going to define the following `Resources`:
   - An S3 bucket for our CloudTrail log files to be stored in
   - A policy for our S3 bucket that allows the CloudTrail service to write to our bucket
   - A CloudTrail *trail*

2. Define an S3 bucket like so. We don't need to give it a name; we'll add the bucket name to the list of `Outputs` later:

```
ExampleTrailBucket:
  Type: AWS::S3::Bucket
```

3. Next, we need to define a policy for our bucket. This section is a little wordy so you may prefer to get this from the code samples instead. This policy essentially allows CloudTrail to do two things to our bucket: `s3:GetBucketAcl` and `s3:PutObject`.

```
ExampleBucketPolicy:
  Type: AWS::S3::BucketPolicy
  Properties:
    Bucket: !Ref ExampleTrailBucket
    PolicyDocument:
      Statement:
      - Sid: AWSCloudTrailAclCheck20150319
        Effect: Allow
        Principal:
          Service: cloudtrail.amazonaws.com
          Action: s3:GetBucketAcl
          Resource: !Join
            - ""
            -
              - "arn:aws:s3:::"
              - !Ref ExampleTrailBucket
      - Sid: AWSCloudTrailWrite20150319
        Effect: Allow
        Principal:
          Service: cloudtrail.amazonaws.com
        Action: s3:PutObject
        Resource: !Join
          - ""
          -
            - "arn:aws:s3:::"
            - !Ref ExampleTrailBucket
            - "/AWSLogs/"
            - !Ref AWS::AccountId
            - "/*"
        Condition:
          StringEquals:
            s3:x-amz-acl: bucket-owner-full-control
```

4. Now we can set up our trail.

One thing to note here is that we use `DependsOn` to make CloudFormation create this trail after it has created the S3 bucket and policy. If you don't do this you'll likely encounter an error when you create the stack because CloudTrail won't be able to access the bucket.

5. Add the `Trail` to your template like so:

```
ExampleTrail:
  Type: AWS::CloudTrail::Trail
  Properties:
    EnableLogFileValidation: true
    IncludeGlobalServiceEvents: true
    IsLogging: true
    IsMultiRegionTrail: true
    S3BucketName: !Ref ExampleTrailBucket
  DependsOn:
    - ExampleTrailBucket
    - ExampleBucketPolicy
```

6. Finally, we're going to output the name of the S3 bucket where our CloudTrail logs will be stored:

```
Outputs:
  ExampleBucketName:
    Value: !Ref ExampleTrailBucket
    Description: Bucket where CloudTrail logs will be stored
```

7. You can go ahead and run your CloudFormation stack using the following command:

```
aws cloudformation create-stack \
  --template-body file://05-auditing-your-aws-account.yaml \
  --stack-name example-cloudtrail
```

How it works...

This template will set up CloudTrail with the following configuration:

- CloudTrail will be turned on for all regions in your account. This is a sensible place to start because it gives you visibility over where your AWS resources are being created. Even if you are the sole user of your AWS account it can be handy to know if you are making API calls to other regions by mistake (it's easy to do). When you create a multi region trail, new regions will automatically be included when they come online with no additional effort on your part.
- Global service events will also be logged. Again this is a sensible default because it includes services that aren't region-specific. CloudFront and IAM are two examples of AWS services that aren't region-specific.

- Log file validation is turned on. With this feature enabled, CloudTrail will deliver a digest file on an hourly basis that you can use to determine if your CloudTrail logs have been tampered with. CloudTrail uses SHA-256 for hashing and signing (RSA). The AWS CLI can be used to perform ad hoc validation of CloudTrail logs.

For a quick view of your CloudTrial logs, with some basic search and filter functionality, you can head to the AWS web console:

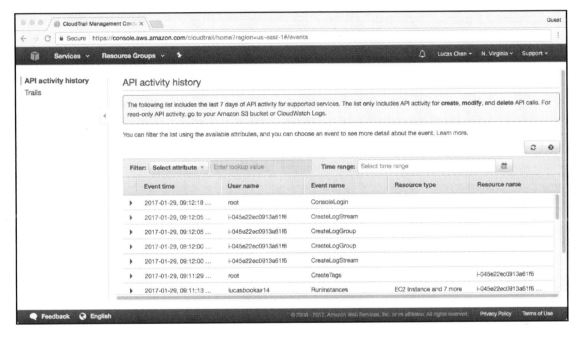

CloudTrail web console

There's more...

- Log files are encrypted using server side encryption in S3. This encryption is transparent to you, but you can opt to encrypt these files with your own **customer master key (CMK)** if you wish.
- API calls are logged by CloudTrail in under 15 minutes.
- Logs are shipping to your S3 bucket every five minutes.
- It's possible to aggregate CloudTrail events across many accounts into a single bucket. This is a pattern often used to log AWS activity into a *SecOps* or similar account for auditing.

- Logging aside, CloudTrail keeps your API activity for seven days.
- You can create more than one trail. You might consider creating a trail for your developers that is separate from the trail consumed by security.
- If a CloudFormation stack creates an S3 bucket and that S3 bucket has objects in it the delete operation will fail if and when you choose to delete the stack. You can manually delete the S3 bucket in the S3 web console if you wish to work around this.

Recommendations with Trusted Advisor

Trusted Advisor covers four main areas and it is designed to give you some guidance around what are considered best practices for your cloud deployment. The areas covered are:

- **Cost Optimization**
- **Performance**
- **Security**
- **Fault Tolerance**

It's available to everyone and free to use—with one fairly large catch. Unless you are paying for Business or Enterprise level support with AWS you only get access to four checks. At the time of publishing there are 55 possible checks.

How to do it...

The good news is you don't need to do anything at all to turn on Trusted Advisor. It's automatically enabled when your AWS account is created and will continue to update for the lifetime of your account.

Go ahead and navigate to the **Trusted Advisor** section of the AWS web console.

How it works...

The four checks provided for free with this service are:

- **Unrestricted ports**: This is a check on the highest risk ports in your security groups. They'll be flagged if they're open to everyone (0.0.0.0/0).
- **IAM usage**: This is a fairly rudimentary check. If there isn't at least one IAM user in your account this check won't pass. It's considered good practice to not use your root login credentials for your AWS account and instead create IAM users with least privilege access.
- **MFA on root account**: This is also a fairly rudimentary check. You need to have MFA enabled for your root login in order for this check to pass. It's obviously a good idea to enable MFA for your IAM users too.
- **Service limits**: This one is quite handy: if you're approaching 80% of your service limits, this check won't pass. For example, it's nice to know if you're about to hit the cap of CloudFormation stacks or EC2 instances before you attempt to create them.

Even though there's only four checks here, these are some of the more useful ones so we'd encourage you to pay attention to them.

The console uses a color scheme to denote the status of each check:

- **Red**: It's recommended that you take action to remedy this check
- **Yellow**: This check requires investigation and possible remediation
- **Green**: This check is passing and needs no attention

Visit the **Preferences** page in the **Trusted Advisor** web console if you'd like to have a weekly report e-mailed to you.

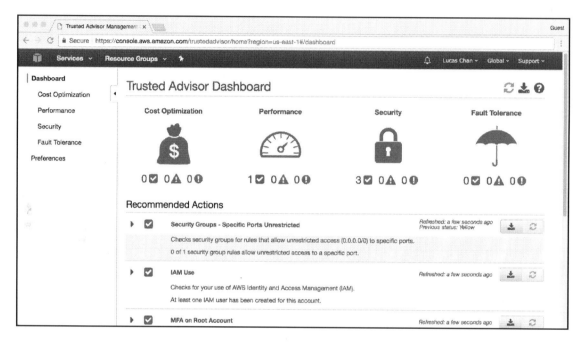

Trusted Advisor console

There's more...

As well as opening up the entire suite of Trusted Advisor checks, a Business or Enterprise level support arrangement gives you access to the following:

- **Notifications**: You are able to have notifications delivered to you at a higher frequency using a number of delivery methods. Since Trusted Advisor is an available source in CloudWatch Events you'll be able to create notifications that can be handled by SNS (e-mail, push, SMS) or even notifications that will trigger Lambda functions.

- **API access**: You'll have access to a number of Trusted Advisor API methods such as `DescribeTrustedAdvisorCheckResult` and `DescribeTrustedAdvisorCheckSummaries`. You can use these to integrate the results from checks into your own dashboards or monitoring systems. You'll also be able to use the APIs to refresh Trusted Advisor checks (after you've taken corrective action on them, for example).
- **Exclusion**: You can selectively mute checks that are failing. You'll sometimes want to do this for things such as RDS instances in your development environments that aren't in multi-AZ mode or don't have backups enabled.

Finally, some of the more useful checks we see for our Business and Enterprise level support customers are:

- **Reserved Instances**: A nice cost optimization if you have a reasonably static workload.
- **Unassociated Elastic IPs**: If IP addresses are not associated with a network interface (on an EC2 instance for example) you will still be charged for them. Also if there are unassociated IPs floating around, that is usually a sign that they are being allocated manually instead of with CloudFormation. Remember that the goal here is for more automation, not less.
- **Idle load balancers**: Again, these cost money and are often easily orphaned in low automation environments.
- **S3 bucket permissions**: It's not always obvious if the permissions on an S3 bucket have been misconfigured. This check helps you avoid unintentionally leaking data.

Creating e-mail alarms

While e-mail alarms may not be the most scalable of all alarms (due to the amount of e-mail most people get), they are the easiest to integrate—almost everyone has an e-mail address!

This recipe uses two AWS services:

- **CloudWatch (CW)**
- **Simple Notification Service (SNS)**

As you will often want to create alarms for metrics after viewing them through the CloudWatch dashboard, this recipe will use the console to create the alarms.

How to do it...

1. In the CloudWatch console, go to the **Alarms** section:

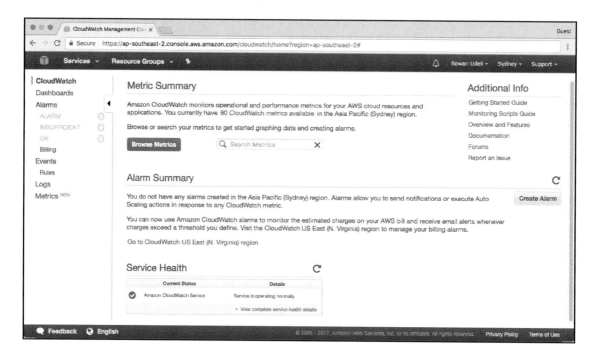

2. Click **Create Alarm** to start the wizard:

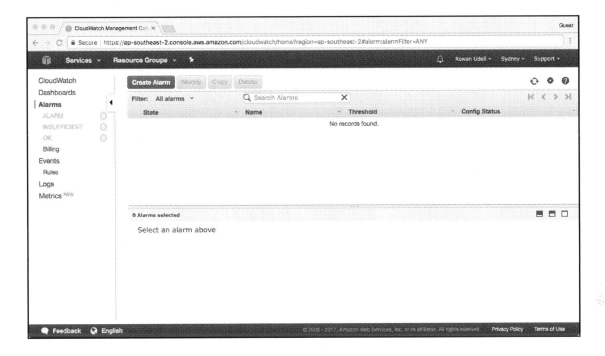

3. Select the metric you are interested in alerting on. In this case, we will choose **By Function Name** under **Lambda Metrics**:

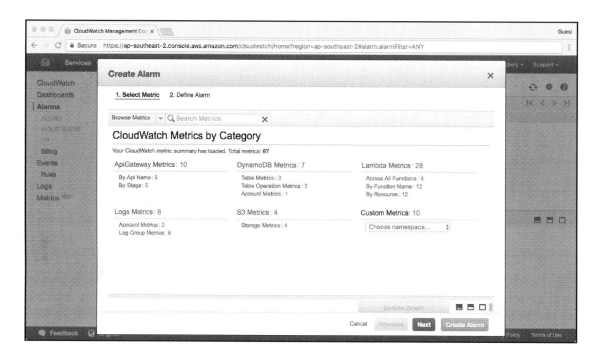

4. Select the specific metric. You can filter by any of the values in the table. In this case, we will select **Errors** and click **Next**:

5. Define the alarm, giving at least a name and a threshold. In this case, we will alert if there are ever *any* errors (such as > 0):

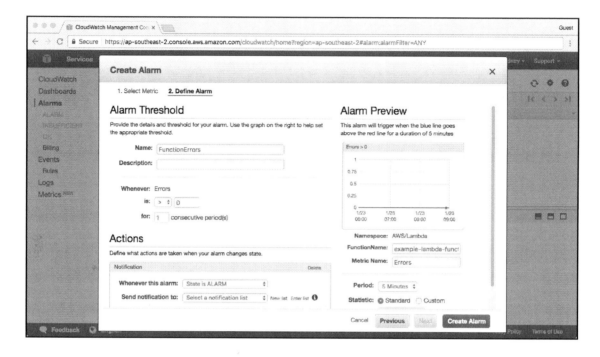

6. In the **Actions** section, create a new list by giving the e-mail address you want to be notified on of a breach, and a topic name (in this example, we use `EmailMe`), and then click **Create Alarm**:

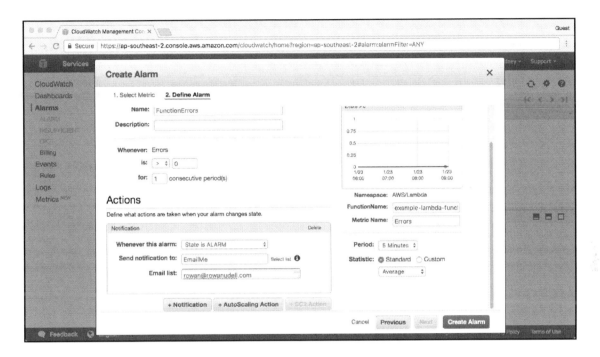

7. You will be asked to confirm the e-mail address, and no notifications will be given until it is verified.

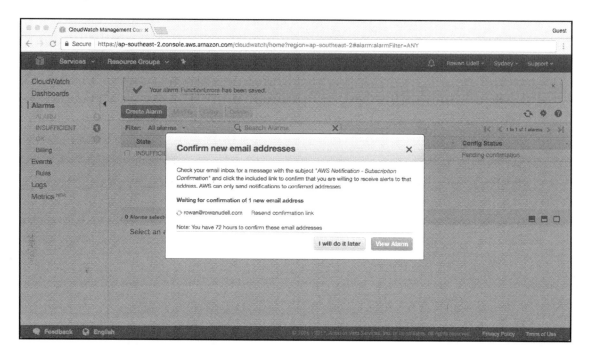

8. The confirmation e-mail will look like this:

9. Once you have clicked on the **Confirm subscription** link in the e-mail, you will see a confirmation message as follows:

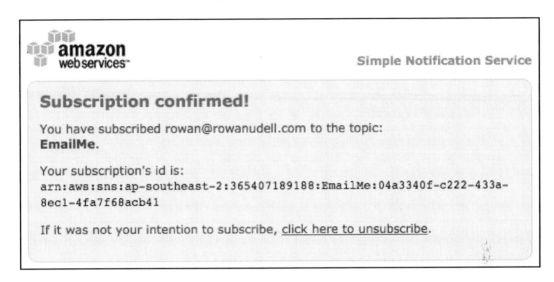

10. Back in the console the status will update, showing that you have successfully confirmed your subscription:

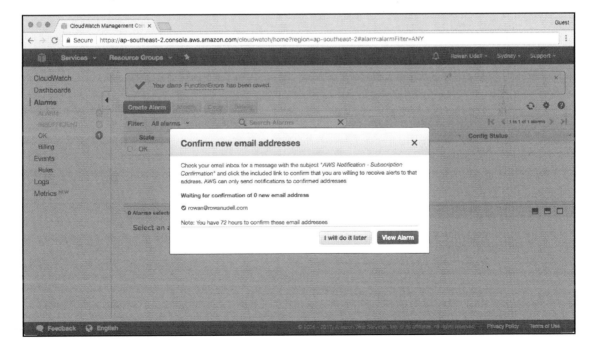

11. You will then see your newly created alarm in the console, and can view its status and history:

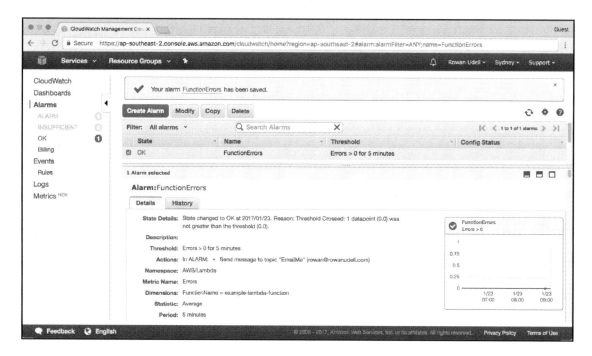

12. In the SNS console, you can see the topic that was created for you as follows:

How it works...

While we normally prefer the CLI (or CloudFormation) for creating AWS resources the wizard for creating alarms does a lot of work for you, so it is a good place to start. Once you know what kinds of alarms you are interested in, you can automate them.

The CloudWatch console is a great place to keep an eye on the performance of your resources. Often when looking at the metrics you might find a scenario that you would want to be notified of, and quickly create an alarm on it.

> While e-mail is probably the easiest way to get started with alarms, it doesn't scale all that well (Do you really want more e-mail?). For very important metrics you might want a CloudWatch dashboard instead, or a different notification protocol/target.

We start by selecting the metric we are interested in; in this case, it is errors from the **example-lambda-function**, but the process would work the same regardless of the metric you select.

You must define a name for the alarm, and you can optionally create a description. One of the most important parts of the alarm is how you define the threshold that will trigger it. You can choose not only the value and comparison operator used (for example, greater than (>), less than (<), greater than or equal to (>=), and so on), but also the number of failing data points that must occur before the alarm is triggered. This can stop you being alerted unnecessarily for temporary *spikes* in metric values. In this scenario we want to know if there are *any* errors, so we set the value to 1.

On the right-hand side you can define the check period and the statistic used (for example, **Average**, **Maximum**, **Minimum**, and so on). You can also see the recent history of the selected metric in the top-right corner. The red line on the graph is where the currently defined threshold will sit, so you can quickly see if the alarm would have been triggered.

In the **Actions** section of the alarm, you define what action will be taken when triggered. While you can select an existing SNS topic, we will define a new one by clicking on **New list**. You are then prompted for the details of the new topic; you must give both a name and an e-mail address to subscribe to the topic.

When you click **Create Alarm,** you will see the status of the subscription. After receiving the e-mail and clicking on the confirmation link, the status will automatically update. It doesn't matter if you navigate away from the window before you confirm the subscription. Just remember that your target e-mail address won't receive any notifications if you do not confirm the subscription.

Viewing the newly created alarm shows its current state, and its recent history. An alarm has three possible states:

- **ALARM**: The metric is over the defined threshold
- **INSUFFICIENT_DATA**: There were not enough data points to determine if the metric is under or over the threshold
- **OK**: The metric is under the defined threshold

You can filter alarms by their state by the links on the side menu, which also show an updated view of how many alarms are in each state.

Behind the scenes, the wizard has created an SNS topic for you. The topic is what handles converting the alarm message to an e-mail, and sending it. Without the SNS topic the alarm would still alert (that is change state), but there would be no way to tell without looking at the metric in the CloudWatch dashboard.

There's more...

This recipe represents the simplest useful configuration of SNS topics and CW alarms, but there is a lot more depth available to you in this pattern.

Existing topics

Instead of choosing **New list** in the wizard, you can use the **Select list** functionality. You then give the name of an existing SNS topic to use, rather than creating a new one.

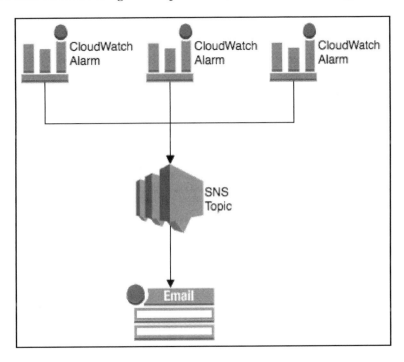

This means you can set up a single topic to push multiple alarms to. In addition to being simpler it also means you only need to confirm the subscription *once*, instead of doing it for each alarm.

Other subscriptions

An SNS topic that notifies an e-mail is the most common subscription, but not the only option. SNS topics can also send notifications to:

- HTTP(S) endpoints
- Amazon SQS
- AWS Lambda
- SMS

See also

- The *Creating monitoring dashboards* recipe

Publishing custom metrics in CloudWatch

Once you get used to using CloudWatch, it is highly likely that you will want to see more than just the built-in AWS metrics.

One of the most common metrics users ask for after starting to run servers in EC2 is memory usage; the built-in metrics for EC2 instances are CPU utilization, network in/out, disk reads/writes, and status—memory is not included by default!

This recipe will show you how to feed the amount of memory inuse on your Linux instances to CloudWatch, so that you can see them alongside the other instance metrics.

 Knowing how utilized (or not) your instances are is a key component in choosing the right instance type to use for your workloads. Getting it wrong can cost you a lot of money!

Getting ready

You will need an EC2 instance running Linux, with the AWS CLI tool installed to perform this recipe. If you use an instance based on AWS Linux, you will have the AWS CLI tool installed for you.

The instance role or credentials you use to run the following commands must have permission to submit metrics to CloudWatch. This is the `CloudWatch:PutMetricData` permission.

How to do it...

1. On the instance, run the following AWS CLI command:

```
aws cloudwatch put-metric-data \
   --metric-name MemoryUsagePercent \
   --namespace CustomMetrics \
   --dimensions InstanceId=`curl -s \
     http://169.254.169.254/latest/meta-data/instance-id` \
   --unit Percent \
   --value `free | grep Mem | awk '{print $3/$2 * 100.0}'`
```

2. Go to the CloudWatch console, and navigate to the **Metrics** dashboard. Your metric will appear under the namespace **CustomMetrics**, **InstanceId**, and the unique ID for the instance, with the metric name **MemoryUsagePercent**.

It can take *up to* 15 minutes for a custom metric to appear in the CloudWatch dashboard (although it usually takes less). Even for the built-in metrics, it may take a minute or two for the metric data to appear in the console.

How it works...

In this recipe, we use the built-in `put-metric-data` AWS CLI command to send our metric to CloudWatch.

We start by defining the metric name and namespace that the values will appear under. This is important because it defines how we will see the metric in the console and dashboards. Names should identify and describe the metric. They do not need to be unique, as the dimension(s) we add will take care of that (we will discuss this later). Namespaces are used to group similar metrics together, like a category. The built-in metrics appear under the namespace `AWS/`. For example, EC2 metrics appear under the `AWS/EC2` namespace.

We then specify a dimension for the metric. A **dimension** is a way to uniquely identify similar metrics. In this case we are using the instance's ID to identify the metric, because the metric is unique to that instance, but we will likely have many instances of the `MemoryUsagePercent` metric (across many EC2 instances). We are obtaining the instance ID by querying (via the `curl` command) the instance metadata service, which is accessed over HTTP on the special IP address `169.254.169.254`.

 There's a lot of other useful information in the instance metadata. See the AWS documentation on instance metadata for more details `http://docs.aws.amazon.com/AWSEC2/latest/UserGuide/ec2-instance-metadata.html`.

Next we specify a percent, because we know what kind of data we are dealing with. This argument can be leftoff if you don't know (or care), as CloudWatch attaches no significance to it (although some other applications may be able to use it, for example, for display).

Finally we specify the value to send. We work this value out dynamically from the output of the `free` command and use `awk` to convert it to a percentage of memory inuse.

Once the metric is being sent to CloudWatch, we can view it in the console. The easiest way is to select your specific metric and view it in the **Metrics** section of the CloudWatch console.

There's more...

This is a good real-world use-case to get started with your own custom metrics, but there's a lot more you can do with them.

Cron

One-off metric values are rarely useful on their own. The real value comes when you can plot and see them over time; how they change, how fast they change, what their range is, and so on.

On Linux you can schedule a command easily with the `cron` command. By putting the AWS CLI commands in a script, and scheduling it with `cron` to run periodically, you can feed metrics consistently to CloudWatch, without the overhead of running a dedicated agent on your instances.

Auto scaling

Instance-based metrics like memory usage become especially useful when collected from all the instances in an auto scaling group.

By collecting instance or even application-specific metrics (for example: number of threads used, internal request duration, and so on) you can make your auto scaling groups increase and decrease in size at the most appropriate times to your workload and performance profile.

To do this, make the auto scaling group name one of the dimensions (you can define multiple dimensions) sent along with your metric value.

Backfilling

You can backfill metrics by running the same command and supplying an additional `--timestamp` argument. The timestamp argument accepts an ISO 8601 date and time stamp in UTC time for example: `2017-01-01T12:00:00.000Z`

Keep in mind that CloudWatch will only retain your metrics for a certain period, decided by the granularity of your metrics. The retention period is:

- Data points with a period of 60 seconds (1 minute) are available for 15 days
- Data points with a period of 300 seconds (5 minute) are available for 63 days
- Data points with a period of 3600 seconds (1 hour) are available for 455 days (15 months)

> While you can send metrics with millisecond precision, the minimum value CloudWatch will store is at the 1 minute level. Anything less than the 1 minute level and CloudWatch will aggregate the values. When aggregated, you can see some additional information about your metric; namely the sample size, minimum and maximum value, and the average of the values.

See also

- The *Creating monitoring dashboards* recipe
- The *Launching an Instance* recipe in `Chapter 4`, *Using AWS Compute*.

Creating monitoring dashboards

The real value of collecting metrics is the ability to spot trends and relationships (often unknown or unexpected) between disparate systems. With this kind of visibility, you are able to identify and troubleshoot issues before they become an incident.

In addition to providing a way to aggregate and view metrics from your systems, the CloudWatch service also makes it easy to create monitoring dashboards so that you can quickly and clearly view the most important metrics.

This recipe uses the AWS console because you cannot create dashboards via CloudFormation or the AWS CLI tool yet.

Getting ready

You will need to have some metrics already present in CloudWatch in order to create a dashboard.

If you have been using AWS services (for example: EC2, RDS, DDB, and so on), then you should have plenty—almost all the AWS services populate metrics in CloudWatch by default.

How to do it...

1. Navigate to the CloudWatch section of the AWS console:

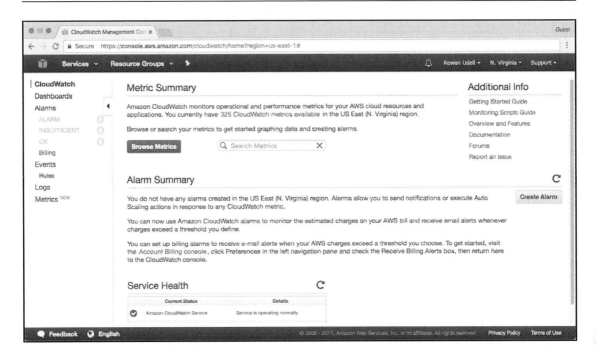

2. Go to the **Dashboards** section of the console via the link on the left-hand menu:

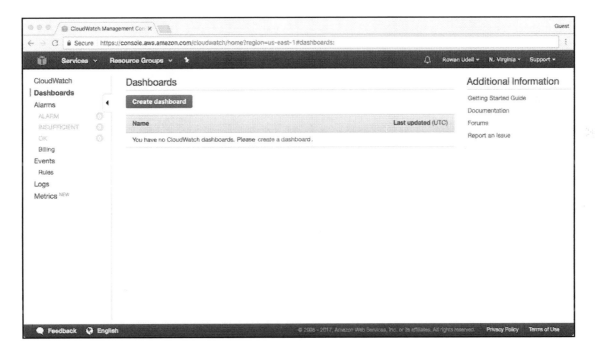

3. Click the **Create Dashboard** button:

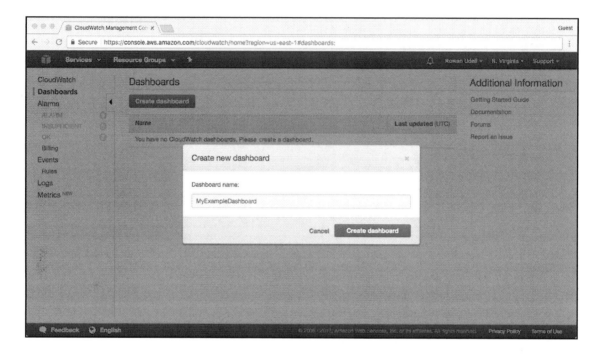

4. Choose the type of widget you want to use to display your metric. In this example, we will choose the most versatile, **Line**:

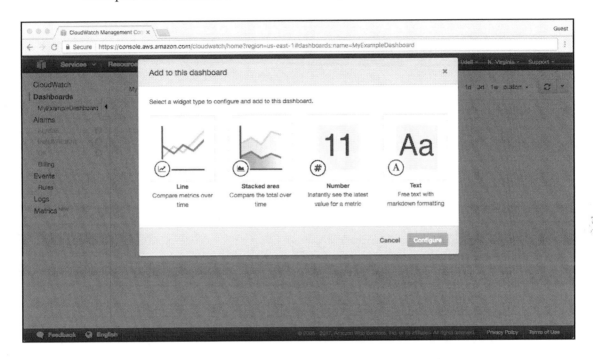

5. Navigate the **All metrics** tab to find the metric(s) you want to include, selecting it by clicking the tick box on the left of the metric details. You will see a preview of the metric(s) and how they will look:

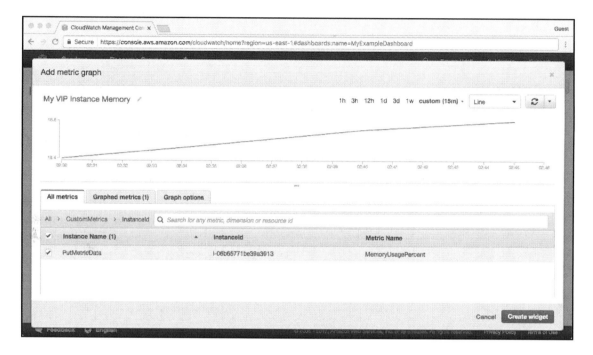

6. Once selected, you can modify how the metric is displayed via the settings on the **Graphed metrics** tab. In this case we have given the widget a name, and changed the **Period** setting for our metric to **1 Minute** to reflect the additional granularity available (You can see that the metric line appears *smoother* because of it).

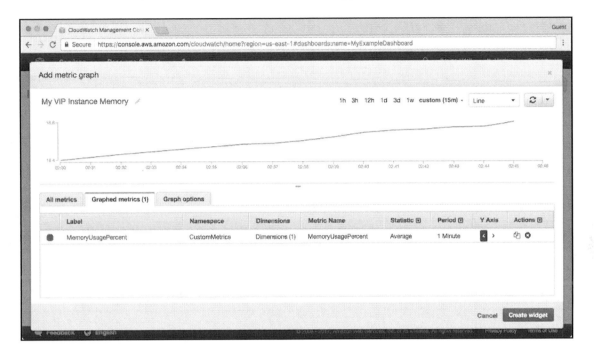

7. Once you click **Create widget,** you will see your widget on the dashboard. Once you click **Save dashboard,** it will appear under the **Dashboards** heading on the left-hand menu:

8. At a dashboard level, you can turn on **Auto refresh** and the refresh frequency interval:

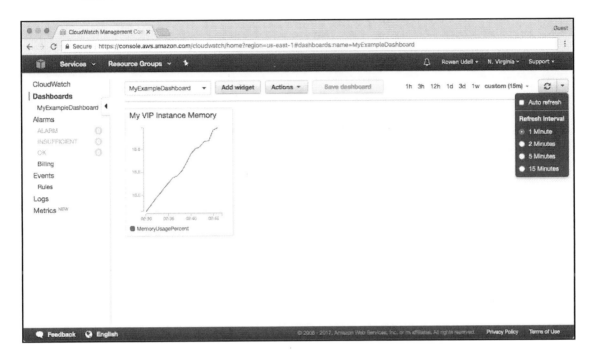

9. You can resize and rearrange your widgets by dragging them. Just remember to click **Save dashboard** to persist any changes:

There's more...

CloudWatch dashboard's value is the ease and simplicity that it allows you to publicize your most important metrics.

 As with any dashboard, make sure that the metrics you choose to display are relevant and actionable. There's no point in displaying a metric if there's no action required when it changes.

Widget types

Line graphs are not the only type of widget that can be displayed in a dashboard. There is also:

- **Stacked area**
- **Number**
- **Text**

Depending on the type of metrics you are collecting or are interested in, you should experiment with different types of widgets to display them. Not all metrics are suited to line graphs.

See also

- The *Publishing custom metrics in CloudWatch* recipe.

Creating a budget

One of the main attractions of using AWS, is its pay-as-you-go model. You only pay for what you use, no more and no less.

Unfortunately, this can sometimes result in what's known as **bill shock** at the end of the month. This happens when you do something that you might not know is a charged service, or you do not know how much is charged for it, and you don't find out until it's too late. Especially when getting started, users may not fully appreciate the cost of the activities they're undertaking.

There are also ways to optimize your costs on AWS, for example, by transferring at slower speeds, removing external access, and so on. All this means that you should be aware of your cost obligations, and manage them in real time. To this end, you can create budgets that help you be aware of your usage and spending.

While you can create budgets via the AWS CLI tool, it is useful to know how the **Billing** dashboard works for administration purposes, so we will use the AWS console for this recipe.

Getting ready

By default, IAM Users do not have access to the billing section of the AWS console. You must perform these steps using the root login details for your account, or enable IAM access for other users, which is a one-off step.

While you should not generally use the root credentials for your AWS account when administering, creating budgets (which should happen only infrequently) is an exception.

 You *should not* be creating access keys for your root account under any circumstances, which is another reason why we use the console (and not the CLI) for this recipe.

How to do it...

1. Log in to the AWS console with your root credentials, and navigate to the **My Billing Dashboard** via the user menu accessed by clicking on your name in the top right:

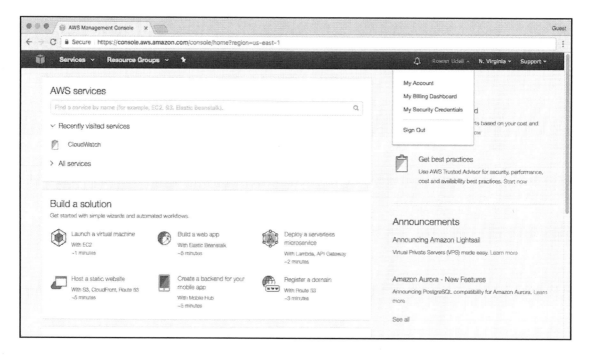

2. The **Billing** dashboard displays your up-to-date usage for the month. Click on **Budgets** in the left-hand menu:

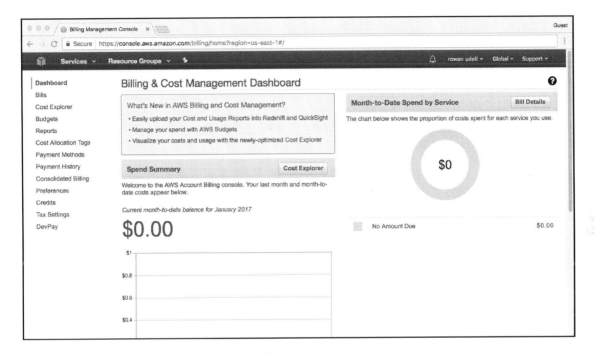

3. When you first arrive at the **Budgets** console, there will be no budgets to display. Click on the **Create budget** button to get started:

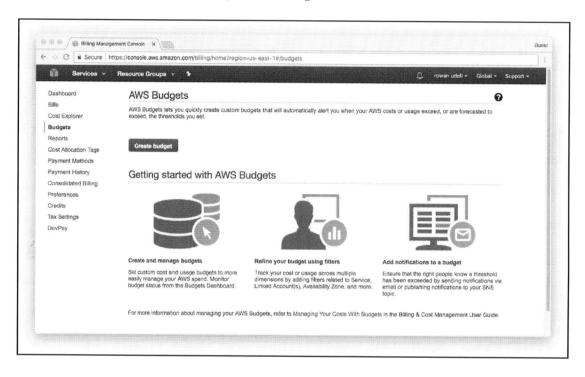

4. Start by filling out the budget details, such as `Cost` for the measurement type, `Monthly` for the period, and the budget amount. Select the **Start date** (which defaults to the first of the current month), and optionally the **End date**. Leave the **End date** field blank to create a rolling budget that is reset each month:

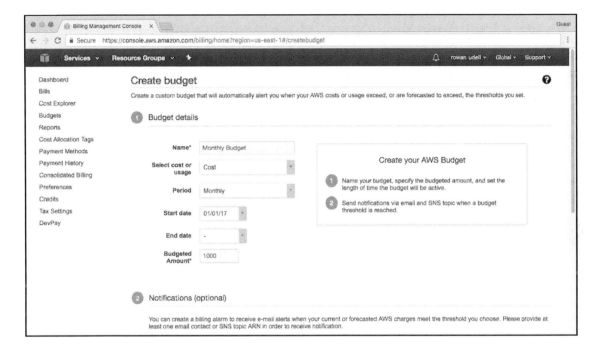

5. Next enter the notification details. This includes the threshold for notification, which we will set to be 80% (of our budget) in forecasted use. For e-mail notifications, simply enter the e-mail addresses you want to receive the notifications. Click **Create** when finished:

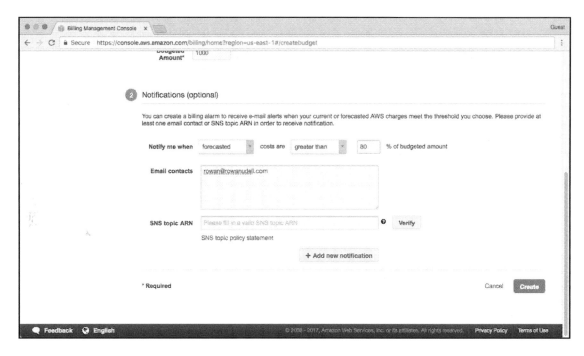

6. You will be returned to the **Budgets** section of the **Billing** dashboard, and you can see your newly created budget:

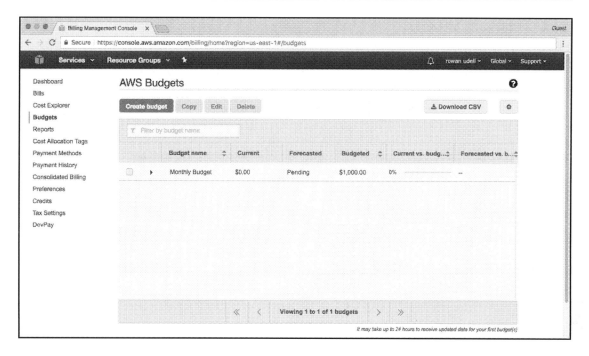

7. For each of the budgets you create, you can select it to view the full details:

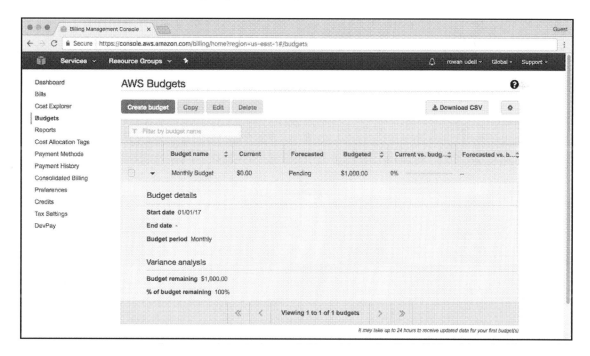

How it works...

The **Billing** dashboard is closely tied to the account itself, which is why it is not part of the regular services in the console. Accessing it via the user menu hints at the special access it requires. Generally, you would configure a budget when you first open a new AWS account, so you don't get any surprises in your bill at the end of the month.

If you get access denied messages in the **Billing** dashboard, it is most likely because you are using an IAM user and IAM access has not been enabled. You must use your root account credentials (such as that you used to create the account), or enable IAM access. IAM access can only be enabled by the root user.

When you first arrive at the billing section, you will see a high-level summary of your usage and expenses. As I performed this example in a new account, there's not much to see at this point. The **Month-to-Date Spend by Service** graph on the right can be particularly useful to find out what the most popular services you use are. This is a great place to start when trying to reduce or optimize your AWS spending.

We then navigate to the budgets section and create a new budget. Most of the details should be self-explanatory, and obvious for the purposes of budgeting. Your main choice is to decide if you want to alert on usage or costs. Cost budgets work against the dollar (or appropriate billing currency) amount you will be charged. Usage budgets work against a selected unit of usage, for example, instance hours or data transfer for EC2. A usage budget can only track one type of usage unit, so you will need to create multiple budgets to track the various units that you might be charged for. This is one reason why we prefer a cost budget, as it takes into account multiple forms of usage.

Specifying e-mail addresses to alert is the simplest way to send any alerts from the budget. For more advanced use cases, you can specify an SNS topic to receive notifications. An example might be if you wanted to receive budget alerts on your phone via an SMS message, or send the alert to a different system automatically (via HTTP/JSON).

Once finished, you can view all your budgets in the dashboard. You can repeat the process to create multiple budgets. This means you can create budgets for forecast usage and actual usage, as well as different time periods.

Feeding log files into CloudWatch logs

CloudWatch logs is a managed, highly durable, log storage system in AWS. It's capable of ingesting logs from many sources. We're going to focus on what is probably the most common use case which is shipping logs off your EC2 instances into CloudWatch logs.

This capability is particularly important in highly dynamic auto scaling environments. Since the lifetime of your EC2 instances can be quite short, any logs which are written only to a local disk will be lost upon instance termination. You'll inevitably find yourself wishing you had access to server logs after an instance has disappeared.

The following pattern we're about to show you allows you to aggregate, search and filter log entries across a number of sources. You can then create custom metrics and trigger alarms based on log activity. Super handy!

In this recipe we're going to:

- Launch an EC2 instance
- Configure it to send logs to CloudWatch logs
- Create a filter based on SSH logins to the instance
- Send ourselves an e-mail alert on filter matches

 This might be something you'd consider doing on your bastion boxes since they will typically be the sole point of SSH access to your environments and it can be a good idea to make a lot of noise if people are logging in to production servers.

Getting ready

We're going to do all of this in us-east-1 with the AWS Linux AMI. If you wish to do this in a different region you'll simply need to provide a different AMI ID to the template we're going to create.

Let's get in to it; you'll need the following:

- The VPC ID of your default VPC in us-east-1. You don't have to use the default VPC, you'll just need to make sure you choose a VPC which has a public subnet (which is configured to assign public IP addresses)
- The subnet ID of the public subnet
- An SSH key pair configured in us-east-1
- An e-mail address we can send alerts to

How to do it...

1. Create a new CloudFormation template. Add the following `Parameters` to it:

```
AmiId:
  Type: AWS::EC2::Image::Id
  Description: AMI ID to launch instances from
  Default: ami-0b33d91d
VpcId:
  Type: AWS::EC2::VPC::Id
  Description: VPC where load balancer and instance will launch
SubnetIDs:
  Type: List<AWS::EC2::Subnet::Id>
  Description: Public subnet where the instance will launch
    (pick at least 1)
KeyPair:
  Type: AWS::EC2::KeyPair::KeyName
  Description: Key to launch EC2 instance with
AlertEmail:
  Type: String
  Description: Email Address which alert emails will be sent to
```

2. Now for the `Resources`, we need to define a `Role` and `InstanceProfile` for our EC2 instance. This will give our server the appropriate permissions to send logs to CloudWatch.

```
ExampleRole:
  Type: AWS::IAM::Role
  Properties:
    AssumeRolePolicyDocument:
      Version: "2012-10-17"
      Statement:
        -
          Effect: Allow
          Principal:
            Service:
              - ec2.amazonaws.com
          Action:
            - sts:AssumeRole
    Path: /
    Policies:
      -
        PolicyName: WriteToCloudWatchLogs
        PolicyDocument:
          Version: "2012-10-17"
          Statement:
```

```
              Effect: Allow
                Action:
                  - logs:CreateLogGroup
                  - logs:CreateLogStream
                  - logs:PutLogEvents
                  - logs:DescribeLogStreams
                Resource: "*"
  ExampleInstanceProfile:
    Type: AWS::IAM::InstanceProfile
    Properties:
      Roles:
        - !Ref ExampleRole
      Path: /
```

3. Our instance will need to live in a security group which allows SSH access, so let's add that now:

```
ExampleEC2InstanceSecurityGroup:
  Type: AWS::EC2::SecurityGroup
  Properties:
    GroupDescription: Security Group for example Instance
    SecurityGroupIngress:
      - IpProtocol: tcp
        CidrIp: "0.0.0.0/0"
        FromPort: 22
        ToPort: 22
    VpcId: !Ref VpcId
```

4. Next we can define our instance. We make sure to use the profile and security group we just created and we also add a small amount of user-data which does the following:

   1. Install the `awslogs` package.

   2. Writes a configuration file which will ship `/var/log/secure` to CloudWatch logs.

   3. Starts the `awslogs` service.

   4. Make the `awslogs` service start on boot (in case of reboot).

```
ExampleEC2Instance:
  Type: AWS::EC2::Instance
  Properties:
    IamInstanceProfile: !Ref ExampleInstanceProfile
    InstanceType: t2.nano
    KeyName: !Ref KeyPair
    UserData:
      Fn::Base64:
```

```
                         Fn::Sub: |
                           #!/bin/bash -ex
                           yum update -y
                           yum install -y awslogs
                           cat << EOF >
                           /etc/awslogs/config/var-log-secure.conf
                           [/var/log/secure]
                           datetime_format = %b %d %H:%M:%S
                           file = /var/log/secure
                           buffer_duration = 5000
                           log_stream_name = {instance_id}
                           initial_position = start_of_file
                           log_group_name = /var/log/secure
                           EOF
                           service awslogs start
                           chkconfig awslogs on
                    ImageId: !Ref AmiId
                    SecurityGroupIds:
                      - Fn::GetAtt: ExampleEC2InstanceSecurityGroup.GroupId
                    SubnetId: !Select [ 0, Ref: SubnetIDs ]
```

5. We're now going to add an SNS topic. This topic will receive alerts and forward them to the e-mail address we're using for alerts:

```
ExampleSNSTopic:
  Type: AWS::SNS::Topic
  Properties:
      Subscription:
        -
          Endpoint: !Ref AlertEmail
          Protocol: email
```

6. Next, we need to filter our /var/log/secure logs for logins. A MetricFilter resource allows us to do this. CloudFormation will throw an error if we refer to a log group which doesn't yet exist, so we add that here too (with a DependsOn reference):

```
ExampleLogGroup:
  Type: AWS::Logs::LogGroup
  Properties:
    LogGroupName: /var/log/secure
    RetentionInDays: 7
ExampleLogsMetricFilter:
  Type: AWS::Logs::MetricFilter
  Properties:
    FilterPattern: '"Accepted publickey for ec2-user from"'
    LogGroupName: /var/log/secure
```

```
MetricTransformations:
  -
    MetricValue: "1"
    MetricNamespace: SSH/Logins
    MetricName: LoginCount
DependsOn: ExampleLogGroup
```

7. The last `Resource` we need is the actual `Alarm`. Add it like so:

```
ExampleLoginAlarm:
  Type: AWS::CloudWatch::Alarm
  Properties:
    AlarmDescription: SSH Login Alarm
    AlarmActions:
    - Ref: ExampleSNSTopic
    MetricName: LoginCount
    Namespace: SSH/Logins
    Statistic: Sum
    Period: 60
    EvaluationPeriods: 1
    Threshold: 0
    ComparisonOperator: GreaterThanThreshold
```

8. Lastly, we'll add the public IP address of our instance to the `Outputs` so we don't need to go to the EC2 web console to look it up:

```
Outputs:
  ExampleEC2InstancePublicIp:
    Value: !GetAtt [ ExampleEC2Instance, PublicIp ]
```

9. Go ahead and launch this CloudFormation stack. You can do it from the AWS CLI like this:

```
aws cloudformation create-stack \
  --template-body \
  file://05-feed-log-files-in-to-cloudwatch-logs.yaml \
  --stack-name example-cloudwatchlogs \
  --capabilities CAPABILITY_IAM \
  --parameters \
  ParameterKey=VpcId,ParameterValue=<your-vpc-id> \
  ParameterKey=SubnetIDs,ParameterValue='<your-subnet-id>' \
  ParameterKey=KeyPair,ParameterValue=<your-ssh-key-name> \
  ParameterKey=AlertEmail,ParameterValue=<your-email-address>
```

10. Before proceeding you'll need to check your e-mail and confirm your subscription to the SNS topic. If you don't do this you won't receive any alerts from CloudWatch:

In the following screenshot, an example of confirmed subscription is illustrated:

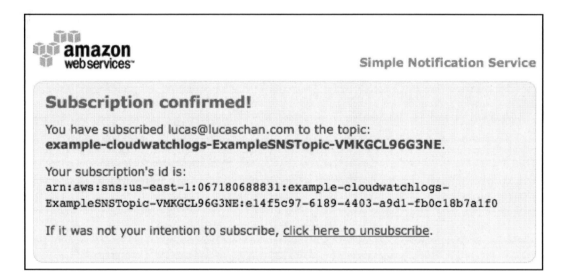

11. Go ahead and SSH to your instance. If your login is successful, you'll see your alarm triggered in the CloudWatch web console:

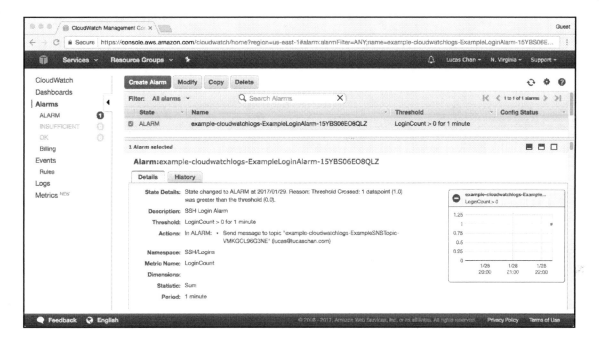

An e-mail will land in your inbox as shown in the following screenshot:

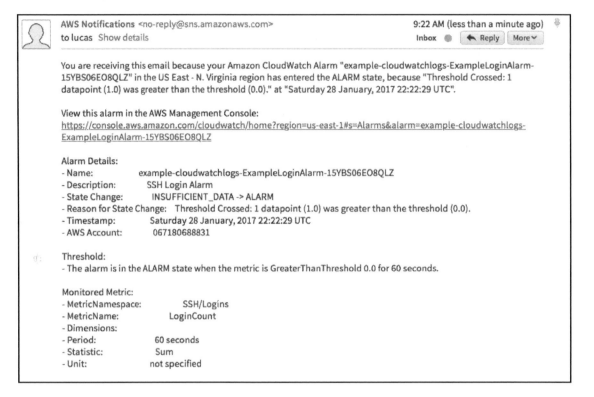

How it works...

It's important that you understand the difference between log streams and log groups.

Log streams are log sequences which come from a single source. This could be an EC2 instance, an application process, or another source within AWS. In our case the name of our log stream is the ID of our EC2 instance. In fact, the CloudWatch logs agent will set the `log_stream_name` to the instance ID by default.

Log groups are collections of log streams with the same properties. In our previous example, the log groups will correspond to `/var/log/secure`. So, we end up with a configuration which looks like:

```
log_group_name = /var/log/secure
log_stream_name = {instance_id}
```

When you install the CloudWatch logs agent, it actually sets up /var/log/messages in exactly the same manner as we've just described:

```
log_group_name = /var/log/messages
log_stream_name = {instance_id}
```

Once the agent has started, it will ship new log entries off the box to CloudWatch logs approximately every 5 seconds.

There's more...

- CloudWatch logs supports ingestion of traditional text-based log entries as well as JSON formatted logs.
- Logs can be ingested from other sources including CloudTrail, IAM, Kinesis Streams and Lambda.
- By default, logs are stored indefinitely. You can customize this time period to suit your needs however.
- Metric filters, like the one we created previously, can be used to graph and chart in the CloudWatch console. Add them to your dashboards as well as your alerting system.
- The CloudWatch web console allows you to test metric filters before you add them. Using this feature will save you a lot of trial and error with CloudFormation. Don't rely on the web console completely however: you should move these metric filters to CloudFormation as soon as you get them right.
- There is a one-one relationship between a log stream and a log source. For example, you can't have multiple instances sending /var/log/secure to the same log stream.
- The non-alarm state for the alarm we've created, will be **INSUFFICIENT_DATA**. This is because our metric filter outputs a value only if a login is detected.

6
Database Services

In this chapter, we will cover:

- Creating a database with automatic failover
- Creating a NAT gateway
- Creating a database read-replica
- Promoting a read-replica to master
- Creating a one-time database backup
- Restoring a database from a snapshot
- Migrating a database
- Calculating DynamoDB performance

Introduction

Having a persistent storage service is a key component of effectively using the AWS cloud for your systems. By ensuring that you have a highly available, fault-tolerant location to store your application state in, you can stop depending on individual servers for your data.

Creating a database with automatic failover

In this recipe, we're going to create a MySQL RDS database instance configured in multi-AZ mode to facilitate automatic failover.

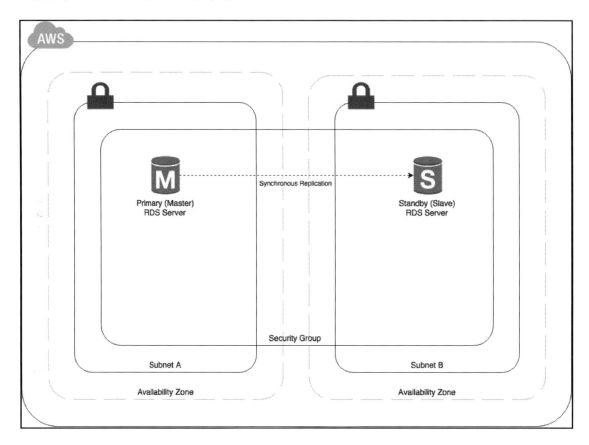

Database with automatic failover

Getting ready

The default VPC will work fine for this example. Once you are comfortable with creating databases, you may want to consider a VPC containing private subnets that you can use to segment your database away from the Internet and other resources (in the style of a three tier application). Either way, you'll need to note down the following:

- The ID of the VPC

- The CIDR range of the VPC
- The IDs of at least two subnets in your VPC. These subnets need to be in different Availability Zones, for example, `us-east-1a` and `us-east-1b`

How to do it...

Create a new CloudFormation template. We're going to add a total of 12 parameters to it:

1. The first three parameters will contain the values we mentioned in the *Getting ready* section:

```
VPCId:
  Type: AWS::EC2::VPC::Id
  Description: VPC where DB will launch
SubnetIds:
  Type: List<AWS::EC2::Subnet::Id>
  Description: Subnets where the DB will launch (pick at least 2)
SecurityGroupAllowCidr:
  Type: String
  Description: Allow this CIDR block to access the DB
  Default: "172.30.0.0/16"
```

2. We're also going to add the database credentials as parameters. This is good practice as it means we're not storing any credentials in our infrastructure source code. Note that the password contains the `NoEcho` parameter set to `true`. This stops CloudFormation from outputting the password wherever the CloudFormation stack details are displayed:

```
DBUsername:
  Type: String
  Description: Username to access the database
  MinLength: 1
  AllowedPattern: "[a-zA-Z][a-zA-Z0-9]*"
  ConstraintDescription: must start with a letter, must
    be alphanumeric
DBPassword:
  Type: String
  Description: Password to access the database
  MinLength: 1
  AllowedPattern: "[a-zA-Z0-9]*"
  NoEcho: true
  ConstraintDescription: must be alphanumeric
```

3. The next block of parameters pertains to cost and performance. They should be mostly self-explanatory. Refer to the AWS documentation on database instance types should you wish to change the instance class for this example. We're supplying a default value of 10 GB for the storage size and choosing a magnetic (standard) volume for the storage type. gp2 offers better performance, but it costs a little more:

```
DBInstanceClass:
  Type: String
  Description: The instance type to use for this database
  Default: db.t2.micro
DBStorageAmount:
  Type: Number
  Description: Amount of storage to allocate (in GB)
  Default: 10
DBStorageType:
  Type: String
  Description: Type of storage volume to use
    (standard [magnetic] or gp2)
  Default: standard
  AllowedValues:
    - standard
    - gp2
```

4. We need to set some additional parameters for our database. These are the MySQL engine version and port. Refer to the AWS documentation for a list of all the available versions. We are setting a default value for this parameter as the latest version of MySQL at the time of writing:

```
DBEngineVersion:
  Type: String
  Description: DB engine version
  Default: "5.7.11"
DBPort:
  Type: Number
  Description: Port number to allocate
  Default: 3306
  MinValue: 1150
  MaxValue: 65535
```

5. Finally, we are going to define some parameters relating to backup and availability. We want our database to run in *multi-AZ* mode, we set this to `true` by default. We also set a backup retention period of 1 day by default; you might want to choose a period larger than this. If you set this value to 0, backups will be disabled (not recommended!):

```
DBMultiAZ:
  Type: String
  Description: Should this DB be deployed in Multi-AZ configuration?
  Default: true
  AllowedValues:
    - true
    - false
DBBackupRetentionPeriod:
  Type: Number
  Description: How many days to keep backups (0 disables backups)
  Default: 1
  MinValue: 0
  MaxValue: 35
```

6. We're done with the parameters for this template; we can now go ahead and start defining our `Resources`. First of all, we want a security group for our DB to reside in. This security group allows inbound access to the database port from the CIDR range we've defined:

```
ExampleDBSecurityGroup:
  Type: AWS::EC2::SecurityGroup
  Properties:
    GroupDescription: Example security group for inbound access to DB
    SecurityGroupIngress:
      - IpProtocol: tcp
        CidrIp: !Ref SecurityGroupAllowCidr
        FromPort: !Ref DBPort
        ToPort: !Ref DBPort
    VpcId: !Ref VPCId
```

7. Next, we need to define a `DBSubnetGroup` resource. This resource is used to declare which subnet(s) our DB will reside in. We define two subnets for this resource so that the primary and standby servers will reside in separate Availability Zones:

```
ExampleDBSubnetGroup:
  Type: AWS::RDS::DBSubnetGroup
  Properties:
    DBSubnetGroupDescription: Example subnet group for example DB
    SubnetIds:
```

```
    - Fn::Select: [ 0, Ref: SubnetIds ]
    - Fn::Select: [ 1, Ref: SubnetIds ]
```

8. Finally, we define our RDS instance resource. We specify it as being a MySQL database and the rest of the properties are made up of the parameters and resources that we've defined previously. Lots of !Ref is required here:

```
ExampleDBInstance:
  Type: AWS::RDS::DBInstance
  Properties:
    AllocatedStorage: !Ref DBStorageAmount
    BackupRetentionPeriod: !Ref DBBackupRetentionPeriod
    DBInstanceClass: !Ref DBInstanceClass
    DBSubnetGroupName: !Ref ExampleDBSubnetGroup
    Engine: mysql
    EngineVersion: !Ref DBEngineVersion
    MasterUsername: !Ref DBUsername
    MasterUserPassword: !Ref DBPassword
    MultiAZ: !Ref DBMultiAZ
    StorageType: !Ref DBStorageType
    VPCSecurityGroups:
      - !GetAtt ExampleDBSecurityGroup.GroupId
```

9. For good measure, we can add an output to this template that will return the hostname for this RDS database:

```
Outputs:
  ExampleDbHostname:
    Value: !GetAtt ExampleDBInstance.Endpoint.Address
```

10. You can provision the database via the CloudFormation web console or use a CLI command like so:

```
aws cloudformation create-stack \
  --stack-name rds1 \
  --template-body \
  file://06-create-database-with-automatic-failover.yaml \
  --parameters \
  ParameterKey=DBUsername,ParameterValue=<username> \
  ParameterKey=DBPassword,ParameterValue=<password> \
  ParameterKey=SubnetIds,"ParameterValue='<subnet-id-a>, \
  <subnet-id-b>'" \
  ParameterKey=VPCId,ParameterValue=<vpc-id>
```

How it works...

In a multi-AZ configuration, AWS will provision a standby MySQL instance in a separate Availability Zone. Changes to your database will be replicated to the standby DB instance in a synchronous fashion. If there is a problem with your primary DB instance AWS will automatically failover to the standby, promote it to be the primary DB, and provision a new standby.

You don't have access to query standby databases directly. So you can't use it to handle all of your read queries, for example. If you wish to use additional database instances to increase read capacity, you'll need to provision a *read-replica*. We'll cover those in a separate recipe.

Backups will always be taken from the standby instance, which means there is no interruption to your DB availability. This is not the case if you opted against deploying your DB in multi-AZ mode.

When you deploy this example it will take roughly 20 minutes or more for the stack to report completion. This is because the RDS service needs to go through the following process in order to provision a fully working multi-AZ database:

- Provision the primary database
- Back up the primary database
- Provision the standby database using the backup from the primary
- Configure both databases for synchronous replication

WARNING

Be careful about making changes to your RDS configuration after you've started writing data to it, especially when using CloudFormation updates. Some RDS configuration changes require the database to be re-provisioned, which can result in data loss. We'd recommend using CloudFormation change sets, which will give you an opportunity to see which changes are about to cause destructive behavior. The CloudFormation RDS docs also provide some information on this.

There's more...

- You can define a maintenance window for your RDS instance. This is the time period when AWS will perform maintenance tasks such as security patches or minor version upgrades. If you don't specify a maintenance window (which we don't in this example), one is chosen for you.

Creating a NAT gateway

Unless required, your instances should not be publicly exposed to the Internet. When your instances are on the Internet, you have to assume that they will be attacked at some stage.

This means most of your workloads should run on instances in private subnets. Private subnets are those that are not connected directly to the Internet.

In order to give your private instances access to the Internet you use **network address translation** (**NAT**). A NAT gateway allows your instances to initiate a connection to the Internet, without allowing connections from the Internet.

Getting ready

For this recipe, you must have the following resources:

- A VPC with an **Internet gateway** (**IGW**)
- A public subnet
- A private subnet route table

You will need the IDs for the public subnet and private subnet route table. Both of these resources should be in the same AZ.

How to do it...

1. Start with the usual CloudFormation template version and description:

```
AWSTemplateFormatVersion: "2010-09-09"
Description: Create NAT Gateway and associated route.
```

2. The template must take the following required parameters:

```
Parameters:
  PublicSubnetId:
    Description: Public Subnet ID to add the NAT Gateway to
    Type: AWS::EC2::Subnet::Id
  RouteTableId:
    Description: The private subnet route table to add the NAT
      Gateway route to
    Type: String
```

3. In the `Resources` section, define an Elastic IP that will be assigned to the NAT gateway:

```
Resources:
  EIP:
    Type: AWS::EC2::EIP
    Properties:
      Domain: vpc
```

4. Create the NAT gateway resource, assigning it the EIP you just defined in the public subnet:

```
NatGateway:
  Type: AWS::EC2::NatGateway
  Properties:
    AllocationId: !GetAtt EIP.AllocationId
    SubnetId: !Ref PublicSubnetId
```

5. Finally, define the route to the NAT gateway and associate it with the private subnet's route table:

```
Route:
  Type: AWS::EC2::Route
  Properties:
    RouteTableId: !Ref RouteTableId
    DestinationCidrBlock: 0.0.0.0/0
    NatGatewayId: !Ref NatGateway
```

How it works...

The parameters required for this recipe are as follows:

- A public subnet ID
- A private subnet route table ID

The public subnet ID is needed to host the NAT gateway, as it must have Internet access. The private subnet route table will be updated with a route to the NAT gateway.

Using the AWS NAT gateway service means that AWS takes care of hosting and securing the service for you. The service will be hosted redundantly in a single AZ.

 You can use the recipe multiple times to deploy NAT gateways in each of your private subnets. Just make sure the public subnet and the private subnet are in the same AZ.

To cater for the unlikely event of an AZ outage (unlikely, but possible) you should deploy a NAT gateway per subnet. This means if one NAT gateway goes offline, instances in the other AZ can continue to access the Internet as normal. You *are* deploying your application in multiple AZs, aren't you?

This recipe will only work if you have created your own private subnets, as the default subnets in a new AWS account are all *public*. Instances in a public subnet have direct access to the Internet (via an IGW), so they do not need a NAT gateway.

See also

- The *Building a secure network* recipe in Chapter 7, *Networking*

Creating a database read-replica

This recipe will show you how to create an RDS read-replica. You can use read-replicas in order to increase the performance of your application by off-loading database reads to a separate database instance. You can provision up to five read-replicas per source DB.

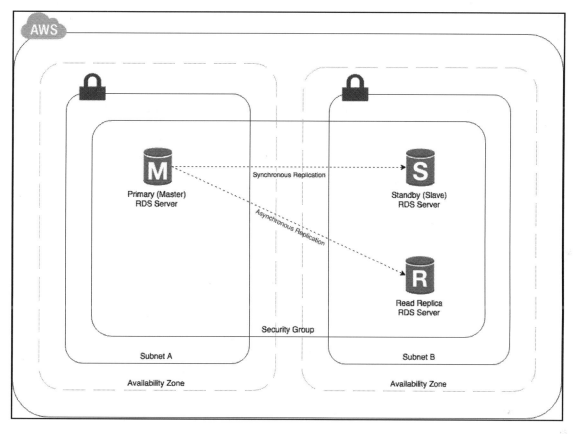

Read-only database slaves

Getting ready

You will need an RDS DB deployed with backup retention enabled. We are going to build upon the DB deployed in the previous *Creating a database with automatic failover* recipe.

You're going to need the following values:

- The identifier for your source RDS instance, for example, `eexocwv5k5kv5z`
- A unique identifier for the read-replicate we're going to create, for example, `read-replica-1`

How to do it...

In the AWS CLI, type this command:

```
aws rds create-db-instance-read-replica \
  --source-db-instance-identifier <source-db-identifier> \
  --db-instance-identifier <unique-identifier-for-replica>
```

How it works...

RDS will now go ahead and create a new read-replica for you.

Some parameters are inherited from the source instance and can't be defined at the time of creation:

- Storage engine
- Storage size
- Security group

The CLI command accepts some parameters that we could have defined, but didn't to keep things simple. They will instead be inherited from the source database. The main two are as follows:

- `--db-instance-class`: The same class as the source instance is used
- `--db-subnet-group-name`: The source instance's subnet group will be used and a subnet is chosen at random (hence, an Availability Zone is chosen at random)

There's more...

- Read-replicas are deployed in a single Availability Zone; there is no standby read-replica.
- It's not possible to enable backups on read-replicas during time of creation. This must be configured afterwards.
- The default storage type is `standard` (magnetic). You can increase performance by choosing `gp2` or using provisioned IOPS.
- It's possible to add MySQL indexes directly to a read-replica to further increase read performance. These indexes are not required to be present on the primary DB.

- Using read-replicas for availability purposes is more of a complimentary DR strategy and shouldn't be used in place of multi-AZ RDS. A multi-AZ configuration gives you the benefit of failure detection and automatic failover.
- It is possible to deploy a read-replica in an entirely different region.
- Unlike the replication between a primary and standby DB (which is synchronous), replication to a read-replica is asynchronous. This means that it's possible for a read-replica to fall behind the primary. Keep this in mind when sending time sensitive read queries to your read-replicas.

Promoting a read-replica to master

We're going to show you how to promote an RDS read-replica to be a primary instance. There are a few reasons you might like to do this:

- To handle a table migration that would typically cause a large amount of downtime, especially when messing with columns or indexes
- Because you need to implement sharding
- Recovery from failure, should you choose not to deploy your existing primary in multi-AZ mode (not recommended)

Getting ready

You're going to need the unique ID, which has been assigned to an RDS read-replica. If you followed the previous *Creating a database with automatic failover*, and *Creating a database read-replica* recipes, then you'll be all set.

It's also a good idea to have backups enabled on this read-replica prior to promoting it. This shortens the promotion process because you won't need to wait for a backup to be taken. You'll want to set the backup retention period to a value between 1 and 8.

Enabling backups on your read-replica will cause it to reboot!

In order to enable backups, you can use the following CLI command:

```
aws rds modify-db-instance \
  --db-instance-identifier <identifier-for-read-replica> \
  --backup-retention-period <days-to-keep-backups-for> \
  --apply-immediately
```

You can drop the `--apply-immediately` parameter if you prefer to wait for the reboot to happen during the configured maintenance window. But you'll still want to wait until after the reboot happens before you continue with the promotion process.

To ensure that you have the most up-to-date data before promotion you'll want to stop all write traffic to the current source primary DB before going ahead. It's also a good idea to make sure that the replication lag on your read-replica is 0 (you can check this in CloudWatch).

How to do it...

1. Run the following command to promote your read-replica to a primary DB instance. This command will cause your read-replica to reboot:

```
aws rds promote-read-replica \
  --db-instance-identifier <identifier-for-read-replica>
```

2. If you wish to then go ahead and configure your new primary RDS instance to run in a multi-AZ configuration then you'll need to run this additional command. Expect to wait a while for this operation to complete:

```
aws rds modify-db-instance \
  --db-instance-identifier <identifier-for-new-primary> \
  --multi-az \
  --apply-immediately
```

Creating a one-time database backup

We're now going to show you how to make a one-off snapshot of your database. You might opt to do this if you have a specific requirement around keeping a point in time backup of your DB. You might also want to take a snapshot for the purpose of creating a new working copy of your dataset.

Getting ready

In order to proceed you're going to need the following:

- The identifier for the RDS instance you wish to back up
- A unique identifier that you'd like to assign to this snapshot

The snapshot identifier has some constraints:

- It needs to start with a letter
- It must not be longer than 255 characters

 If your primary database isn't running in a multi-AZ configuration then be aware that creating a snapshot will cause an outage. In a multi-AZ configuration the snapshot is taken on the standby instance so no outage occurs.

How to do it...

Type the following AWS CLI command to initiate the creation of a snapshot. You'll need to wait for a few minutes for the snapshot to complete before you can use it:

```
aws rds create-db-snapshot \
  --db-instance-identifier <primary-rds-id> \
  --db-snapshot-identifier <unique-id-for-snapshot>
```

Restoring a database from a snapshot

We'll now talk through how to restore a database from a snapshot. This process creates a new database that will retain a majority of the configuration of the database that the snapshot was taken from.

Getting ready

You'll need the following pieces of information:

- The ID of the snapshot you wish to restore from
- A name or identifier that you wish to give to the database we're about to create

AWS does not allow RDS services in your account to share the same identifier. If the source database is still online you'll need to make sure to choose a different identifier (or rename the source database).

How to do it...

1. Type the following command:

```
aws rds restore-db-instance-from-db-snapshot \
  --db-snapshot-identifier <name-of-snapshot-to-restore > \
  --db-instance-identifier <name-for-new-db> \
  --db-subnet-group-name <your-db-subnet-group> \
  --multi-az
```

2. You may have noticed that this command creates a new database in the default security group. This happens because the `restore-db-instance-from-db-snapshot` doesn't accept a security group ID as a parameter. You'll have to run a second command to assign a nondefault security group to the new database:

```
aws rds modify-db-instance \
  --db-instance-identifier <name-of-newly-restored-db> \
  --vpc-security-group-ids <id-of-security-group>
```

 The `modify-db-instance` command will return an error unless the state of the target database is `available`.
Also, security group names aren't valid with this command; you'll need to use a security group ID instead, for example, `sg-7603d50a`.

There's more...

The previous command includes the parameter for enabling multi-AZ on the new DB. If you'd like the new DB to be running in single-AZ mode only then can you simply remove this flag.

Migrating a database

In this recipe, we will use **Database Migration Service** (**DMS**) to move an external database into **Relational Database Service** (**RDS**).

Unlike many of the other recipes, this will be performed manually through the web console.

Most database migrations are one-off, and there are many steps involved. We suggest that you first perform the process manually via the console before automating it, if required (which you can do with the AWS CLI tool or SDKs).

Getting ready

For this recipe you will need the following:

- An external database
- An RDS database instance

The source database in this example is called **employees**, so substitute your own database name as required.

Both databases must be accessible from the replication instance that will be created as part of the recipe. The simplest way to do this is to allow access to the databases from the Internet, but obviously this has security implications.

How to do it...

1. Navigate to the DMS console:

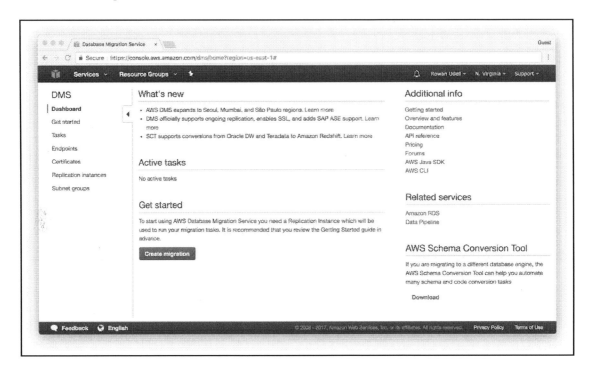

2. Click on **Create Migration** to start the migration wizard:

3. Specify the details for your replication instance. Unless you have a specific VPC configuration, the defaults will be fine:

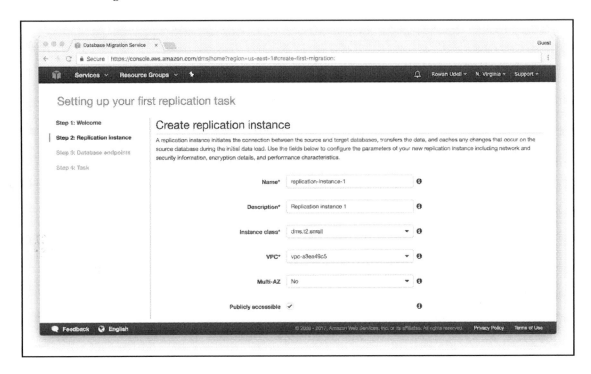

4. While waiting for the replication instance to be ready, fill out the source and target endpoint information, including server hostname and port, and the username and password to use when connecting:

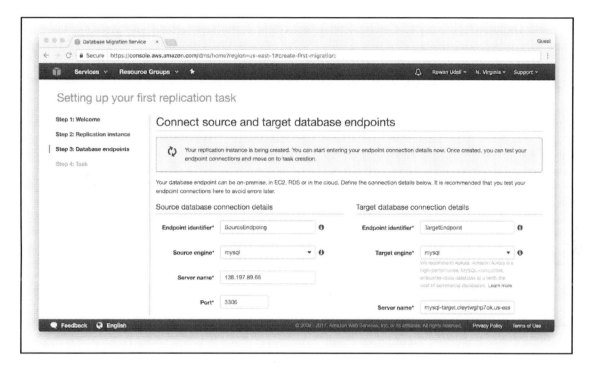

5. Once the instance is ready, the interface will update and you can proceed:

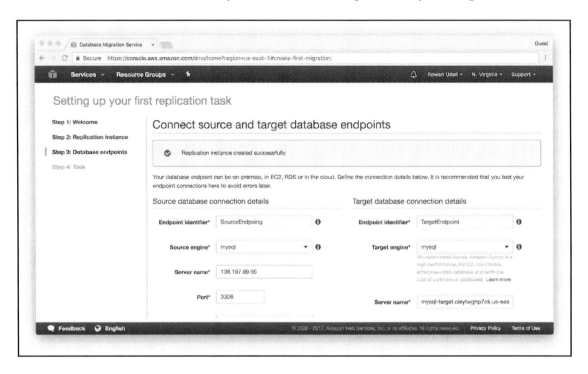

6. In order to confirm and create the source and target endpoints, click on the **Run test** button for each of your databases:

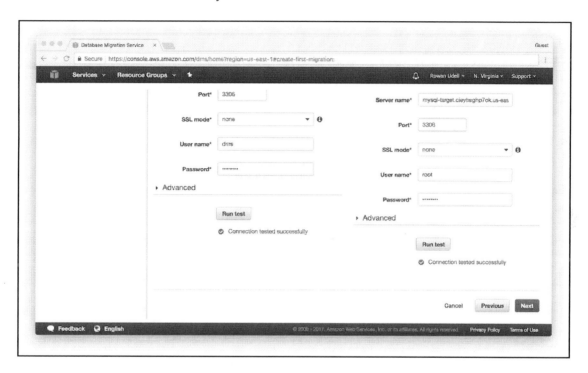

7. After the endpoints have been successfully tested and created, define your task. In this recipe, we will simply migrate the data (without ongoing replication):

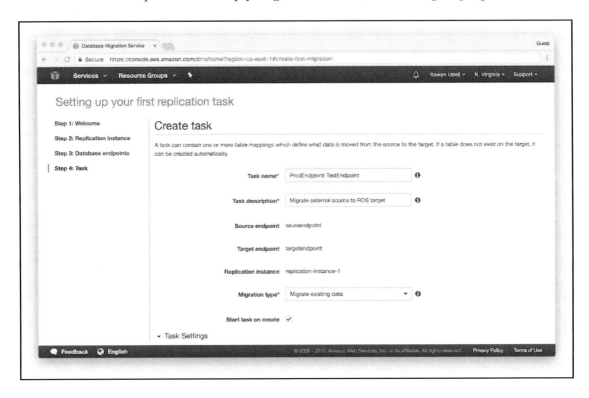

8. For simplicity, drop the tables in the target database (which should be empty) to ensure parity between the databases:

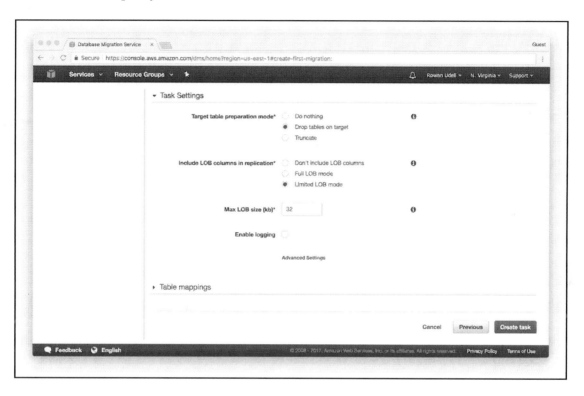

9. Finally, define the mappings between the two databases. In this case, we will migrate all the tables (by using the wildcard %) in the **employees** database on the source:

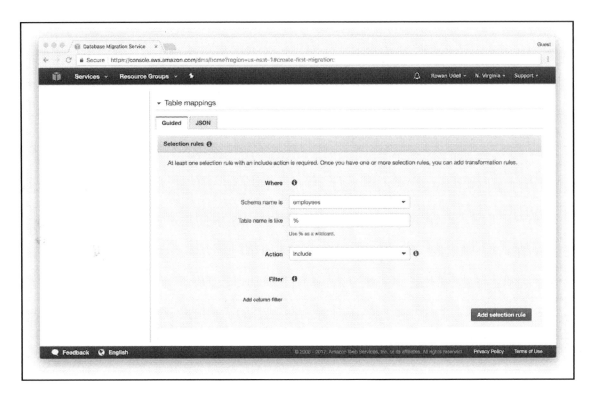

10. Once you click **Add selection rule** you will see your rule in the selection rules list:

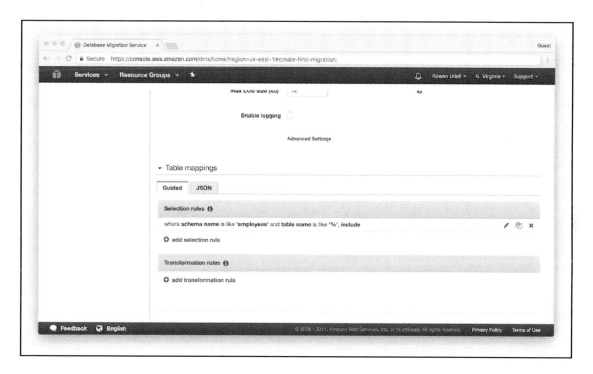

11. Once the task is defined you have finished the wizard. You will then see the task being created:

12. Once the status of the task is **Ready** you can select it and click on the **Start/Resume** button:

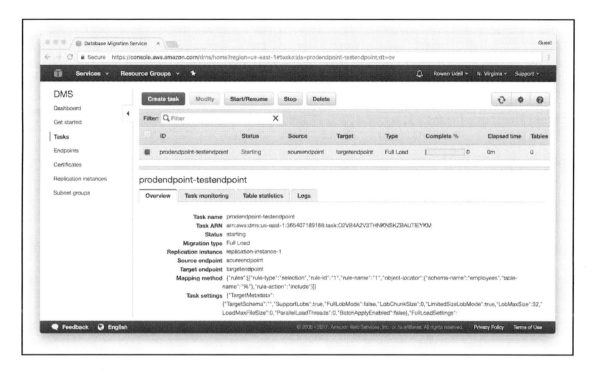

13. When complete, you will see the task's details updated in the console:

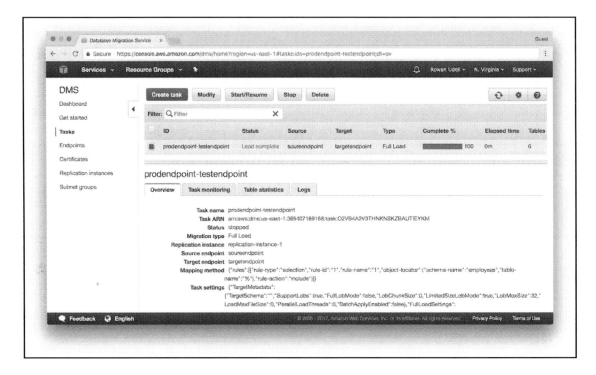

How it works...

At a high level, this is what the DMS architecture looks like:

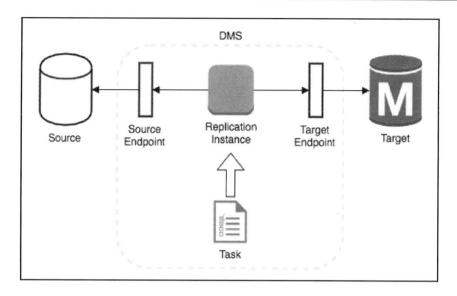

Both the **Source** and **Target** databases are external to **DMS**. They are represented internally by endpoint resources that are references to the databases. Endpoints can be reused between different tasks if needed.

This recipe starts by defining the replication instance details. Keep in mind that the DMS migration process works best when the migration/transform between the two databases is kept *in memory*. This means that for larger jobs you should allocate a more powerful instance. If the process needs to temporarily write data to disk (such as swap) then the performance and throughput will be much lower. This can have flow-on effects, particularly for tasks that include ongoing replication.

Next, the two endpoints are defined. It is very important to verify your endpoint configuration by using the built-in testing feature so that your tasks do not fail later in the process. Generally, if the connectivity test fails, it is one of two main issues:

- Network connectivity issues between the replication instance and the database. This is particularly an issue for on-premise databases, which are usually specifically restricted from being accessed externally.
- User permissions issues: For example, in the case of MySQL, the root user cannot be used to connect to the database externally, so this default user cannot be used.

Defining the task involves defining your migration type. The recipe uses the simplest type; migrate tables. This means that the data will be copied between the two databases, and will be complete when the data is propagated. We also get to define the behavior on the target database. For simplicity, we have configured the task to drop the tables in the target database ensuring that the two databases look as similar as possible, even if the tables are renamed, or the table mappings change. For the task table mappings we use the wildcard symbol % to match all tables in the source database. Obviously, you could be more selective if you only wanted to match a subset of your data.

Once the replication instance, endpoints, and task are defined the wizard ends and you are returned to the DMS console. After the task is finished creating it can be started.

As it is a *migrate existing data-type* task, it will complete once all the data has been propagated to the target database.

There's more...

This is obviously a simple example of what DMS can do. There are other features and performance aspects that you should consider in more advanced scenarios.

Database engines

While this example uses two MySQL databases, it is possible to migrate from one database engine to a complete database engine, for example, Oracle to MySQL. Unfortunately, this can be a complex process, and while this functionality is very useful it is beyond the scope of this recipe. Due to the differences in the various engines, there are some limitations on what you can migrate and transform.

 See the *AWS Schema Conversion Tool* documentation for more details on what can be migrated between different database engines.

Ongoing replication

There are also some limits around the ongoing propagation of data—only table data can be migrated. Things such as indexes, users, and permissions cannot be replicated continually.

Multi-AZ

For ongoing replication tasks, you may want to create a multi-AZ replication instance so that the impact of any interruptions of services are minimized. Obviously you will need to have a similarly configured (such as multi-AZ) RDS instance as your target to get the full benefit!

 For best performance, when setting up your replication instance you should make sure it is in the *same* AZ as your target RDS instance.

Calculating DyanmoDB performance

DynamoDB (DDB) is the managed NoSQL database service from AWS.

As DDB pricing is based on the amount of read and write capacity units provisioned, it is important to be able to calculate the requirements for your use case.

This recipe uses a written formula to estimate the required **read capacity units** (**RCU**) and **write capacity units** (**WCU**) that should be allocated to you DDB table.

It is also crucial to remember that while new partitions will be automatically added to a DDB table, they cannot be automatically taken away. This means that excessive partitioning can cause long-term impacts to your performance, so you should be aware of them.

Getting ready

All of these calculations assume that you have chosen a good partition key for your data. A good partition key ensures the following:

- Data is evenly spread across all the available partitions
- Read and write activity is spread evenly in time

Unfortunately, choosing a good partition key is very data-specific, and beyond the scope of this recipe.

All reads are assumed to be strongly consistent.

How to do it...

1. Start with the size of the items, in **kilobytes (KB)**:

   ItemSize = Size of the items (rows) in KB

2. Work out the required number of RCUs required by dividing the number by 4, and rounding up:

   RCU Per Item = ItemSize / 4 (rounded up)

3. Define the expected number of read operations per second. This is one of the numbers you will use to provision your table with:

   *Required RCU = Expected Number of Reads * RCU Per Item*

4. Divide the number by *3,000* to calculate the number of DDB partitions required to reach the capacity:

   Read Partitions = Required RCU / 3,000

5. Next, work out the write capacity required by dividing the item size by *1*, and rounding up:

   WCU Per Item = ItemSize / 1 (rounded up)

6. Define the expected number of write operations per second. This is one of the numbers you will use to provision your table with:

   *Required WCU = Expected Number of Writes * WCU Per Item*

7. Divide the number by *1,000* to calculate the number of DDB partitions required to reach the capacity:

   Write Partitions = Required WCU / 1,000

8. Add these two values to get the capacity partitions required (rounding up to a whole number):

   Capacity Partitions = Read Partitions + Write Partitions (rounded up)

9. Work out the minimum number of partitions required by the amount of data you plan to store:

Size Partitions = Total Size in GB / 10 (rounded up)

10. Once you have the partition requirements for your use case, take the maximum of your previous calculations:

Required Partitions = Maximum value between Capacity Partitions and Size Partitions

11. Since your allocated capacity is spread evenly across partitions, divide the RCU and WCU values to get the per-partition performance of your table:

Partition Read Throughput = Required RCU / Required Partitions

Partition Write Throughput = Required WCU / Required Partitions

How it works...

Behind the scenes, DDB throughput is controlled by the number of partitions that are allocated to your table. It is important to consider how your data will be spread across these partitions to ensure you get the performance you expect *and have paid for*.

We start this recipe by calculating the size of the items in your database, for throughput purposes. DDB has a minimum size it will consider, and even if an operation uses less than this size, it is rounded up in terms of allocated throughput used. The minimum size depends on the type of operation:

- Read operations are calculated in 4-K blocks
- Write operations are calculated in 1-K blocks

We then work out what the required RCU and WCU is, based on the expected number of operations. These values are what can then be used to provision the DDB table, as they represent the minimum required throughput (in optimal conditions).

Once you have these values, you can use them to provision your table.

Next, we calculate the throughput per partition key. These calculations rely on knowing what the performance of each partition is expected to be. The numbers 3,000 (for RCUs) and 1,000 (for WCUs) represent the capacity of a single DDB partition. By expressing the capacity in terms of partition performance (reads and writes) and adding them together we get the minimum number of partitions required from a capacity point of view.

We then do the same calculation for total data size. Each DDB partition can handle up to 10 GB of data. Any more than that will need to be split between multiple partitions.

 The specific values for partition capacity (for reads, writes, and size) have been stable for a while, but may change in the future. Double-check that the current values are the same as used here for complete accuracy.

Once we have the minimum partitions for both capacity and size, we take the highest value and work with that. This ensures we meet both the capacity and size requirements.

Finally, we take the provisioned capacity and divide it by the number of partitions. This gives us the throughput performance for each partition key, which we can then use to confirm against our use case.

There's more...

There are many nuances to using DDB efficiently and effectively. Here are some of the more important/impactful things to note.

Burst capacity

There is a burst capacity available to tables that go over their allocated capacity. Unused read and write capacity can be retained for up to five minutes (such as 300 seconds, for calculation purposes). Relying on this capacity is not good practice, and it will undoubtedly cause issues at some stage in the future.

Metrics

DDB tables automatically send data to CloudWatch metrics. This is the quickest and easiest way to confirm that your calculations and provision capacity are meeting your needs. It also helps you keep an eye on your usage to track your throughput needs over time. All metrics appear in the *AWS/DynamoDB* namespace. Some of the most interesting metrics for throughput calculations are as follows:

- `ConsumedReadCapacityUnits`
- `ConsumedWriteCapacityUnits`
- `ReadThrottleEvents`
- `WriteThrottleEvents`

There are other metrics available; see the *Amazon DynamoDB Metrics and Dimensions* documentation for more details.

Eventually consistent reads

Using eventually consistent reads (as opposed to strongly consistent reads) *halves* the RCU requirements for calculation purposes. In this recipe, we have used strongly consistent reads because it works with all workloads, but you should confirm that your use case actually requires it. Use eventually consistent reads if it does not.

By reducing the required provisioned capacity for reads, you effectively reduce your *cost* for using DDB.

7
Networking

In this chapter, we will cover:

- Building a secure network
- Creating a NAT gateway
- Canary deployment via DNS
- Hosting a domain
- Routing based on location with failover
- Network logging and troubleshooting

Introduction

Networking is a foundational component of using other AWS services such as EC2, RDS, and others. Using constructs such as VPCs and NAT gateways gives you the capability and confidence to secure your resources at a networking level. At a DNS level, Route 53 provides connectivity to your users in a responsive and fault-tolerant way that ensures the best performance in a variety of scenarios.

Building a secure network

In this recipe, we're going to build a secure network (VPC) in AWS. This network will consist of two public and private subnets split across two Availability Zones. It will also allow inbound connections to the public subnets for the following:

- SSH (port 22)
- HTTP (port 80)
- HTTPS (port 443)

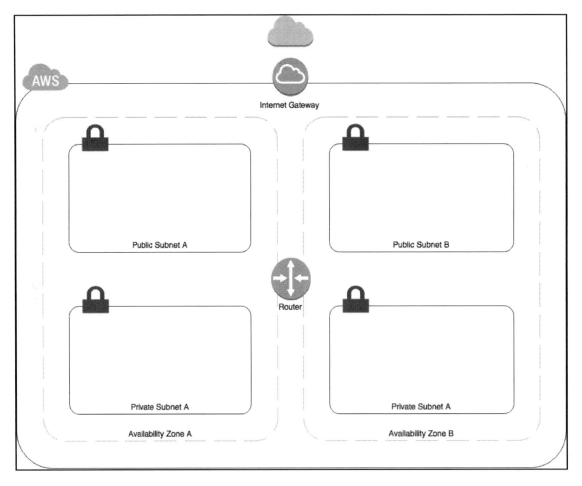

Building a secure network

Getting ready

Before we proceed, you're going to need to know the names of at least two Availability Zones in the region we're deploying to. The recipes in this book will typically deploy to `us-east-`, so to get things moving you can just use the following:

- `us-east-1a`
- `us-east-1b`

 When you create an AWS account, your zones are randomly allocated. This means that `us-east-1a` in your account isn't necessarily the same data center as `us-east-1a` in my account.

How to do it...

Go ahead and create a new CloudFormation template for our VPC. Just a heads-up: this will be one of the larger templates that we'll create in this book:

1. The first two `Parameters` correspond to the Availability Zones we discussed previously. We don't provide any default values for these parameters, to maintain region portability:

```
Parameters:
  AvailabilityZone1:
    Description: Availability zone 1 name (e.g. us-east-1a)
    Type: AWS::EC2::AvailabilityZone::Name
  AvailabilityZone2:
    Description: Availability zone 2 name (e.g. us-east-1b)
    Type: AWS::EC2::AvailabilityZone::Name
```

2. The shell of our VPC has now been created. At this point, it's not connected to the Internet, so it's not entirely useful to us. We need to add an Internet gateway and attach it to our VPC. Go ahead and do that, as follows:

```
Resources:
  # VPC & subnets
  ExampleVPC:
    Type: AWS::EC2::VPC
    Properties:
      CidrBlock: !Ref VPCCIDR
      EnableDnsSupport: true
      EnableDnsHostnames: true
```

```
        Tags:
          - { Key: Name, Value: Example VPC }
    PublicSubnetA:
      Type: AWS::EC2::Subnet
      Properties:
        AvailabilityZone: !Ref AvailabilityZone1
        CidrBlock: !Ref PublicSubnetACIDR
        MapPublicIpOnLaunch: true
        VpcId: !Ref ExampleVPC
      Tags:
        - { Key: Name, Value: Public Subnet A }
    PublicSubnetB:
      Type: AWS::EC2::Subnet
      Properties:
        AvailabilityZone: !Ref AvailabilityZone2
        CidrBlock: !Ref PublicSubnetBCIDR
        MapPublicIpOnLaunch: true
        VpcId: !Ref ExampleVPC
      Tags:
        - { Key: Name, Value: Public Subnet B }
    PrivateSubnetA:
      Type: AWS::EC2::Subnet
      Properties:
        AvailabilityZone: !Ref AvailabilityZone1
        CidrBlock: !Ref PrivateSubnetACIDR
        VpcId: !Ref ExampleVPC
      Tags:
        - { Key: Name, Value: Private Subnet A }
    PrivateSubnetB:
      Type: AWS::EC2::Subnet
      Properties:
        AvailabilityZone: !Ref AvailabilityZone2
        CidrBlock: !Ref PrivateSubnetBCIDR
        VpcId: !Ref ExampleVPC
      Tags:
        - { Key: Name, Value: Private Subnet B }
```

3. The remaining `Parameters` define the IP address ranges for the following:
    - The entire VPC
    - The public subnets (A and B)
    - The private subnets (A and B)

4. The default values we provide for the subnets will allocate 512 IP addresses to each subnet:

AWS reserves a small number of IP addresses in your IP space for AWS-specific services. The VPC DNS server is one such example of this. It's usually located at the second (*.2) IP address in the block allocated to your VPC.

```
VPCCIDR:
  Description: CIDR block for VPC
  Type: String
  Default: "172.31.0.0/21" # 2048 IP addresses
PublicSubnetACIDR:
  Description: CIDR block for public subnet A
  Type: String
  Default: "172.31.0.0/23" # 512 IP address
PublicSubnetBCIDR:
  Description: CIDR block for public subnet B
  Type: String
  Default: "172.31.2.0/23" # 512 IP address
PrivateSubnetACIDR:
  Description: CIDR block for private subnet A
  Type: String
  Default: "172.31.4.0/23" # 512 IP address
PrivateSubnetBCIDR:
  Description: CIDR block for private subnet B
  Type: String
  Default: "172.31.6.0/23" # 512 IP address
```

5. Now we can start to define `Resources`. We'll start by defining the VPC itself, as well as the two public and two private subnets inside it:

```
# Internet Gateway
ExampleIGW:
  Type: AWS::EC2::InternetGateway
  Properties:
    Tags:
      - { Key: Name, Value: Example Internet Gateway }
IGWAttachment:
  Type: AWS::EC2::VPCGatewayAttachment
  DependsOn: ExampleIGW
  Properties:
    VpcId: !Ref ExampleVPC
    InternetGatewayId: !Ref ExampleIGW
```

6. We need to create a couple of route tables. The first one we'll focus on is the public route table. We'll assign this route table to the two public subnets we've created. This route table will have just one route in it, which will direct all Internet-bound traffic to the Internet gateway we created in the previous step:

```
# Public Route Table
# Add a route for Internet bound traffic pointing to our IGW
# A route for VPC bound traffic will automatically be added
PublicRouteTable:
  Type: AWS::EC2::RouteTable
  Properties:
    VpcId: !Ref ExampleVPC
    Tags:
      - { Key: Name, Value: Public Route Table }
PublicInternetRoute:
  Type: AWS::EC2::Route
  DependsOn: IGWAttachment
  Properties:
    RouteTableId: !Ref PublicRouteTable
    GatewayId: !Ref ExampleIGW
    DestinationCidrBlock: "0.0.0.0/0"
RouteAssociationPublicA:
  Type: AWS::EC2::SubnetRouteTableAssociation
  Properties:
    RouteTableId: !Ref PublicRouteTable
    SubnetId: !Ref PublicSubnetA
RouteAssociationPublicB:
  Type: AWS::EC2::SubnetRouteTableAssociation
  Properties:
    RouteTableId: !Ref PublicRouteTable
    SubnetId: !Ref PublicSubnetB
```

7. We'll create the private route table in a similar fashion. Since the private subnet is isolated from the Internet, we won't add a route to the Internet gateway. Note that if you were to follow the NAT gateway recipe in this book, it will require a route table as an input parameter—this is the route table you want to add NAT routes to:

```
# Private Route Table
# We don't add any entries to this route table because there is
  no NAT gateway
# However a route for VPC bound traffic will automatically be added
PrivateRouteTable:
  Type: AWS::EC2::RouteTable
  Properties:
    VpcId: !Ref ExampleVPC
    Tags:
```

```
      - { Key: Name, Value: Private Route Table }
PrivateSubnetAssociationA:
  Type: AWS::EC2::SubnetRouteTableAssociation
  Properties:
    RouteTableId: !Ref PrivateRouteTable
    SubnetId: !Ref PrivateSubnetA
PrivateSubnetAssociationB:
  Type: AWS::EC2::SubnetRouteTableAssociation
  Properties:
    RouteTableId: !Ref PrivateRouteTable
    SubnetId: !Ref PrivateSubnetB
```

8. We can now focus on the security aspects of our network. Let's focus on the public subnets. These are the subnets you'll add your load balancers to; you'll also add things such as bastion boxes and NAT gateways. So we need to add a **Network ACL (NACL)** with several entries:

   - Allow outbound traffic to all ports. Outbound access is unrestricted from hosts in our public subnets.

   - Allow inbound traffic to ephemeral ports (above 1024). This ensures that packets returned to us from our outbound connections are not dropped.

   - Allow inbound access to low port numbers for SSH, HTTP, and HTTPS (22, 80, and 443):

```
# Public NACL
PublicNACL:
  Type: AWS::EC2::NetworkAcl
  Properties:
    VpcId: !Ref ExampleVPC
    Tags:
      - { Key: Name, Value: Example Public NACL }
# Allow outbound to everywhere
NACLRulePublicEgressAllowAll:
  Type: AWS::EC2::NetworkAclEntry
  Properties:
    CidrBlock: "0.0.0.0/0"
    Egress: true
    Protocol: 6
    PortRange: { From: 1, To: 65535 }
    RuleAction: allow
    RuleNumber: 100
    NetworkAclId: !Ref PublicNACL
# Allow outbound to VPC on all protocols
NACLRulePublicEgressAllowAllToVPC:
  Type: AWS::EC2::NetworkAclEntry
  Properties:
```

```
        CidrBlock: !Ref VPCCIDR
        Egress: true
        Protocol: -1
        RuleAction: allow
        RuleNumber: 200
        NetworkAclId: !Ref PublicNACL
  # Allow inbound from everywhere to ephemeral ports
    (above 1024)
  NACLRulePublicIngressAllowEphemeral:
    Type: AWS::EC2::NetworkAclEntry
    Properties:
      CidrBlock: "0.0.0.0/0"
      Protocol: 6
      PortRange: { From: 1024, To: 65535 }
      RuleAction: allow
      RuleNumber: 100
      NetworkAclId: !Ref PublicNACL
  # Allow inbound from everywhere on port 22 for SSH
  NACLRulePublicIngressAllowSSH:
    Type: AWS::EC2::NetworkAclEntry
    Properties:
      CidrBlock: "0.0.0.0/0"
      Protocol: 6
      PortRange: { From: 22, To: 22 }
      RuleAction: allow
      RuleNumber: 200
      NetworkAclId: !Ref PublicNACL
  # Allow inbound from everywhere on port 443 for HTTPS
  NACLRulePublicIngressAllowHTTPS:
    Type: AWS::EC2::NetworkAclEntry
    Properties:
      CidrBlock: "0.0.0.0/0"
      Protocol: 6
      PortRange: { From: 443, To: 443 }
      RuleAction: allow
      RuleNumber: 300
      NetworkAclId: !Ref PublicNACL
  # Allow inbound from everywhere on port 80 for HTTP
  NACLRulePublicIngressAllowHTTP:
    Type: AWS::EC2::NetworkAclEntry
    Properties:
      CidrBlock: "0.0.0.0/0"
      Protocol: 6
      PortRange: { From: 80, To: 80 }
      RuleAction: allow
      RuleNumber: 400
      NetworkAclId: !Ref PublicNACL
  # Allow inbound from VPC on all protocols
```

```
NACLRulePublicIngressAllowFromVPC:
  Type: AWS::EC2::NetworkAclEntry
  Properties:
    CidrBlock: !Ref VPCCIDR
    Protocol: -1
    RuleAction: allow
    RuleNumber: 500
    NetworkAclId: !Ref PublicNACL
NACLAssociationPublicSubnetA:
  Type: AWS::EC2::SubnetNetworkAclAssociation
  Properties:
    NetworkAclId: !Ref PublicNACL
    SubnetId: !Ref PublicSubnetA
NACLAssociationPublicSubnetB:
  Type: AWS::EC2::SubnetNetworkAclAssociation
  Properties:
    NetworkAclId: !Ref PublicNACL
    SubnetId: !Ref PublicSubnetB
```

9. We need to do the same for our private subnets. These subnets are somewhat easier to deal with. They should *only* be allowed to talk to hosts within our VPC, so we just need to add some NACLs allowing inbound and outbound traffic to our VPCs IP range:

```
# Private NACL
PrivateNACL:
  Type: AWS::EC2::NetworkAcl
  Properties:
    VpcId: !Ref ExampleVPC
    Tags:
      - { Key: Name, Value: Example Private NACL }
# Allow all protocols from VPC range
NACLRulePrivateIngressAllowVPC:
  Type: AWS::EC2::NetworkAclEntry
  Properties:
    CidrBlock: !Ref VPCCIDR
    Protocol: -1
    RuleAction: allow
    RuleNumber: 100
    NetworkAclId: !Ref PrivateNACL
# Allow TCP responses from everywhere
NACLRulePrivateIngressAllowEphemeral:
  Type: AWS::EC2::NetworkAclEntry
  Properties:
    CidrBlock: "0.0.0.0/0"
    Protocol: 6
    PortRange: { From: 1024, To: 65535 }
```

```
        RuleAction: allow
        RuleNumber: 200
        NetworkAclId: !Ref PrivateNACL
# Allow outbound traffic to everywhere, all protocols
NACLRulePrivateEgressAllowVPC:
  Type: AWS::EC2::NetworkAclEntry
  Properties:
    CidrBlock: "0.0.0.0/0"
    Egress: true
    Protocol: -1
    RuleAction: allow
    RuleNumber: 100
    NetworkAclId: !Ref PrivateNACL
NACLAssociationPrivateSubnetA:
  Type: AWS::EC2::SubnetNetworkAclAssociation
  Properties:
    NetworkAclId: !Ref PrivateNACL
    SubnetId: !Ref PrivateSubnetA
NACLAssociationPrivateSubnetB:
  Type: AWS::EC2::SubnetNetworkAclAssociation
  Properties:
    NetworkAclId: !Ref PrivateNACL
    SubnetId: !Ref PrivateSubnetB
```

10. Finally, we'll add some Outputs to our template. These outputs are usually candidates for feeding into other templates or components of automation:

```
Outputs:
  ExampleVPC:
    Value: !Ref ExampleVPC
  PublicSubnetA:
    Value: !Ref PublicSubnetA
  PublicSubnetB:
    Value: !Ref PublicSubnetB
  PrivateRouteTable:
    Value: !Ref PrivateRouteTable
  PublicRouteTable:
    Value: !Ref PublicRouteTable
  PrivateSubnetA:
    Value: !Ref PrivateSubnetA
  PrivateSubnetB:
    Value: !Ref PrivateSubnetB
```

11. You can go ahead and create your VPC in the web console or via the CLI using the following command:

```
aws cloudformation create-stack \
  --stack-name secure-vpc \
  --template-body file://07-building-a-secure-network.yaml \
  --parameters \
  ParameterKey=AvailabilityZone1,ParameterValue=<az-1> \
  ParameterKey=AvailabilityZone2,ParameterValue=<az-2>
```

How it works...

When you run this template, AWS will go ahead and create an isolated, secure network just for you. While it contains a number of resources and concepts which will be familiar to network administrators, it's essentially an empty shell, which you can now go ahead and populate.

For example, each VPC contains a virtual router. You can't see it and you can't log into it to perform any special configuration, but you can customize its behavior by modifying the route tables in this template.

The NACLs we've deployed are not stateful and should *not* be considered a substitution for security groups. NACLs are *complementary* to security groups, which are stateful and frankly much easier to change and manage than NACLs. While the NACLs in our recipe allow everywhere (0.0.0.0/0) to make inbound connections to port 22, for example, you'll want to use security groups to lock this down to a specific IP range (your corporate data center, for example).

There's more...

Actually, there's a *lot* more. Despite the amount of code in this recipe, we've really only covered the basics of what's possible with VPCs and networking in AWS. Here are some of the main VPC topics you'll encounter as you progress with your VPC usage:

- **Direct Connect**: This is a method of connecting your DC to your VPC using a private, dedicated pipe. Doing this often provides better network performance, and may also be cheaper than a VPN connection over the Internet.
- **Virtual Private Gateway** (**VPN**): You can configure your VPC to connect to your corporate DC over the Internet via VPN. This requires that you run supported VPN hardware in your DC.
- IPv6 support was added recently. We've left it out to keep things simple.

- **VPC endpoints**: This feature exposes AWS endpoints inside your VPC so that you don't have to route traffic over public Internet to consume them. Only S3 is supported at the time of writing.
- **VPC peering**: You can peer a VPC to one or more VPCs so that (unencrypted) traffic can flow between them. The IP ranges must not clash and, while the peering is free, you will still need to pay for traffic between VPCs. Transitive peering isn't supported, so if you need traffic to traverse VPCs you'll require a VPN/routing appliance of some kind. Cross-account VPC peering is supported (we use this feature quite often), but cross-region peering isn't yet available.
- **VPC sizing**:
    - IPv4: You can deploy networks between sizes /28 and /16.
    - IPv6: Your VPCs will be fixed in size at /56.
    - Once your VPC has been deployed you can't change its size. If you run out of IP space, your only option is to deploy a larger VPC and migrate everything (ouch!), or you can perhaps mitigate your problem with VPC peering.

- **VPC flow-logs**: You will want to enable VPC flow-logs in order to monitor traffic and do any kind of network debugging.
- Multicast traffic isn't supported.
- Subnets must reside in a single availability zone; they can't span Availability Zones.
- **Elastic Load Balancers** (**ELBs**) can scale out to use a lot of private IP addresses if you are sending a large amount of traffic through them. Keep this in mind when you're sizing your subnets.
- The number of VPCs you can deploy is limited to five per region, per account. You can request to increase this limit if necessary. Internet gateways have the same limit, and increasing one limit increases the other.
- The *default* VPC:
    - First and foremost, the default VPC is created automatically for you when you create your account. It has some different properties and behaviors to the VPCs you create for yourself.
    - If you try to launch an EC2 instance without specifying a subnet ID, AWS will attempt to launch it in your default VPC.

- It consists of only public subnets. These subnets are configured to provide a public IP address to all instances by default.
- It's possible to delete the default VPC in a region. If you do this by mistake, or have simply decided that you'd like to undo this action, you'll need to log a support ticket with AWS to have them create a new one for you.

See also...

- The *Creating a NAT gateway* recipe

Creating a NAT gateway

Unless required, your instances should not be publicly exposed to the Internet. When your instances are on the Internet, you have to assume they will be attacked at some stage.

This means most of your workloads should run on instances in private subnets. Private subnets are those that are not connected directly to the Internet.

In order to give your private instances access to the Internet, you use **network address translation (NAT)**. A NAT gateway allows your instances to initiate a connection *to* the Internet, without allowing connections *from* the Internet.

Getting ready

For this recipe, you must have the following existing resources:

- A VPC with an **Internet gateway (IGW)**
- A public subnet
- A private subnet route table

You will need the IDs for the public subnet and private subnet route table. Both of these resources should be in the same AZ.

How to do it...

1. Start with the usual CloudFormation template version and description:

```
AWSTemplateFormatVersion: "2010-09-09"
Description: Create NAT Gateway and associated route.
```

2. The template must take the following required parameters:

```
Parameters:
  PublicSubnetId:
    Description: Public Subnet ID to add the NAT Gateway to
    Type: AWS::EC2::Subnet::Id
  RouteTableId:
    Description: The private subnet route table to add the NAT
    Gateway route to
    Type: String
```

3. In the `Resources` section, define an **Elastic IP (EIP)** that will be assigned to the NAT gateway:

```
Resources:
  EIP:
    Type: AWS::EC2::EIP
    Properties:
      Domain: vpc
```

4. Create the NAT gateway resource, assigning it the EIP you just defined in the public subnet:

```
NatGateway:
  Type: AWS::EC2::NatGateway
  Properties:
    AllocationId: !GetAtt EIP.AllocationId
    SubnetId: !Ref PublicSubnetId
```

5. Finally, define the route to the NAT gateway and associate it with the private subnet's route table:

```
Route:
  Type: AWS::EC2::Route
  Properties:
    RouteTableId: !Ref RouteTableId
    DestinationCidrBlock: 0.0.0.0/0
    NatGatewayId: !Ref NatGateway
```

6. Save the template with a known filename; for example, `07-nat-gateway.yaml`.
7. Launch the template with the following CLI command:

```
aws cloudformation create-stack \
  --stack-name nat-gateway \
  --template-body file://07-nat-gateway.yaml \
  --parameters \
  ParameterKey=RouteTableId,ParameterValue=<route-table-id> \
  ParameterKey=PublicSubnetId,ParameterValue=<public-subnet-id>
```

How it works...

The parameters required for this recipe are as follows:

- A public subnet ID
- A private subnet route table ID

The public subnet ID is needed to host the NAT gateway, which must have Internet access. The private subnet route table will be updated with a route to the NAT gateway.

Using the AWS NAT gateway service means that AWS takes care of hosting and securing the service for you. The service will be hosted redundantly in a single AZ.

> You can use this recipe multiple times to deploy NAT gateways in each of your private subnets. Just make sure the public subnet and the private subnet are in the same AZ.

In the unlikely (but possible) event of an AZ outage, you should deploy a NAT gateway per subnet. This means that if one NAT gateway goes offline, instances in the other AZ can continue to access the Internet as normal. You are deploying your application in multiple subnets, aren't you?

This recipe will only work if you have created your own private subnets, as the default subnets in a new AWS account are all *public*. Instances in a public subnet have direct access to the Internet (via an IGW), so they do not need a NAT gateway.

See also

- The *Building a secure network* recipe

Canary deployment via DNS

Canary deployment is a popular deployment method in the cloud. It allows you to deploy new versions of your resources alongside your old resources, gradually and selectively directing parts of your traffic to the new resource.

By directing a small portion of your traffic to your new resources, you can get valuable real-world data and metrics. This means you don't need to engage in a *big bang* deployment—where you switch over all of your traffic at once.

It also gives you more flexibility in terms of troubleshooting and monitoring; if you see errors for your new resources, you can redirect the traffic back to your old resources while you investigate.

In this recipe, we will create the resources necessary to do a DNS-based canary deployment, and cut traffic from one resource to another (that is, old to new).

Getting ready

This recipe requires a few things to be in place:

- A Route 53 hosted zone for your domain suffix
- Existing DNS records for your *old* and *new* resources/endpoints

How to do it...

1. In a new file, define the template version and description:

```
AWSTemplateFormatVersion: "2010-09-09"
Description: Create a weighted DNS setup for canary deployments.
```

2. Start the `Parameters` section and the required parameters:

```
Parameters:
  HostedZoneName:
    Type: String
    Description: The hosted zone to create records in

  DomainName:
    Type: String
    Description: The domain name to create in the hosted zone
```

```
OldResource:
  Type: String
  Description: The older resource domain name

NewResource:
  Type: String
  Description: The newer resource domain name
```

3. Include the optional parameters (such as those with defaults) in the `Parameters` section:

```
OldWeight:
  Type: Number
  Default: 1
  Description: The ratio of requests to send to the older endpoint

NewWeight:
  Type: Number
  Default: 0
  Description: The ratio of requests to send to the newer endpoint
```

4. Start the `Resources` section of the template, and define your record set group:

```
Resources:
  RecordSetGroup:
    Type: AWS::Route53::RecordSetGroup
    Properties:
      HostedZoneName: !Ref HostedZoneName
      Comment: Canary deployment record set group
      RecordSets:
        - Name: !Join [ ".", [ Ref: DomainName, Ref:
            HostedZoneName ] ]
          Type: CNAME
          TTL: "300"
          SetIdentifier: Old
          Weight: !Ref OldWeight
          ResourceRecords:
            - !Ref OldResource
        - Name: !Join [ ".", [ Ref: DomainName, Ref:
            HostedZoneName ] ]
          Type: CNAME
          TTL: "300"
          SetIdentifier: New
          Weight: !Ref NewWeight
          ResourceRecords:
            - !Ref NewResource
```

5. Save the template with a known filename; for example, `07-canary-deployments.yaml`.

6. Launch the template with the following CLI command:

```
aws cloudformation create-stack \
  --stack-name canary \
  --template-body file://07-canary-deployments.yaml \
  --parameters \
  ParameterKey=DomainName,ParameterValue=<your-domain-name> \
  ParameterKey=OldResource,ParameterValue=<old-resource-dns> \
  ParameterKey=NewResource,ParameterValue=<new-resource-dns> \
  ParameterKey=HostedZoneName,ParameterValue=<your-hosted-zone>
```

7. When ready, update the stack to change (just) the domain weighting with the following CLI command:

```
aws cloudformation update-stack \
  --stack-name canary \
  --parameters \
  ParameterKey=HostedZoneName,UsePreviousValue=true \
  ParameterKey=DomainName,UsePreviousValue=true \
  ParameterKey=OldResource,UsePreviousValue=true \
  ParameterKey=NewResource,UsePreviousValue=true \
  ParameterKey=OldWeight,ParameterValue=0 \
  ParameterKey=NewWeight,ParameterValue=1 \
  --use-previous-template
```

How it works...

This template focuses on utilizing the features of a Route 53 record set group, and the most useful properties have been parameterized.

The value for your `DomainName` parameter will be created as multiple CNAME records in your hosted zone (as set in `HostedZoneName`), one for each of your resources, old and new.

The `OldResource` and `NewResource` parameters represent the target domain names that the incoming requests will be shared between.

Once the stack is deployed, you will be able to go to your domain name and see your *old* resource. By default, this template will send all traffic to the old resource endpoint.

Once you've verified the setup is working correctly, you can start to deploy by updating the stack to send *some* of your requests to the new resource.

Changing the resource record set's weightings via the CLI is quite involved, as it requires passing a complex JSON object as an argument. It is much simpler and safer to simply update the existing CloudFormation stack you deployed, changing just the weighting parameters that are already present.

With the `update-stack` command, the new weightings will be propagated to your record set group members (without interruption) and the new distribution of traffic will start taking effect.

For the parameters without default values, you must explicitly tell CloudFormation to use the previous values, as well as the template body supplied previously.

Remember that the distribution will be determined by the target's weight divided by the total weight value of all targets. This means you can easily *turn off* a target by setting its weight to 0, regardless of the other weight values. In this recipe, we have used 0 and 1 as simple values to illustrate the impact, but you can (and should) use more fine-grained parameters.

Hosting a domain

In this recipe, we'll show you how to host a domain in Route 53 and add some records to it:

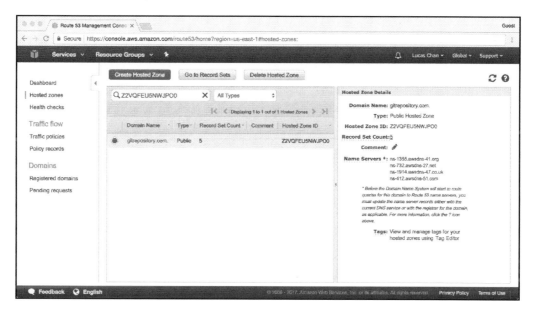

Hosting a domain

Getting ready

You technically don't need to have registered a domain name in order to proceed with this recipe, but it sure helps if you have a real domain that you can use.

How to do it...

1. Create a new CloudFormation template and add the following `Parameter` to it:

```
Parameters:
  DomainName:
    Description: Your domain name (example.org)
    Type: String
```

2. Next we need to add a `HostedZone` resource to our template, as follows:

```
Resources:
  DNSHostedZone:
    Type: AWS::Route53::HostedZone
    Properties:
      Name: !Ref DomainName
```

3. You're now ready to go ahead and create your hosted zone in Route 53. You can do so via the CloudFormation web console, or use the following CLI command:

```
aws cloudformation create-stack \
  --stack-name example-hosted-zone \
  --template-body file://07-hosting-a-domain.yaml \
  --parameters \
  ParameterKey=DomainName,ParameterValue=<your-domain-name>
```

How it works...

This will create a hosted zone in Route 53. Once the stack has finished creating, go and find it in the web console. You'll see that there are a number of name servers associated with it. These are the name servers to use if you wish to proceed with delegating your domain name to AWS's Route 53 servers using your domain name registrar's control panel.

There's more...

A hosted zone with no DNS records will be of limited use to you. Here are some examples of records that you may wish to add to your template:

```
DNSRecords:
  Type: AWS::Route53::RecordSetGroup
  Properties:
    HostedZoneId:
      Ref: DNSHostedZone
    RecordSets:
    - Name: !Ref DomainName
      Type: A
      TTL: 60
      ResourceRecords:
        - "127.0.0.1"
    - Name: !Ref DomainName
      Type: MX
      TTL: 60
      ResourceRecords:
        - "10 smtp.example.org"
        - "20 smtp.example.org"
    - Name: !Ref DomainName
      Type: TXT
      TTL: 60
      ResourceRecords:
        - '"v=spf1 include:spf.example.org ?all"'
```

Some items of note:

For the priority in MX records, add the number at the start of the record followed by a space.

For TXT records such as spf entries, which are typically required to be quoted, you can surround double quotes with single quotes.

Here's how they look in the Route 53 web console:

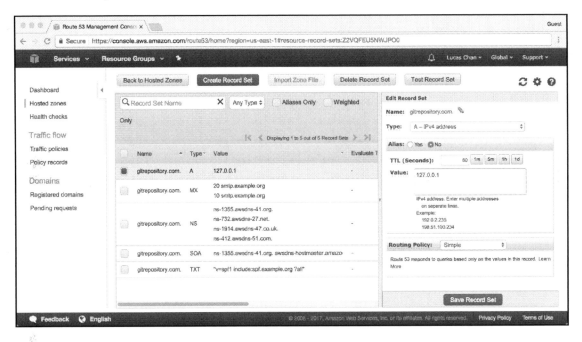

Hosting a domain

See also...

- The *Hosting a static website* recipe in Chapter 3, *Storage and Content Delivery*

Routing based on location with failover

In this recipe, we're going to show you two Route 53 routing policies:

- Geolocation routing
- Failover routing

In fact, we're actually going to combine these two policies together. A perusal of the AWS documentation might lead you to believe that this isn't particularly common practice, but understand that by combining routing policies, you can do great things for your performance and availability.

Getting ready

Given that we're demonstrating a failover task, you'll want to set up two ELBs before we proceed. We're going to assume you're doing this in different regions, but this isn't strictly necessary. These ELBs will need to accept HTTP connections (on port 80 of course) and have at least one instance attached to them (which is passing its health check and serving content).

 The *Creating security groups* recipe in Chapter 4, *Using AWS Compute* deployed in two different regions, should fit the bill nicely.

You'll also need a domain name that you'd like to create as a new hosted zone in Route 53. You technically don't need to delegate this domain to Route 53 from your registrar, so you can complete this recipe with any domain you choose. Just remember that using a real domain you can delegate to Route 53, which will save you messing with your localhost's file or DNS setup in order to test this recipe.

In summary, you'll need the following:

- The DNS names for both ELBs
- The hosted zone IDs for both ELBs
- A domain name of your choosing

How to do it...

1. Go ahead and create a new CloudFormation template. We'll add some `Parameters` for the items we've mentioned previously:

```
Parameters:
  DomainName:
    Description: Your domain name (example.org)
    Type: String
  LoadBalancerDNSNameRegionA:
    Description: The DNS name of your ELB in region A
    Type: String
  LoadBalancerHostedZoneRegionA:
    Description: The Hosted Zone ID of your ELB in region A
    Type: String
  LoadBalancerDNSNameRegionB:
    Description: The DNS name of your ELB in region B
    Type: String
  LoadBalancerHostedZoneRegionB:
    Description: The Hosted Zone ID of your ELB in region B
    Type: String
```

2. The first `Resource` we want is the `HostedZone` resource for our domain name. Add it to your template as follows:

```
Resources:
  DNSHostedZone:
    Type: AWS::Route53::HostedZone
    Properties:
      Name: !Ref DomainName
```

3. In order to have failover happen automatically, we're going to need to set up some health checks. We want health checks on the ELBs in both regions:

```
RegionAHealthCheck:
  Type: AWS::Route53::HealthCheck
  Properties:
    HealthCheckConfig:
      FailureThreshold: 3
      FullyQualifiedDomainName: !Ref LoadBalancerDNSNameRegionA
      Port: 80
      RequestInterval: 30
      ResourcePath: "/"
      Type: HTTP
    HealthCheckTags:
      - { Key: Name, Value: Region A Health Check }
```

```
RegionBHealthCheck:
  Type: AWS::Route53::HealthCheck
  Properties:
    HealthCheckConfig:
      FailureThreshold: 3
      FullyQualifiedDomainName: !Ref LoadBalancerDNSNameRegionB
      Port: 80
      RequestInterval: 30
      ResourcePath: "/"
      Type: HTTP
    HealthCheckTags:
      - { Key: Name, Value: Region B Health Check }
```

4. We're now going to create four record sets for your domain:

   - a.<your-domain>-PRIMARY

   - b.<your-domain>-PRIMARY

   - a.<your-domain>-SECONDARY (failover to b)

   - b.<your-domain>-SECONDARY (failover to a)

5. These records correspond to ELB A and ELB B (or *site* A and B, if that term makes more sense to you), and they will allow each region to fail over to the other if the health check fails.

6. Let's start with the primary records for both ELBs:

```
RegionAPrimary:
  Type: AWS::Route53::RecordSet
  Properties:
    Name: !Join [ ., [ a, Ref: DomainName ] ]
    Type: A
    HostedZoneId: !Ref DNSHostedZone
    AliasTarget:
      HostedZoneId: !Ref LoadBalancerHostedZoneRegionA
      DNSName: !Ref LoadBalancerDNSNameRegionA
    Failover: PRIMARY
    SetIdentifier: primary-region-a
    HealthCheckId: !Ref RegionAHealthCheck
RegionBPrimary:
  Type: AWS::Route53::RecordSet
  Properties:
    Name: !Join [ ., [ b, Ref: DomainName ] ]
    Type: A
    HostedZoneId: !Ref DNSHostedZone
    AliasTarget:
      HostedZoneId: !Ref LoadBalancerHostedZoneRegionB
      DNSName: !Ref LoadBalancerDNSNameRegionB
```

```
        Failover: PRIMARY
        SetIdentifier: primary-region-b
        HealthCheckId: !Ref RegionBHealthCheck
```

7. Now add the secondary (failover) records:

```
RegionAFailover:
  Type: AWS::Route53::RecordSet
  Properties:
    Name: !Join [ ., [ a, Ref: DomainName ] ]
    Type: A
    HostedZoneId: !Ref DNSHostedZone
    AliasTarget:
      HostedZoneId: !Ref LoadBalancerHostedZoneRegionB
      DNSName: !Ref LoadBalancerDNSNameRegionB
      Failover: SECONDARY
      SetIdentifier: secondary-region-a
RegionBFailover:
  Type: AWS::Route53::RecordSet
  Properties:
    Name: !Join [ ., [ b, Ref: DomainName ] ]
    Type: A
    HostedZoneId: !Ref DNSHostedZone
    AliasTarget:
      HostedZoneId: !Ref LoadBalancerHostedZoneRegionA
      DNSName: !Ref LoadBalancerDNSNameRegionA
      Failover: SECONDARY
      SetIdentifier: secondary-region-b
```

8. Now we're going to add the root/apex record for our domain. For the purposes of this recipe, we're going to send requests originating from North America to region/ELB A, and requests from the rest of the world to region/ELB B:

```
NorthAmericaGeolocation:
  Type: AWS::Route53::RecordSet
  Properties:
    Name: !Ref DomainName
    Type: A
    HostedZoneId: !Ref DNSHostedZone
    AliasTarget:
      HostedZoneId: !Ref DNSHostedZone
      DNSName: !Join [ ., [ a, Ref: DomainName ] ]
    GeoLocation:
      ContinentCode: NA # North America
    SetIdentifier: geolocation-region-a
RestOfWorldGeolocation:
  Type: AWS::Route53::RecordSet
  Properties:
```

```
Name: !Ref DomainName
Type: A
HostedZoneId: !Ref DNSHostedZone
AliasTarget:
  HostedZoneId: !Ref DNSHostedZone
  DNSName: !Join [ ., [ b, Ref: DomainName ] ]
GeoLocation:
  CountryCode: "*" # Rest of world
SetIdentifier: geolocation-region-b
```

9. That's it! You can now run this CloudFormation template in the AWS web console or via the CLI, as follows:

```
aws cloudformation create-stack \
  --stack-name geolocation-failover \
  --template-body file://07-routing-based-on-location.yaml \
  --parameters \
  ParameterKey=DomainName,ParameterValue=gitrepository.com \
  ParameterKey=LoadBalancerDNSNameRegionA,ParameterValue=<elb-a> \
  ParameterKey=LoadBalancerHostedZoneRegionA, \
  ParameterValue=<elb-zoneid-a> \
  ParameterKey=LoadBalancerDNSNameRegionB,ParameterValue=<elb-b> \
  ParameterKey=LoadBalancerHostedZoneRegionB, \
  ParameterValue=<elb-zoneid-b>
```

How it works...

We've effectively constructed a small decision tree, as follows:

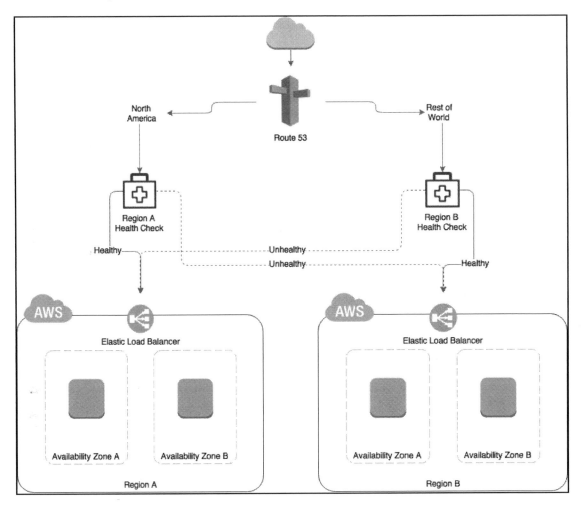

Route 53 flow

In order to test this for yourself, you'll need to have some way of performing DNS responses from other regions. In the following screenshots, we have provisioned a machine using AWS workspaces in North America (left), while our actual location is in Australia (right).

Normal operation (geolocation routing)

Under normal operation, our North American user (left) will connect to region A, which, for practical reasons, we've deployed in `us-east-1`, although it could be in any region. Our Australian user (right) will connect to region B, which is the region we've designated as being for the *rest of the world*. Again, for practical reasons, we deployed this site to the `ap-southeast-2` region:

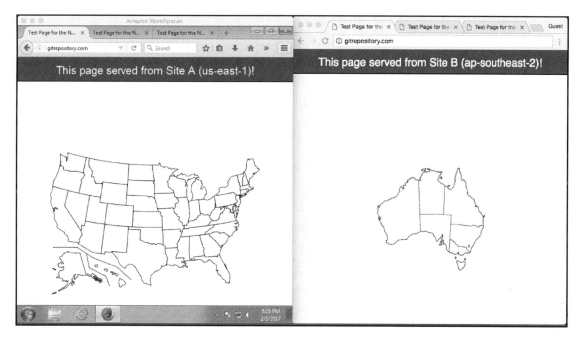

Left: Region A served to North American user. Right: Region B served to Australian user.

Region A failure

To simulate a failure of region A, we'll simply stop the web server, which is attached to the ELB as follows:

```
[root@ip-172-30-0-153 ec2-user]# service nginx stop
Stopping nginx:                                    [  OK  ]
```

After a short period, the web console will show that the health check for region A is failing:

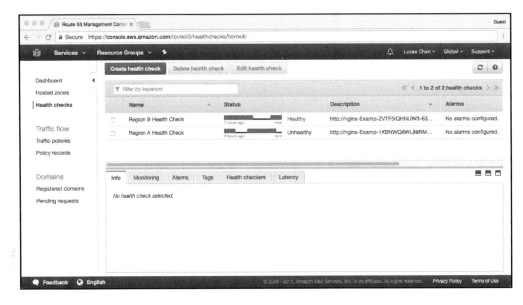

Region A failing health check

Our North American user (left) now sees region B instead:

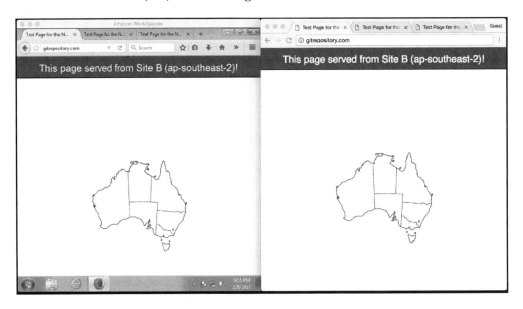

Left: Region B served to North American users due to failover. Right: Region B served to Australian users as normal.

Region B failure

We'll now flip the script and simulate the same scenario in region B. This time, the web server in this region is stopped, but the server in region A is healthy:

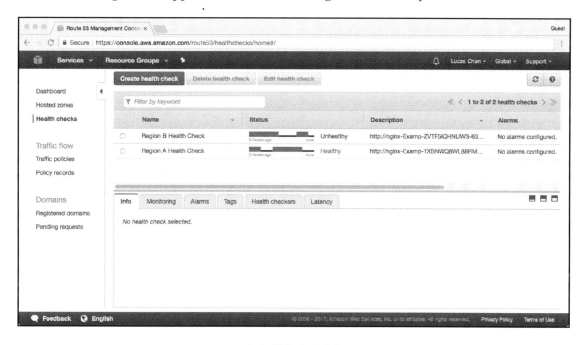

Region B failing health check

Region A content will now be shown to both North American users and those designated as the *rest of the world* (including Australia):

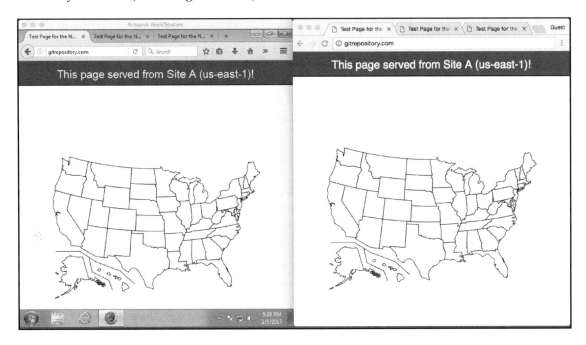

Left: Region A served to North American users as normal. Right: Region A served to Australian users due to failover.

There's more...

Route 53 offers a couple of other useful routing policies, so you should have a think about which best suits you:

- **Latency-based routing**: This policy makes the Route 53 DNS servers respond to you with IP addresses that provide the lowest latency. This will not necessarily be the endpoint geographically closest to you.
- **Weighted routing**: This allows you to divvy up your traffic between endpoints based on a weighting system. You might have a 50/50 split between two regions, or you may elect to have a 90/10 ratio instead.

See also...

- The *Hosting a static website* recipe in `Chapter 3`, *Storage and Content Delivery*
- The *Creating security groups* recipe in `Chapter 4`, *Using AWS Compute*

Network logging and troubleshooting

One of the benefits of using virtualized infrastructure is that you can get a level of introspection that is difficult or costly with physical hardware. Being able to quickly switch on logging at a network-device level is an extremely useful feature, especially when getting used to the interactions between VPCs, subnets, NACLs, routing, and security groups.

In this recipe, we will turn on logging for our network resources. You could do this all the time, to give yourself another layer for monitoring and auditing, or you could selectively enable it during troubleshooting, saving yourself any additional datastorage charges.

Getting ready

For this recipe, you must have a VPC to log activity on.

How to do it...

1. Start by defining the template version and description:

```
AWSTemplateFormatVersion: "2010-09-09"
Description: Flow logs for networking resources
```

2. Define the `Parameters` for the template. In this case, it is just the `VpcId` to turn logging on for:

```
Parameters:
  VpcId:
    Type: String
    Description: The VPC to create flow logs for
```

3. Create the `Resources` section of the template and define the log group to use to send our flow-logs to:

```
Resources:
  LogGroup:
    Type: AWS::Logs::LogGroup
    DeletionPolicy: Delete
    Properties:
      LogGroupName: LogGroup
```

4. Next we define the IAM role that will give the flow-logs service permission to write the logs:

```
IamRole:
  Type: AWS::IAM::Role
  Properties:
    AssumeRolePolicyDocument:
      Version: "2012-10-17"
      Statement:
        -
          Effect: Allow
          Principal:
            Service: vpc-flow-logs.amazonaws.com
          Action: sts:AssumeRole
    Policies:
      -
        PolicyName: CloudWatchLogsAccess
        PolicyDocument:
          Version: "2012-10-17"
          Statement:
            -
              Action:
                - logs:CreateLogGroup
                - logs:CreateLogStream
                - logs:PutLogEvents
                - logs:DescribeLogGroups
                - logs:DescribeLogStreams
              Effect: Allow
              Resource: "*"
```

5. Finally, we define the flow-log itself:

```
FlowLog:
  Type: AWS::EC2::FlowLog
  DependsOn: LogGroup
  Properties:
    DeliverLogsPermissionArn: !GetAtt IamRole.Arn
```

```
LogGroupName: LogGroup
ResourceId: !Ref VpcId
ResourceType: VPC
TrafficType: ALL
```

6. Save the template, and give it a known filename such as `07-flow-logs.yaml`.

7. Create the flow-logs and associated resources by creating the template with the following command:

```
aws cloudformation create-stack \
  --stack-name VpcFlowLogs \
  --template-body file://07-flow-logs.yml \
  --capabilities CAPABILITY_IAM \
  --parameters ParameterKey=VpcId,ParameterValue=<your-vpc-id>
```

8. Once launched (and assuming you have network activity), you will be able to see your flow-log in the CloudWatch logs console.

How it works...

The only parameter required for this template is the VPC ID to target. We specifically target a VPC to turn on flow-logging for, because it gives us the most *bang for buck*. While you can enable flow-logs for subnets and **Elastic Network Interfaces** (**ENIs**) individually, if you enable them on a VPC you get flow-logs for all the networking resources contained in that VPC—which includes subnets and ENIs.

In the resources section, we start by explicitly defining the log group to *hold* the flow-logs. If you don't create the log group yourself (and specify it in your flow-log resource configuration), a log group will be created for you. This means that you will still be able to use flow-logs, but the log group won't be managed by CloudFormation and will have to be maintained (for example, deleted) manually. We have also set a **deletion policy** of *delete* for our log group. This means it will be deleted if the CloudFormation stack is deleted, which is fine for a demonstration such as this. If using in a *real* environment (such as production), remove the `DeletionPolicy` property and its value.

 By default, CloudWatch log groups are *not* deleted when the stack that created them is deleted. This lets you retain any important logs, but it can incur an ongoing cost.

Next we define the IAM role to use. Via the `AssumeRolePropertyDocument` value, we give the AWS flow-logs service permission to assume this role. Without this access, the flow-logs service cannot access the account. In the `Policies` property, we give the role permission to create and update log groups and streams.

Finally, now that we have created the dependent resources, we define the flow-log resource itself. You don't need to define the resources in order of dependencies, but it is usually easier to read if you do. In the resource, we also define a `DependsOn` relationship to the log group we defined earlier, so that the log group is ready to receive the flow-logs when it is created.

The final step is to launch the template you have created, passing the VPC ID as parameter. As this template creates an IAM role to allow the VPC service to send logs to CloudWatch logs, the command to create the stack must be given the `CAPABILITY_IAM` flag to signify that you are aware of the potential impact of launching this template.

There's more...

Turning on logging is just the start of the troubleshooting process. There are a few other things you should be aware of when using flow-logs.

Log format

Once logging is enabled, you can view the logs in the CloudWatch logs console. Here is a summary of the type of information you will see in the flow-log (in order):

- The VPC flow-logs version
- The AWS account ID
- The ID of the network interface
- The source IPv4 or IPv6 address
- The destination IPv4 or IPv6 address
- The source port of the traffic
- The destination port of the traffic
- The IANA protocol number of the traffic
- The number of packets transferred
- The number of bytes transferred
- The start time of the capture window (in Unix seconds)
- The end time of the capture window (in Unix seconds)

- The action associated with the traffic; for example, ACCEPT or REJECT
- The logging status of the flow-log; for example, OK, NODATA, or SKIPDATA

 To identify the protocol, check the protocol number field against the IANA protocol numbers list at http://www.iana.org/assignments/protocol-numbers/protocol-numbers.xhtml.

Updates

You cannot update the configuration of an existing flow-log; you must delete it and recreate it if you want to change any settings associated. This is another reason why it is good to explicitly create and manage the associated log group.

Omissions

Some traffic is not captured by the flow-logs service, as follows:

- Traffic to the Amazon DNS server (x.x.x.2 in your allocated range)
- Traffic for Amazon Windows license activation (obviously only applicable to Windows instances)
- Traffic to and from the instance metadata service (that is, IP address 169.254.169.254)
- DHCP traffic
- Traffic to the reserved VPC IP address for the default VPC router (x.x.x.1 in your allocated range)

See also

- The *Building a secure network* recipe

8
Security and Identity

In this chapter, we will cover:

- Federating with your AWS account
- Creating SSL certificates
- Active Directory as a service
- Creating users
- Creating instance roles
- Cross-account user roles
- Storing secrets

Introduction

Security is one of the most critical areas of using the cloud. It's important to get it right because good security practices reinforce themselves, leading to a virtuous cycle of capabilities and control.

There are many tools and AWS services to ensure that your cloud-based infrastructure is as secure—if not more secure—than your own resources.

AWS IAM is the backbone of security in AWS. It provides incredibly granular levels of permissions to allow (and deny) specific users access to your resources.

Federating with your AWS account

This recipe will show you how to federate identities from your Active Directory and use AD groups and IAM roles to provide different levels of access to multiple AWS accounts.

At a high level, we're going to have an AWS account that is designated as an Auth Account. Users will log in to this account and be assigned a role. This role will have next to no privileges because we don't want them doing anything in the **Auth Account**. However, they will be able to use role switching to access another AWS account; we'll call this the **App Account**.

This is a reasonably common pattern whereby users will have access to a number of AWS accounts and use role switching to jump between them—all using credentials that are verified against an AD backend and a level of access that is derived from AD groups.

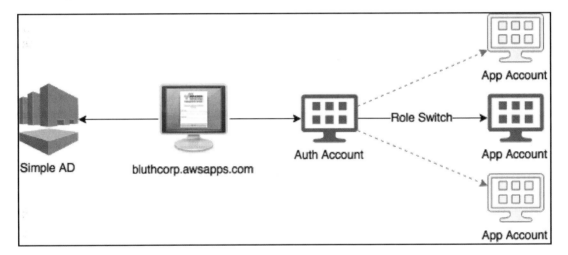

Federation

Getting ready

You'll need the following before we can proceed:

- An instance of Simple AD. Refer to the *Active Directory as a service* recipe.
- The name of an access URL, which your users will use to log in (that is, `https://bluthcorp.awsapps.com`).
- Two AWS accounts. One of these will be your *Auth Account*, the other will be your *App Account*.
- A Windows server in your VPC, joined to your Simple AD domain, with Remote Server Admin Tools installed so we can manage groups and users.

> If you launch the Windows server using the launch wizard, it will give you the option of joining the domain at boot time. Note that the server will need to be running with an instance role that will have the following two AWS Managed Policies: **AmazonEC2RoleForSSM** and **AmazonSSMReadOnlyAccess**.

How to do it...

This recipe is split up in to five parts:

- Active Directory configuration
- Auth Account policy configuration
- Auth Account role configuration
- Simple AD Directory configuration
- App Account role configuration

Active Directory configuration

Our first task will be to create the necessary groups in Active Directory:

1. Go ahead and create a group called AWSPowerUser, as shown in the following screenshot:

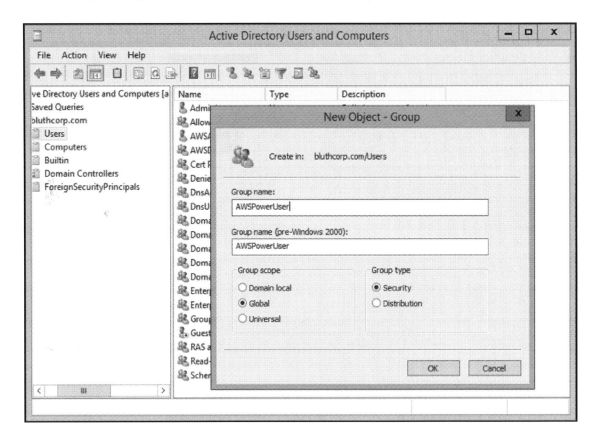

2. Do the same for the `AWSReadOnly` group:

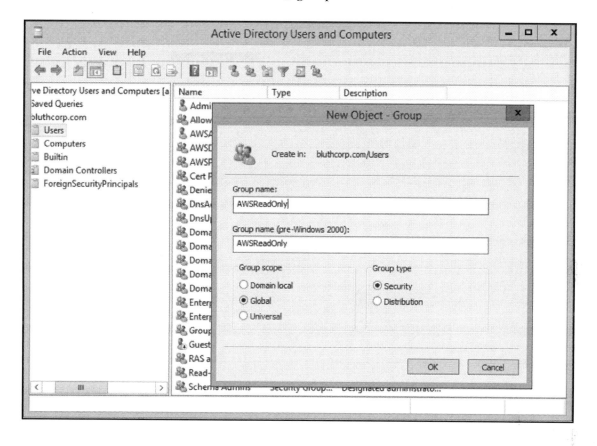

3. We're now going to create a couple of users. The first one is `Lucille`, as shown in the following screenshot:

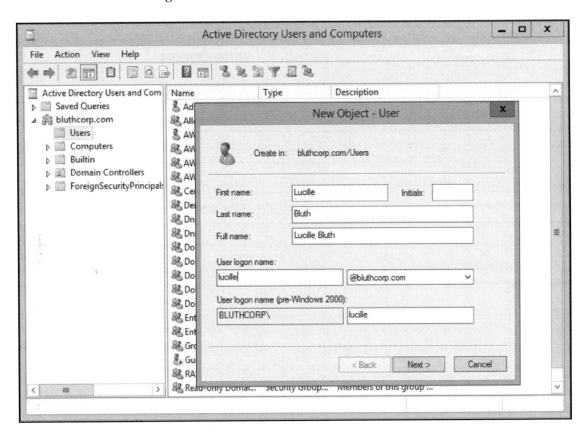

4. The next user will be `Buster`. Let's add him now:

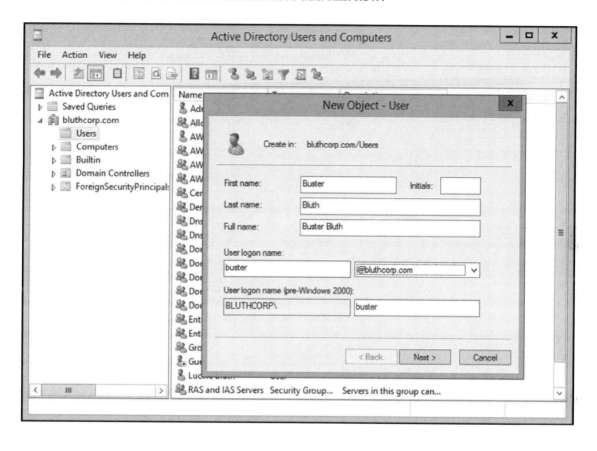

5. `Lucille` is going to be our power user, so we'll add her to the `AWSPowerUser` group:

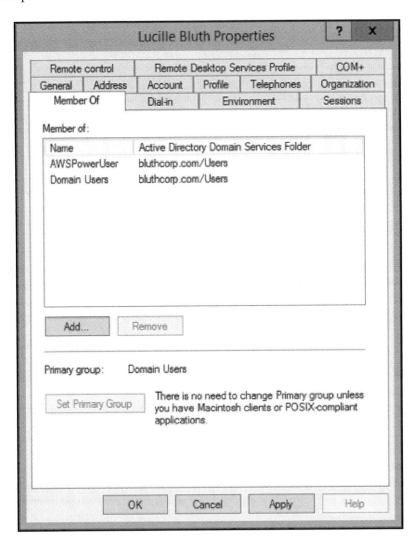

6. We don't really trust `Buster` at all. True to his name, he's prone to breaking things. Let's add him to the `AWSReadOnly` group:

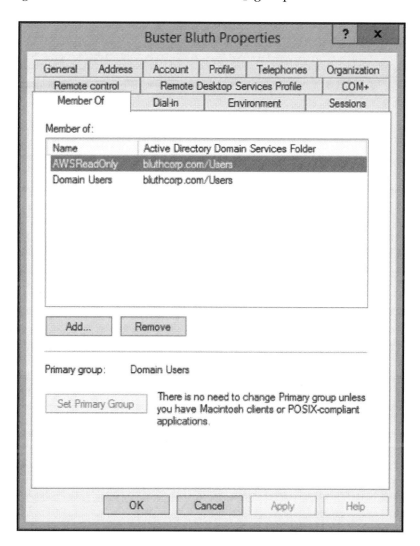

Auth Account policy configuration

We now we need to create a policy in our Auth Account. Remember that this is the account that the users `Lucille` and `Buster` will initially log in to when visiting the AWS console. We actually want to give them extremely limited access to this account. In fact, the only thing we're going to let them do is attempt to switch to a role in the application account.

1. Visit the IAM console in the Auth Account and create a new policy:

> AWS refers to this type of policy as a *Customer Managed Policy*.

2. Call this policy `AllowAssumeRole`. Give it a description to help you remember what it's for. Then apply the following policy document. You are going to want to make sure the account number of the App Account is added to your policy:

```
{
    "Version": "2012-10-17",
    "Statement": [
        {
```

```
        "Sid": "Stmt1487396837000",
        "Effect": "Allow",
        "Action": [
            "sts:AssumeRole"
        ],
        "Resource": [
            "arn:aws:iam::<app-acct-number>:role/*"
        ]
    }
  ]
}
```

Auth Account policy config

Auth Account role configuration

Now we're going to create two roles. These roles will correspond to the groups we defined in Active Directory:

- AWSPowerUser: CanAssumePowerUser
- AWSReadOnly: CanAssumeReadOnly

1. Start by creating the CanAssumePowerUser role first:

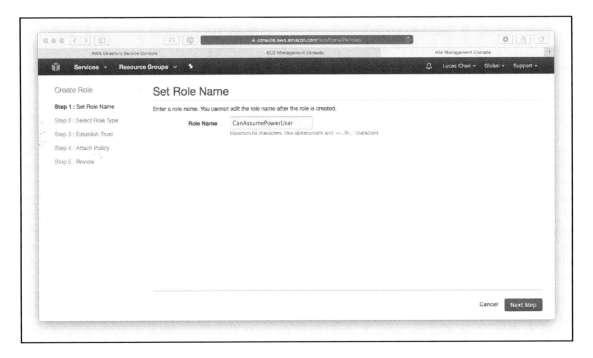

2. We want this role to be an **AWS Directory Service** role, so be sure to select it before proceeding:

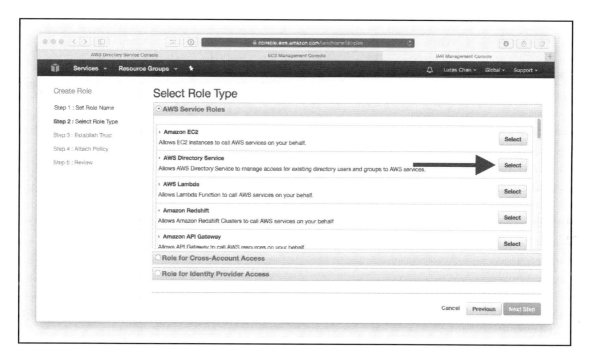

3. Attach the `AllowAssumeRole` policy we have already created to this role:

Hint: You can filter the roles using the search box to make finding them easier.

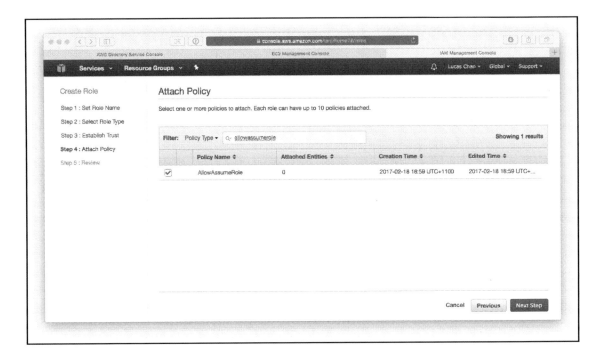

4. Click **Create Role** to confirm:

5. Now go ahead and do exactly the same for the `CanAssumeReadOnly` role. Again, attach the `AllowAssumeRole` policy we created earlier:

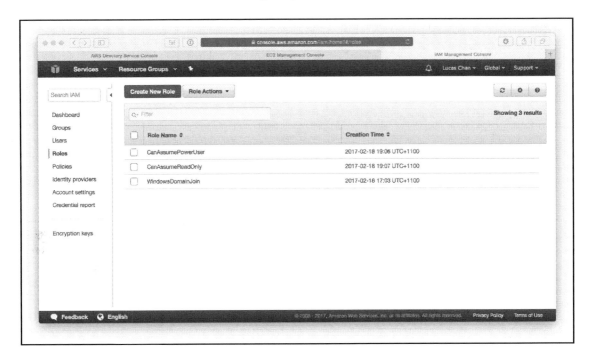

Simple AD configuration

We now need to go through the process of enabling user accounts in the directory to log in to the AWS management console.

1. Point your browser to the **AWS Directory Service Console** and edit the configuration of your Simple AD directory. Enter the access URL you've chosen:

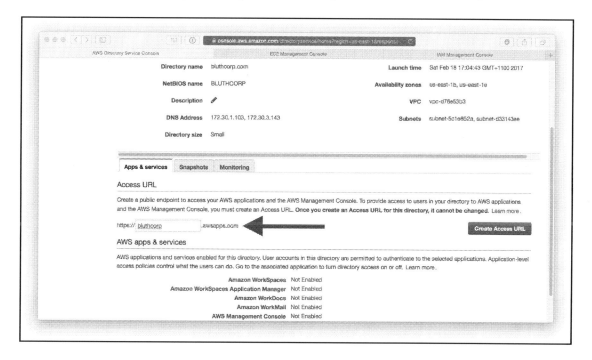

2. We now want to enable the **AWS Management Console** for this service. Click on it to proceed to the next step:

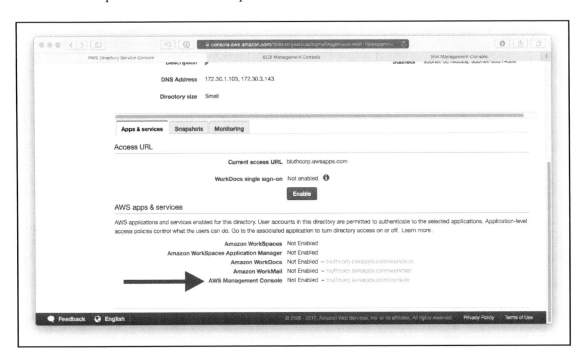

3. We've already created roles and assigned a policy to them. So select **Use Existing Role**, as shown in the following screenshot:

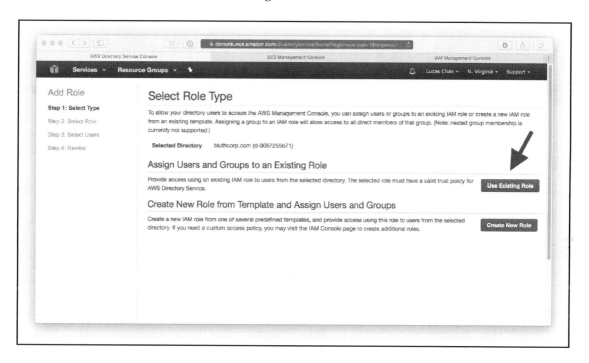

4. Start with the `CanAssumePowerUser` role. We need to map it to the `AWSPowerUser` group we created in AD (the one `Lucille` resides in):

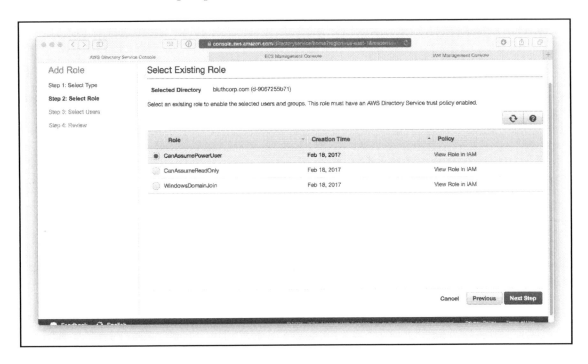

5. Search for `AWSPowerUser` and then proceed to the next step:

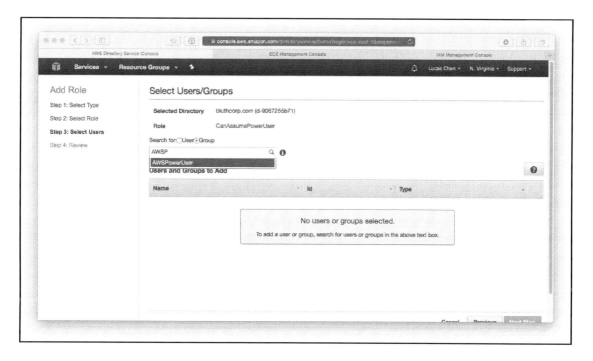

6. You now need to repeat these steps for the `CanAssumeReadOnly` role. Map it to the `AWSReadOnly` role we created in AD:

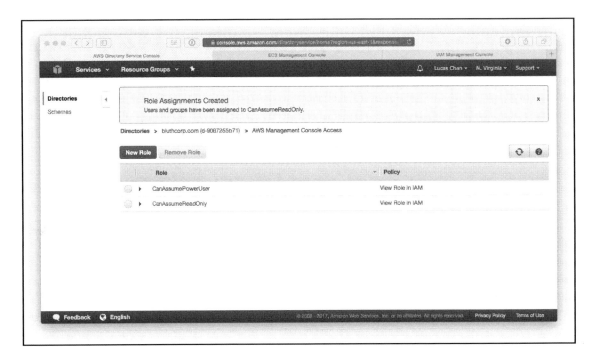

App Account role configuration

It's now time to configure our application account. In it, we need to create some new roles and then set up a trust relationship between those new roles and the roles we created in our Auth Account:

1. Start by going to the IAM console in the Auth Account and creating a new role. This role will be `PowerUserRole`:

2. This role will be of the **Role for Cross-Account Access** kind. Make sure to select this type:

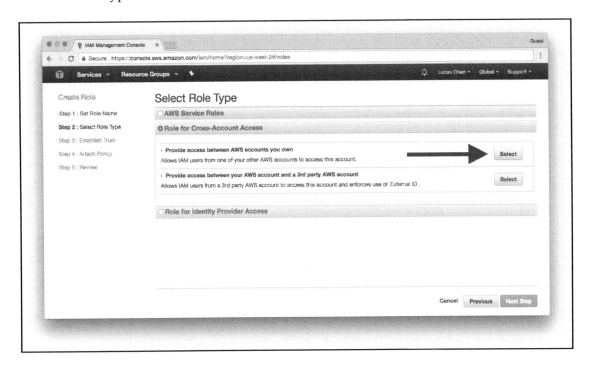

3. You'll be prompted to enter an AWS **Account ID**. This is the account ID of the Auth Account:

4. For this role, we are going to use the AWS Managed Policy for `PowerUserAccess`, so go ahead and attach this policy now:

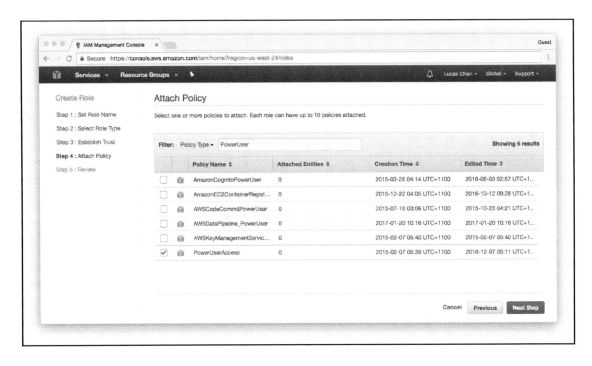

5. Click **Create Role** on the confirmation page and we're ready for the next step:

6. AWS will automatically create a trust relationship on our behalf. Unfortunately, it's not quite right, so we need to edit it:

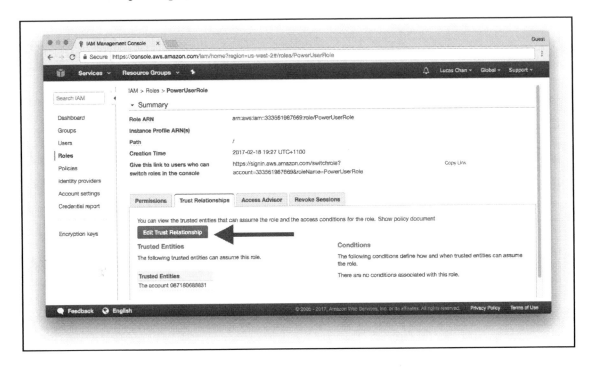

7. We want anyone who has the `CanAssumePowerUser` role in our Auth Account to be able to assume `PowerUserRole` in our App Account. So we need to make a small change to the trust relationship like so (remember to replace the account IDs with your own):

```
{
    "Version": "2012-10-17",
    "Statement": [
        {
            "Effect": "Allow",
            "Principal": {
                "AWS": "arn:aws:iam::<auth-account-number>:
                    role/CanAssumePowerUser"
            },
            "Action": "sts:AssumeRole"
        }
    ]
}
```

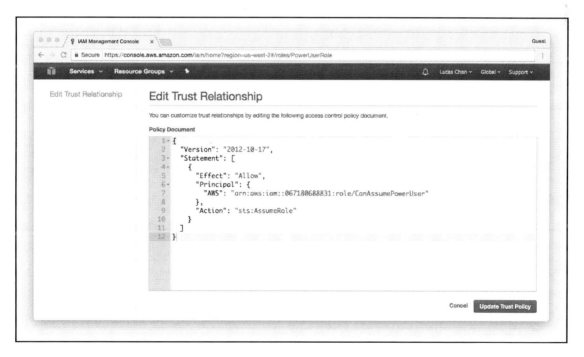

8. Repeat these steps by creating a role called `ReadOnlyRole` and attach the AWS Managed `ReadOnlyAccess` policy to it:

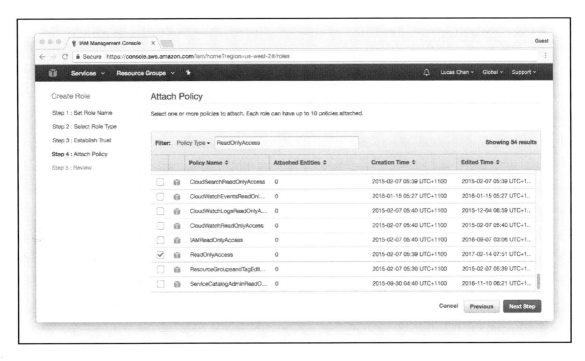

9. Again, we want to update the trust policy. Here we're going to allow both `CanAssumePowerUser` and `CanAssumeReadOnly` to switch to the `ReadOnlyRole`. This will be useful for administrators who would want to avoid accidents while clicking around the console:

```
{
    "Version": "2012-10-17",
    "Statement": [
        {
            "Effect": "Allow",
            "Principal": {
                "AWS": "arn:aws:iam::<auth-account-number>:
                    role/CanAssumeReadOnly"
            },
            "Action": "sts:AssumeRole"
        },
        {
            "Effect": "Allow",
            "Principal": {
                "AWS": "arn:aws:iam::<auth-account-number>:
```

```
                    role/CanAssumePowerUser"
            },
            "Action": "sts:AssumeRole"
        }
    ]
}
```

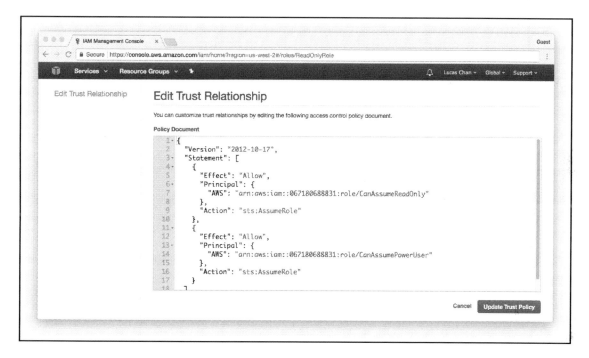

App Account role config

That was our final step. It's now time to test it out.

How it works...

1. Visit the access URL you assigned to your Simple AD directory (for example, `https://bluthcorp.awsapps.com/console`). Log in with the credentials of the user `Lucille` so we can test out our `PowerUserRole`:

2. If you click around the AWS console, you'll notice you don't really have access to do anything at all. This is because you're currently bound by a policy that only allows you to assume a role (in the application account). So, let's try doing that. Click on your account name in the top-right corner and choose **Switch Role**:

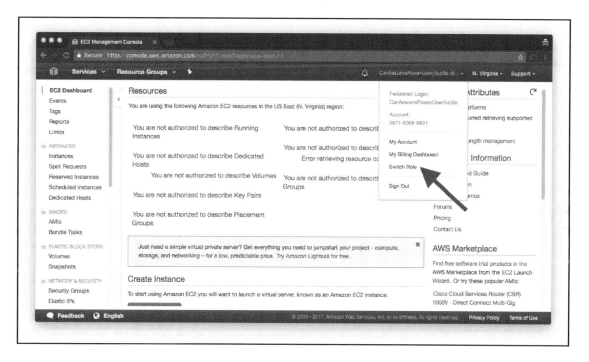

3. On the next page, you want to enter the account ID of the application account and the role you wish to assume: `PowerUserRole`. Clicking **Switch Role** here will log you in to the application account under `PowerUserRole`:

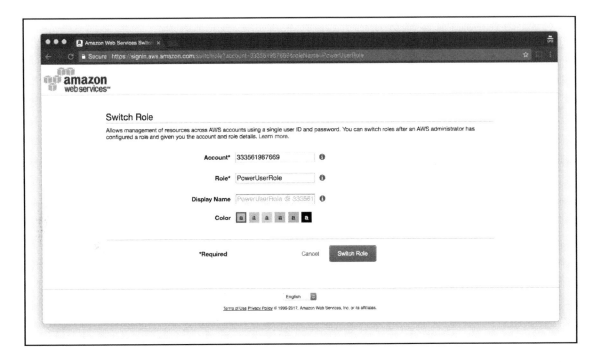

4. You should now have an active session under `PowerUserRole` in the application account. You'll recall that we assigned a `PowerUserAccess` policy to this role. So you should be free to do almost anything in this account using the profile of the user, `Lucille` (notable exceptions being IAM and organizations management). If you click on your name again, you'll see details about which role was assigned to you when you logged in and which role is currently active:

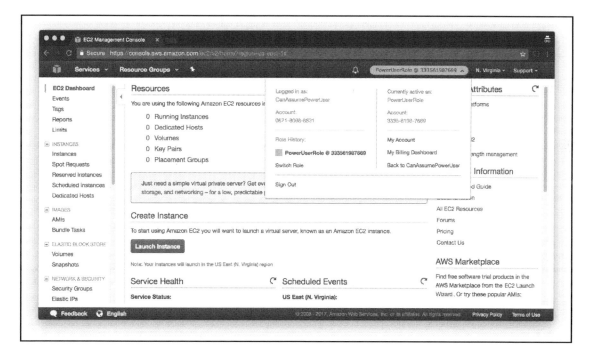

5. Try switching to the `ReadOnlyRole`. Verify that you aren't able to create any resources, perhaps by trying to create a new EC2 key pair or by creating an empty security group:

6. Log out and go back to the access URL for Simple AD. Sign in with the credentials of the user, `Buster`. Again, you'll see you don't have access to do much in the Auth Account:

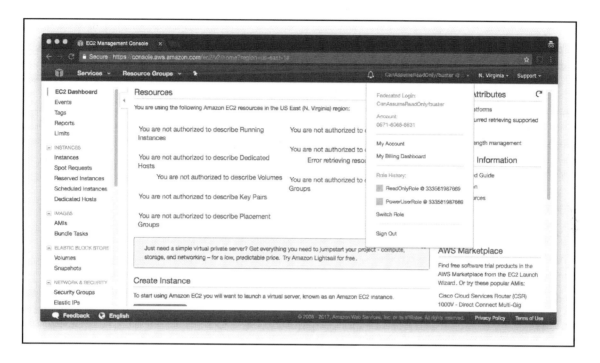

7. You should be able to switch to the `ReadOnlyRole` in the application account. Try it now to make sure it works. You can use the **Role History** shortcut to avoid typing in the account number and role name again:

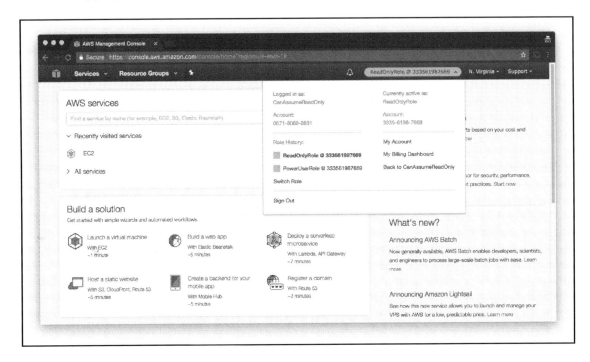

8. Finally, try switching `Buster` to `PowerUserRole` in the application account. `Buster` definitely shouldn't have access to it and you should see an error page that looks like this:

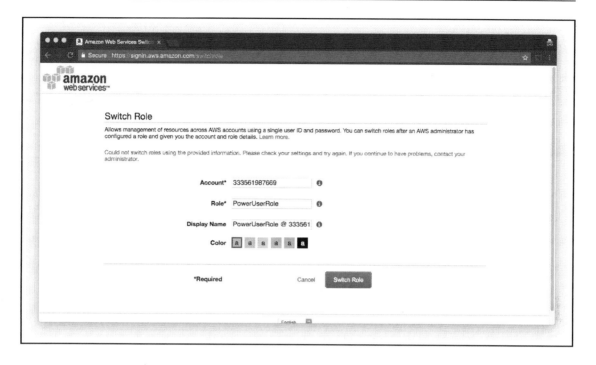

There's more...

- Exactly the same setup can be achieved with your existing Active Directory installation, even if it resides outside AWS in your data center. You will need to swap out Simple AD for AD Connector:

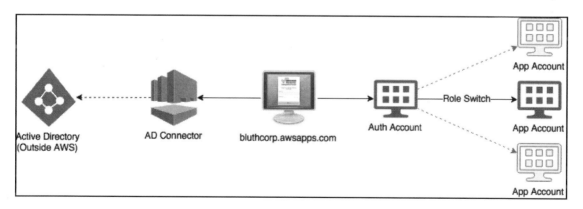

Federation with AD Connector

- You can also use ADFS and SAML 2.0 to enable federation to AWS from your existing AD installation. This would negate the need for users to log in to the console using a `*.awsapps.com` domain and would also negate the need for an Auth account.

See also

- The *Active Directory as a service* recipe

Creating SSL certificates

SSL-based communications are now becoming the de facto standard—insecure methods are no longer *good enough*.

AWS provides the **AWS Certificate Manager** (**ACM**) service to provision AWS-backed SSL certificates that you can use with your AWS resources, such as **Elastic Load Balancers** (**ELBs**) and CloudFront.

ACM is free to use! There's nothing to pay for the certificates themselves. You pay for the underlying resources you use with them as normal.

How to do it...

1. Run the CLI command, including the domain name you want the certificate for (you can use `*` as a wildcard):

```
aws acm request-certificate --domain-name <your-domain>
```

2. You can now see the request in the ACM console, but note the request is pending:

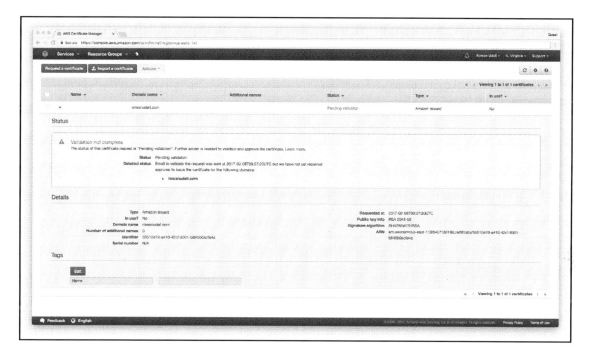

3. Check your domain administration e-mail(s). You will receive a confirmation of the request that will look like the following message:

4. Once you approve the request, you will be given a confirmation message:

Amazon Web Services (AWS) has received a request to issue an SSL certificate for rowanudell.com. You are listed as one of the authorized representatives for this domain name. Your authorization is required prior to issuing this certificate.

Verify that the domain name, AWS account ID, and certificate identifier below correspond to a request from you or a person authorized to request certificates for this domain name.

Domain name	rowanudell.com
AWS account number	3654-0718-9188
AWS Region	us-east-1
Certificate identifier	59510e19-a410-42cf-8901-b845b0acfe4a

Review the information presented above and click **I Approve** only if you recognize the request and the account requesting it. By clicking **I Approve**, you authorize Amazon to request a certificate for the above domain name.

I Approve

If you choose not to approve this request, close this page.

If you have concerns about the validity of this request, forward the email you received with a brief explanation of your concern to: validation-questions@amazon.com

5. You can now see that the certificate is ready to use in the AWS ACM console:

Success!

You have approved an SSL/TLS certificate for the domain name rowanudell.com

Domain name	rowanudell.com
AWS account number	3654-0718-9188
AWS Region	us-east-1
Arn	arn:aws:acm:us-east-1:365407189188:certificate/59510e19-a410-42cf-8901-b845b0acfe4a

Once all the domain names in the certificate request are approved, the authorized AWS account holder can review the certificate via the AWS Management Console, CLI, or API, or provision the certificate for use with integrated services, such as Amazon CloudFront or Elastic Load Balancing. For more information refer to the AWS Certificate Manager User Guide.

6. Use the **Identifier** value to apply the certificate to your resources:

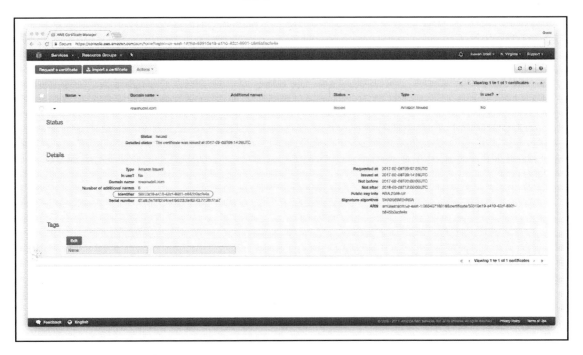

How it works...

Using the CLI tool is the quickest and easiest way to create a certificate request. Create the certificate in the region you plan to use it in; that is where your ELB(s) are located.

 If you plan to use your certificate with CloudFront, you must create it in the `us-east-1 region`.

After the request has been created, AWS will confirm the request is valid by sending approval e-mails to various standard e-mail addresses, based on conventions and the WHOIS information for your domain. Approval e-mails will be sent to the following:

- The domain registrant
- The technical contact
- The administrative contact

- And the following addresses:
  - administrator@<your-domain>
  - hostmaster@<your-domain>
  - postmaster@<your-domain>
  - webmaster@<your-domain>
  - admin@<your-domain>

You must accept at least one of the approvals before you can use your certificate.

Once approved, you can use the **Identifier** value in the configuration of your other resources, such as EC2 ELB(s) and CloudFront distributions.

There's more...

While ACM makes getting SSL certificates for your application trivial, there are a few limitations to be aware of.

EC2 instances

You'll notice in the documentation that only ELBs and CloudFront are supported by ACM certificates. You cannot put an ACM certificate directly on an EC2 instance.

While this is a limitation, in practice it's not a big issue. Generally, you wouldn't want to expose your instances to the Internet directly—they should be behind an ELB/ALB for security, performance, and management reasons. If you are serving static assets, CloudFront is going to be much more secure, and performs better at a lower cost.

Importing certificates

You can import your own certificates in to ACM, so that they can be used with your ELB(s) and CloudFront. This might be done because you have already purchased a certificate from a third-party provider, or require a particular signing authority.

CloudFormation

You can also request certificates as part of the CloudFormation stack. This is great for ensuring each of your resources has a specific certificate, unique to each deployment.

Here is a sample snippet of CloudFormation YAML to create a certificate, similar to the preceding example in this recipe:

```
Resources:
  MyCertificate:
    Type: "AWS::CertificateManager::Certificate"
    Properties:
      DomainName: <your-domain>
```

Active Directory as a service

This recipe will show you how to deploy an AWS **Simple Active Directory (Simple AD)** service.

Simple AD is powered by Samba 4 and is a Microsoft Active Directory compatible managed service. It will work with many applications that require Active Directory support and provides a large range of the commonly used Active Directory features, including the following:

- User accounts
- Single sign-on (Kerberos)
- Group memberships
- Domain joining

It also integrates with other services provided by AWS, such as the following:

- AWS Management Console
- WorkMail
- WorkDocs
- WorkSpaces and WorkSpaces Application Manager

AWS manages backup and restoration of the directory for you in the form of daily snapshots and the ability to perform point-in-time recovery.

Features that aren't supported include the following:

- Trust relationships with other AD domains
- DNS dynamic updates
- Schema extensions
- MFA
- LDAPS

- PowerShell AD cmdlets
- Transfer of FSMO roles

The ideal scenario for Simple AD usage is when you don't require advanced AD features and you're supporting less than 5,000 users. If either of these isn't true, you will want to look at AWS' fully fledged Microsoft Active Directory service. Brace yourself for some added complexity and much higher cost if you choose this path, however.

Getting ready

Before going ahead, we'll need the following pieces of info:

- The FQDN for your directory (for example, `http://megacorp.com/`).
- A password for administering your directory. This password corresponds to the `Administrator` user that will be created on your behalf. Note that the password needs to be between 8-64 characters and will also need to contain one character from three of the following four groups:
    - Lowercase letters
    - Uppercase letters
    - Numbers
    - Non-alphanumeric characters
- The ID of the VPC we're deploying to.
- The IDs of two subnets in this VPC. These subnets need to be in different Availability Zones.
- The size of the directory you'd like to deploy. You can choose between *Small* and *Large*.

A domain controller is going to be deployed in each of the two subnets you've chosen. They'll be communicating between each other on a fairly large number of ports. Ideally, these subnets would exist in the same *tier* in your VPC and by extension would not have any NACLs which would stop the controllers from talking with each other.

> If, for some reason, you're restricting traffic using NACLs within your VPC tiers, you will want to refer to the AWS docs for a list of which ports to allow.
> For more details, visit
> `http://docs.aws.amazon.com/directoryservice/latest/admin-guide/prereq_simple.html`.

How to do it...

1. Create a new CloudFormation template file. We'll start by populating it with `Parameters` that correspond to all the requirements we mentioned before:

```
AWSTemplateFormatVersion: '2010-09-09'
Parameters:
  FullyQualifiedName:
    Description: The fully qualified name for the directory
      (e.g. megacorp.com)
    Type: String
    AllowedPattern: '^([a-zA-Z0-9]+[\\.-])+([a-zA-Z0-9])+$'
  Password:
    Description: The password for the directory Administrator
    Type: String
    NoEcho: true
  VpcId:
    Description: The ID of the VPC to deploy to
    Type: AWS::EC2::VPC::Id
  SubnetIds:
    Description: Subnets where the directory will be deployed to
      (pick at least 2)
    Type: List<AWS::EC2::Subnet::Id>
  DirectorySize:
    Description: The size of the directory to deploy
    Type: String
    AllowedValues:
      - Small
      - Large
```

2. Next, we define our `Resources`. Even though two Simple AD domain controllers are being deployed, we only need to create one resource here:

```
Resources:
  ExampleDirectory:
    Type: AWS::DirectoryService::SimpleAD
    Properties:
      Name: !Ref FullyQualifiedName
      Password: !Ref Password
      Size: !Ref DirectorySize
      VpcSettings:
        SubnetIds:
          - !Select [ 0, Ref: SubnetIds ]
          - !Select [ 1, Ref: SubnetIds ]
        VpcId: !Ref VpcId
```

3. You can now go ahead and run this template in the CloudFormation web console, or via the CLI like this:

```
aws cloudformation create-stack \
  --stack-name example-directory \
  --template-body file://08-active-directory-as-a-service.yaml \
  --parameters \
  ParameterKey=FullyQualifiedName,ParameterValue=<fqdn> \
  ParameterKey=Password,ParameterValue=<password> \
  ParameterKey=VpcId,ParameterValue=<vpd-id> \
  "ParameterKey=SubnetIds,ParameterValue='<subnet-1>,<subnet-2>'" \
  ParameterKey=DirectorySize,ParameterValue=<Small/Large>
```

How it works...

It will take several minutes to create the directory. Once the **Status** becomes **Active**, you may proceed with further setup and integration tasks. Your directory listing page will eventually show a directory listing that looks similar to this:

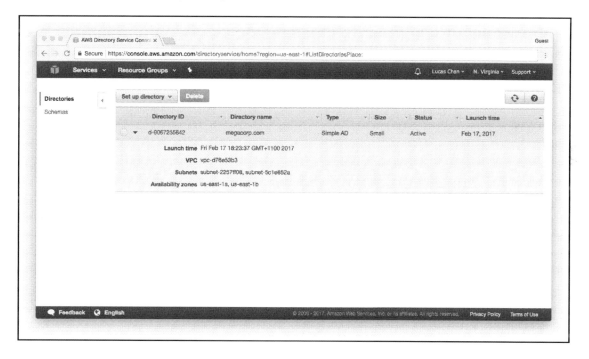

Clicking on the directory ID will reveal more detailed information about your directory, like so:

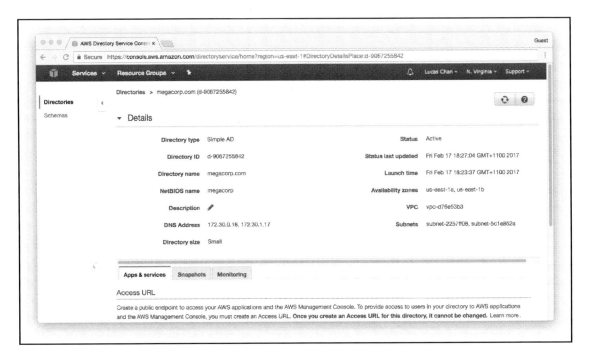

There's more...

- The password for the `Administrator` account can't be retrieved or reset. Be sure to keep this password somewhere safe.
- You may notice an additional security group appear in your EC2 console. This group is necessary for the directory controllers (although you won't see these appear as EC2 instances in your console).
- The directory will contain an account with the prefix `AWSAdminD-`. This account is necessary for AWS to perform maintenance tasks such as backup and FSMO role transfers. Removing this account or changing its password is almost certainly a bad idea.

See also

- The *Building a secure network* recipe in `Chapter 7`, *Networking*.

Creating users

Before we introduce this recipe, we need to talk briefly about **Identity and Access Management (IAM)**. It's free and is enabled on every account. It allows you to create groups and users and allows you to control exactly what they can and can't do using policy assignment.

By default, groups and users will have no permissions until you assign them either an *AWS Managed Policy* or a *Customer Managed Policy* (one which you manage). You'll want to use AWS Managed Policies as much as possible to avoid having to create and maintain your own.

 There's a third kind of policy called an **Inline Policy**. Use this sparingly. In fact, the only time we typically see it is in CloudFormation templates.

You pretty much never want to assign a policy directly to a user. If you go down this path, you'll create a lot of work for yourself in the future. Instead, you want to apply policies to groups and then assign users to those groups. Fortunately, it's a pretty easy process and we're about to walk you through it.

The IAM dashboard provides a URL that your IAM users can use to log in to the web console (if you've assigned them a password and given them access to do so). You can also customize this *IAM sign-in link* if necessary. Don't forget to give this URL to any IAM users you create so they know where to go to sign in.

It will look something like this until you customize it:

```
https://<account-id>.signin.aws.amazon.com/console
```

Now, jump right in. There's no excuse for not using IAM. Start today!

Getting ready

All you need to proceed is the CLI tools installed with a profile which can call the AWS IAM API. If you don't have this, you can follow along with the recipe steps using the AWS web console instead as the process is the same.

How to do it...

1. Create a new group by running this CLI command:

   ```
   aws iam create-group --group-name <group-name>
   ```

2. The output looks like this:

   ```
   {
       "Group": {
         "Path": "/",
         "GroupId": "AGPAIHM2XJ2ELQTNYBFQQ",
         "Arn": "arn:aws:iam::067180688831:group/PowerUsers",
         "GroupName": "PowerUsers"
       }
   }
   ```

3. The group doesn't have permissions to do anything yet, so you'll need to attach a policy to it. You can do it with this command (which unfortunately doesn't provide any feedback if it successfully runs):

   ```
   aws iam attach-group-policy \
     --group-name <group-name> \
     --policy-arn <policy-arn>
   ```

4. You can find the **Amazon Resource Name (ARN)** for the policy you'd like to attach in the AWS IAM web console. You can also run the following CLI command to get a list of policies:

   ```
   aws iam list-policies
   ```

5. In this example, we're dealing with PowerUsers so we want to attach the following ARN, which maps to the AWS Managed Policy for power users:

   ```
   arn:aws:iam::aws:policy/PowerUserAccess
   ```

6. Now we can go ahead and create a new user by running this CLI command:

```
aws iam create-user --user-name <new-username>
```

7. You'll get a response that looks like this:

```
{
   "User": {
      "UserName": "lucille.bluth",
      "Path": "/",
      "CreateDate": "2017-02-19T06:16:50.558Z",
      "UserId": "AIDAIU5P6ESCGYTVGACFE",
      "Arn": "arn:aws:iam::07180688831:user/lucille.bluth"
   }
}
```

8. If you wish to give this user access to the web console, you'll need to create a login profile for them. You can do it like so:

```
aws iam create-login-profile --user-name <username> \
   --password <password> \
   --password-reset-required
```

9. Forcing a password reset here is probably good practice. The API should respond to you like so:

```
{
   "LoginProfile": {
      "UserName": "lucille.bluth",
      "CreateDate": "2017-02-19T06:29:06.244Z",
      "PasswordResetRequired": true
   }
}
```

10. To give the API access to the user, they'll need a set of API keys. Generate them with this command:

```
aws iam create-access-key --user-name <username>
```

11. The output will look something like this:

```
{
    "AccessKey": {
        "UserName": "lucille.bluth",
        "Status": "Active",
        "CreateDate": "2017-02-19T06:59:45.273Z",
        "SecretAccessKey": "abcdefghijklmnopqrstuvwxyz",
        "AccessKeyId": "AAAAAAAAAAAAAAAAAAAA"
    }
}
```

12. Access keys can only be retrieved once. There is no way to fetch them again after they've been generated and shown to you. If you lose your access keys, you'll have to regenerate a new set of keys.

13. This user still doesn't have any permissions to do anything; this is because they don't yet belong to a group. Let's add them to the group we created in step 1:

```
aws iam add-user-to-group \
  --group-name <group-name> \
  --user-name <username>
```

 Note that unfortunately this command doesn't return any output either. You can verify whether or not this worked by running this command:

```
aws iam list-groups-for-user --user-name <username>
```

14. You should see something like this:

```
{
    "Groups": [
        {
            "Path": "/",
            "CreateDate": "2017-02-19T07:24:46Z",
            "GroupId": "AGPAIHM2XJ2ELQTNYBFQQ",
            "Arn": "arn:aws:iam::067180688831:group/PowerUsers",
            "GroupName": "PowerUsers"
        }
    ]
}
```

There's more...

This pretty much covers the basics of how to create IAM groups and users and assign policies to them. Here are some of the IAM tips and gotchas we've run into over the years:

- Users can exist in more than one group. Use this to your advantage.
- Groups, however, cannot exist within other groups.
- Users can have more than one set of API keys. This is necessary when they need to perform key rotation.
- You can (and should) define a strong password policy for your IAM users.
- The `PowerUserAccess` policy is good but does not allow IAM access. At first this might not seem to be a problem; however, if you are bound by this policy you will encounter issues when running CloudFormation stacks that create IAM roles for EC2 instances, for example.
- IAM is a global service, meaning that users and groups are global, not region-specific. By default, a user can use AWS services in any region.
- EC2 key pairs are region-specific and not specific to an IAM user. In other words, IAM users don't have SSH keys associated with them.
- Your IAM username and password (and access keys) won't provide you with SSH or RDP access to running instances. Credentials for these services are managed separately.
- You can assign up to 10 policies to a group or user.
- You should also consider enabling MFA on IAM user accounts for added security. This is used primarily for accessing the web console but you can also configure your policies so that MFA will be required for API calls too. You can choose between hardware and software tokens. A good rule of thumb is to use software tokens for IAM users and hardware tokens for root logins. MFA via SMS is due to arrive soon and is currently in public preview.

See also

- The *Federating with your AWS account* recipe
- The *Cross-account user roles* recipe

Creating instance roles

This recipe is reasonably short but it contains a really important concept to anyone who is new to the AWS platform. Understanding and utilizing IAM roles for EC2 will significantly reduce your exposure to lost credentials and probably help you sleep a little better at night too. In a nutshell, instance roles help you get AWS credentials off your servers and out of your code base(s).

Roles contain one or more policies. We're going to create a role that has some AWS Managed Policies as well as an Inline Policy. As the name would suggest, an AWS Managed Policy is a policy that is created and fully controlled by AWS. The Inline Policy is going to be created by us and will be embedded in our role definition.

The AWS Managed Policies we'll use will allow read-only access to the S3 and EC2 APIs. The Inline Policy we'll create will allow write access to CloudWatch logs. We'll talk through why you would or wouldn't choose a Managed Policy later in this recipe.

How to do it...

1. Create a new CloudFormation template file and add the first `Resource`. This is going to be our role that contains references to the managed policies, and also our Inline Policy:

```
AWSTemplateFormatVersion: '2010-09-09'
Resources:
  ExampleRole:
    Type: AWS::IAM::Role
    Properties:
      AssumeRolePolicyDocument:
        Version: "2012-10-17"
        Statement:
          -
            Effect: Allow
            Principal:
              Service:
                - ec2.amazonaws.com
            Action:
              - sts:AssumeRole
      ManagedPolicyArns:
        - arn:aws:iam::aws:policy/AmazonS3ReadOnlyAccess
        - arn:aws:iam::aws:policy/AmazonEC2ReadOnlyAccess
      Path: /
      Policies:
```

```
          PolicyName: WriteToCloudWatchLogs
          PolicyDocument:
            Version: "2012-10-17"
            Statement:
              -
                Effect: Allow
                Action:
                  - logs:CreateLogGroup
                  - logs:CreateLogStream
                  - logs:PutLogEvents
                  - logs:DescribeLogStreams
                Resource: "*"
```

2. We now need to create an `InstanceProfile` resource. A profile encapsulates a single IAM role and, roughly speaking, that's all it's used for. A profile can contain only a single IAM role, so it's not clear why AWS has built this extra layer of abstraction; presumably they have plans to give profiles of other properties aside from roles:

```
ExampleInstanceProfile:
  Type: AWS::IAM::InstanceProfile
  Properties:
    Roles:
      - !Ref ExampleRole
    Path: /
```

3. For convenience, we'll add some `Outputs` that will provide the profile name and ARN to us after the stack is created:

```
Outputs:
  ExampleInstanceProfile:
    Value: !Ref ExampleInstanceProfile
  ExampleInstanceProfileArn:
    Value: !GetAtt ExampleInstanceProfile.Arn
```

4. You can now create your instance role CloudFormation web console or via the CLI like this:

```
aws cloudformation create-stack \
  --stack-name example-instance-profile \
  --template-body file://08-creating-instance-roles.yaml \
  --capabilities CAPABILITY_IAM
```

This role can now be assigned to your EC2 instances. The *Feeding log files in to CloudWatch logs* recipe in `Chapter 5`, *Management Tools*, shows how you can define a role and assign it to an EC2 instance at launch using CloudFormation.

How it works...

How on earth does this solve the problem of hardcoded AWS API keys? Well, something really interesting happens when you assign a role to an EC2 instance. The metadata for that instance will return a set of short-lived API keys. You can retrieve these keys by sending an HTTP request to the metadata URL (this is a service EC2 instances can use to fetch information about themselves):

```
http://169.254.169.254/latest/meta-data/iam/security-credentials/<role
name>
```

The output of a curl request to this URL will look something like this:

```
{
  "Code" : "Success",
  "LastUpdated" : "2017-02-17T11:14:23Z",
  "Type" : "AWS-HMAC",
  "AccessKeyId" : "AAAAAAAAAAAAAAAAAAAA",
  "SecretAccessKey" : "zzzzzzzzzzzzzzzzzzzzzzzzzzzzzzzzzzzzzzzz",
  "Token" : "token",
  "Expiration" : "2017-02-17T12:14:23Z"
}
```

If you take the `AccessKeyId` and `SecretAccessKey` returned in the response, you can use them to query the AWS API. The policies applied to the instance based on the role assigned to it will determine exactly what API actions the instance is able to perform using these keys.

The really fun part is that you don't have to worry too much about handling these keys at all (although it's really useful to know how all this works under the hood). For example, the AWS CLI tools will automatically fetch these keys for you prior to running any CLI commands. The same goes for the AWS SDKs.

Take a scenario where your developers are building an application that needs to fetch files from S3. As long as they are using the AWS SDK to do this and the application is running on an EC2 instance that has been assigned a role containing a policy that allows files to be fetched from S3, then no credentials are required by the application whatsoever! The SDK will take care of the queries to the metadata service for you.

The AWS SDKs are available for almost every widely used language, so there's no excuse for keeping hardcoded AWS credentials in config files or source code.

You will see your instances roles listed in the IAM console under the `Roles` section:

Clicking on the role will reveal further details, such as the policies that have been assigned to it:

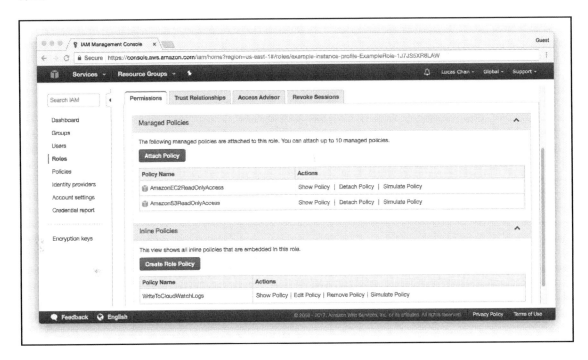

There's more...

- IAM is a global service. This means that the roles and policies you create will be available in every region.
- You'll find all the available AWS Managed Policies in the AWS web console. There's quite a few of them so don't be afraid to use the search bar.
- There's a third kind of policy called a Customer Managed Policy. These are policies which are managed by you and will appear in the AWS console amongst the AWS Managed Policies.
- As of February 2017, it is possible to attach an IAM role to an existing/running EC2 instance. This previously wasn't the case and the role could only be assigned at the time the instance launched.
- AWS automatically and periodically rotates the credentials returned by the metadata service.

- It's not always appropriate to use an AWS Managed Policy. For example, if a server needs to write to CloudWatch logs, it may be tempting to assign it the AWS Managed Policy that provides full access. If you do this, however, you'll also be giving the server access to delete log groups and streams. This is almost certainly undesirable. You'll want to inspect the policies before you apply them and defer to an Inline or Customer Managed Policy where appropriate. The principle of least privilege applies here.

See also

- The *Feeding log files in to CloudWatch logs* recipe in `Chapter 5`, *Management Tools*

Cross-account user roles

Using multiple accounts to provision your resources (for example, development and production environments) provides a form of *blast radius* protection—even in a worst-case scenario, any issues or damages are limited to the account they occur in, not your entire AWS presence.

Creating and assuming roles across accounts is the best way to manage access to multiple accounts. Specific roles provide a clear and explicit declaration of permissions that can be easily reviewed, and revoked if needed.

This recipe provides a way to scale your access across many accounts, without compromising your security.

Getting ready

This recipe assumes you already have two AWS accounts created and ready to go.

In one account (the **source** account, referred to as *Account A*) you will need an IAM user.

While you will need to use your account's root credentials to set up the first role in an account, *do not* use them on a day-to-day basis. The root account has permissions to do anything in your account, and should only be used when necessary.

How to do it...

1. Start a new template with a version and description:

    ```
    AWSTemplateFormatVersion: "2010-09-09"
    Description: This template creates a role that can be assumed
      from another account.
    ```

2. The template will take one parameter—the source account that can assume the role:

    ```
    Parameters:
      SourceAccountNumber:
        Type: String
        Description: The AWS account number to grant access to assume
          the role.
        AllowedPattern: "[0-9]+"
        MaxLength: "12"
        MinLength: "12"
    ```

3. The role itself will consist of the trust role and a sample policy:

    This role has full access to the target account.

    ```
    Resources:
      CrossAccountRole:
        Type: "AWS::IAM::Role"
        Properties:
          Path: "/"
          AssumeRolePolicyDocument:
            Version: "2012-10-17"
            Statement:
              - Sid: ""
                Action: "sts:AssumeRole"
                Effect: Allow
                Principal:
    ```

```
            AWS:
                !Sub "arn:aws:iam::${SourceAccountNumber}:root"
        Policies:
          - PolicyName: DoEverything
            PolicyDocument:
              Version: "2012-10-17"
              Statement:
                - Action:
                    - "*"
                  Effect: Allow
                  Resource: "*"
                  Sid: DoEverything
```

4. Finally, we create an output that will make it easy to retrieve the target role ARN:

```
Outputs:
  RoleARN:
    Description: The Role ARN that can be assumed by the
      other account.
    Value: !GetAtt CrossAccountRole.Arn
```

5. Save the template with a known name, for example `08-target-account-role.yaml`.

6. Deploy the role to the target account (that is, **Account B**) by using the CLI tool:

```
aws cloudformation create-stack \
  --stack-name CrossAccountRole \
  --template-body file://src/08-target-account-role.yaml \
  --parameters \
  ParameterKey=SourceAccountNumber, \
  ParameterValue=<your-source-account-number> \
  --capabilities CAPABILITY_IAM
```

7. Get (just) the target role ARN from the outputs of your CloudFormation stack:

```
aws cloudformation describe-stacks \
  --stack-name CrossAccountRole \
  --query 'Stacks[0].Outputs[0].OutputValue' \
  --output text
```

8. In your source account (that is, **Account A**) confirm that you can assume the target role by manually invoking the CLI tool:

```
aws sts assume-role \
  --role-arn <your-target-role-arn> \
  --role-session-name CrossAccountRole
```

How it works...

While cross-account roles are extremely useful for administering multiple AWS accounts, they're not the most intuitive thing to configure. Here's a diagram that illustrates the resources and their interactions:

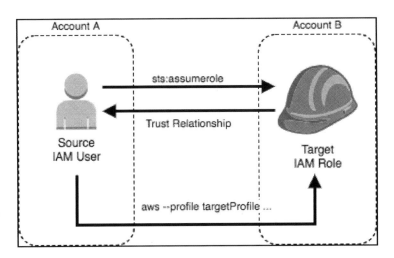

The first few steps of this recipe are simply creating the **Target IAM Role** in a clear and repeatable way using CloudFormation.

You must explicitly call out the AWS account number that will be allowed to assume this role. If you want to allow multiple accounts to assume the role, simply add more statements to the `AssumeRolePolicyDocument` property of the role.

The sample policy created in this template gives full access to the target account (because the `Action` and `Resource` are both set to *). You should adjust this as appropriate for your needs.

Defining an output value that returns the IAM role's ARN will make it easier to get the generated ID later in the recipe.

We then launch the template in the target account. As this template creates IAM resources, you must supply the `--capabilities CAPABILITY_IAM` argument. If you don't have any existing IAM users that can launch it, use the AWS web console (after logging in with your root credentials). This means you don't need to bother creating IAM users in the target account.

Once you have deployed the template, you will no longer need to log in to the account manually—you can just assume the newly created role from the trusted (source) account. Using an IAM role in the target account means that your day-to-day access does not require multiple passwords, which takes work to manage and store securely. You only need to have one password—the password of your source IAM user.

After the stack has finished creating (which shouldn't take long, as it's only creating one resource), you can quickly extract the target role's ARN with a `describe-stacks` call, combined with a specifically-crafted `--query` argument. The JMESPath query `Stacks[0].Outputs[0].OutputValue` gets the `OutputValue` property of the first output in the first stack returned, which we know will be the target role ARN because there is only one output in the template.

Finally, the sample `assume-role` command will return the credentials for the target role (that is, `ACCESS_KEY_ID` and `SECRET_ACCESS_KEY`). You can then use this in an API call, via the CLI tool or one of the SDKs. Keep in mind that these tokens will be short-lived.

See the next section for a more convenient way to use the credentials with the CLI tool by creating profiles.

There's more...

Just as there are multiple ways to use roles, there are multiple ways to utilize cross-account roles.

AWS CLI profiles

One of the easiest ways to use a cross-account role is configuring it as a profile for the AWS CLI tool to use. This means you can quickly and easily switch accounts just by changing the profile you use when executing your commands.

To do this, you must define the target role in the CLI configuration file. With this configuration, it is assumed that your `default` profile is in the source account (that is, Account A).

Add the following snippet to the `~/.aws/config` file on Linux and Mac computers, and `C:\Users\[USERNAME]\.aws\config` file on Windows:

```
[profile accountb]
role_arn = <your-target-account-role-arn>
source_profile = default
```

To use switch roles, all you need to do is pass the `--profile` argument along with your command:

```
aws --profile accountb ...
```

See also

- The *Creating users* recipe.

Storing secrets

A common mistake new administrators make when getting started with Infrastructure-as-Code is committing secrets (passwords, access keys, and so on) in their repositories. While this makes their infrastructure repeatable, it also makes it much more likely their credentials will be compromised. Once something is in version control, it's hard and annoying to remove it (that's the point of version control!). Even if you do remove it, it's almost impossible to know if it has already been viewed/copied by someone unintended.

In this recipe, we will introduce and use the open source tool, **Unicreds**.

 Unicreds is a Golang port of the Python tool, Credstash: `https://github.com/fugue/credstash`.
While the functionality is very similar, Unicreds has the benefit of being cross-platform and dependency-free!

Since this pattern is completely backed by AWS services, it removes the need to manage (and worry about) password vaults, shared passwords, and committing sensitive information to SCM.

You might even use Unicreds to store non-secret information, because it provides a convenient way to store and share settings without the need to run or maintain any servers!

Getting ready

You must have Unicreds present on your target system.

As it is written in Golang, it is easily distributed as a standalone binary application—no installer or dependencies are required.

 Releases for all platforms are available at
https://github.com/Versent/unicreds/releases.

These commands assume your default profile has the permission to create KMS keys and DynamoDB tables. You can override the profile used by passing the `--profile` argument with all of the commands in the recipe. You must also have your AWS region setting configured.

How to do it...

1. Create a KMS key, and take note of the Key ID returned:

   ```
   aws kms create-key --query 'KeyMetadata.KeyId' --output text
   ```

2. Create an alias for the key:

    Unicreds uses the `alias/credstash` alias to make it compatible with Credstash.

   ```
   aws kms create-alias --alias-name 'alias/credstash' \
   --target-key-id "<your-key-id>"
   ```

3. Set up the resources required by Unicreds:

   ```
   unicreds setup
   ```

4. Store a secret using the `put` command:

   ```
   unicreds put foo bar
   ```

5. Get the secret using the `get` command:

```
unicreds get foo
```

How it works...

Here is a high-level diagram that illustrates the components involved in theses Unicreds commands:

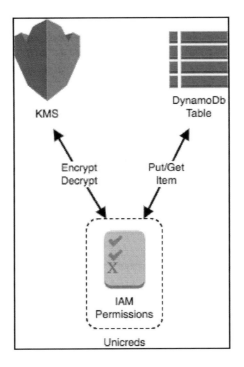

We start this recipe by creating the key that will be used to encrypt the secrets in KMS. Note that we never get to see this key—it only exists in KMS. All you can do is request that KMS encrypts or decrypts data with it for you.

It is possible to import your own key in to KMS (so that you could decrypt the secrets outside of AWS if you needed to), but this is not required for Unicreds to work. The `create-key` command returns the GUID for the key, which will be used in the following steps.

Aliases make it much easier to deal with KMS keys. You can use them in most commands in place of the full key ARN. More importantly, it makes it obvious which key you are dealing with so that you can quickly, easily, and confidently assign access permissions.

The default alias for the key used with Unicreds is `alias/credstash`. While this might seem a bit confusing at first, it means that Unicreds is backward-compatible with Credstash. You can choose your own alias; you will simply need to override it when you give your other commands (such as `setup`, `put`, and so on).

The `setup` command creates the required resources in your AWS account. This effectively means creating a DynamoDB table to store the secrets in.

Once everything is set up, you can start storing secrets using Unicreds. In this example, the secret is stored with the (highly original) key `foo` and the value `bar`.

At this stage, you can go to DynamoDB in the AWS console and see the stored value in the `credential-store` table. You can also change the name of the DDB table used when you run the `credstash setup` command, if you want to.

Once there's a secret stored, you can retrieve it with the `get` command. It's important to remember that there's no need to do this from the same machine you stored it from. As long as the AWS user/role has sufficient permission to use the KMS service and access the DDB table, they will be able to retrieve the secret.

There's more...

Unicreds leverages the built-in functionality of AWS, so you get an enterprise-grade solution without the overhead of needing to run your own servers. Here are some other useful things you can do to make your secrets even more secure.

Key aliases

Creating multiple KMS keys—and referring to them with unique aliases—is a great way to limit the access to put/get secrets to specific applications or teams.

Instead of using the default `alias/credstash` alias, you could give a team their own alias and be confident that they aren't going to see or write to anyone else's secrets.

Secret reader role

Due to the fine-grained nature of IAM permissions, you can easily segment the type of different access roles get to your AWS resources.

With the following IAM policy, you can ensure that the user/role can only read secret values (using a specific key and table), but they can never set or change them:

```
{
  "Version": "2012-10-17",
  "Statement": [
    {
      "Action": [
        "kms:Decrypt"
      ],
      "Effect": "Allow",
      "Resource": "arn:aws:kms:us-east-1:<your-account-id>:
        key/<your-key-id>"
    },
    {
      "Action": [
        "dynamodb:GetItem",
        "dynamodb:Query",
        "dynamodb:Scan"
      ],
      "Effect": "Allow",
      "Resource": "arn:aws:dynamodb:us-east-1:<your-account-id>:
        table/credential-store"
    }
  ]
}
```

Secret writer role

The flip side to the secret reader role is the secret writer.

Add this snippet to the relevant IAM policy section of a role to give it the ability to set secret values, but not retrieve them:

```
{
  "Version": "2012-10-17",
  "Statement": [
    {
      "Action": [
        "kms:GenerateDataKey"
      ],
```

```
      "Effect": "Allow",
      "Resource": "arn:aws:kms:us-east-1:<your-account-id>:
        key/<your-key-id>"
    },
    {
      "Action": [
        "dynamodb:PutItem"
      ],
      "Effect": "Allow",
      "Resource": "arn:aws:dynamodb:us-east-1:<your-account-id>:
        table/credential-store"
    }
  ]
}
```

The put-file command

You can put entire files in to storage with Unicreds. Just use the `put-file` command:

```
unicreds put-file foo bar.txt
```

Versioning

While storing your secrets securely is a great start, it is still good practice to change/rotate your passwords, keys, and other secrets regularly.

Unicreds has built-in support for versioning, which means you can update your secrets while still keeping records of previous versions.

When you put to the same secret name multiple times, Unicreds will automatically create new versions for the values. You can get a specific version of secret by providing a version argument with a `get` or `put` command:

```
unicreds get foo 1
```

See also

- The *Creating users* recipe

9
Estimating Costs

In this chapter, we will cover:

- Calculating costs
- Estimating CloudFormation template costs
- Purchasing reserved instances
- Estimating total cost of ownership

Introduction

One of the hardest things to get used to when starting with AWS is that you pay for almost everything that you use. One of the biggest benefits of AWS is that you only pay for what you use. This makes it hard to quickly answer the *how much is it going to cost?* question that often arises when people first start using AWS; they don't know exactly what they currently use!

In a *traditional* infrastructure or data center setup, many costs are paid during the initial outlay or in annual contracts. As AWS has no upfront fees, and few long-term commitments, so the usual thought process around costs is turned on its head.

There are a number of helpful tools to get a better estimate of your AWS usage costs. Don't forget that every AWS service page has a pricing section. While some pricing models can be a bit confusing at the start, it quickly makes sense.

Calculating costs

AWS Simple Monthly Calculator is a website application provided to help you estimate and forecast your AWS costs. By listing the resources you expect to consume you can calculate your pay-as-you-go costs, which is how AWS bills you—there's no upfront costs involved.

Getting ready

In order to use the AWS Simple Monthly Calculator effectively, you need to already know the specific services and resources that you will use on a monthly basis.

You also need to know specifics about things such as monthly data transfer and the amount of data you will need to store. In AWS, you get charged for data in and out of AWS (for example, visitors to your website), but not between AWS services (for example, EC2 instances to RDS databases).

How to do it...

1. Go to the calculator website, `http://calculator.s3.amazonaws.com/index.html`:

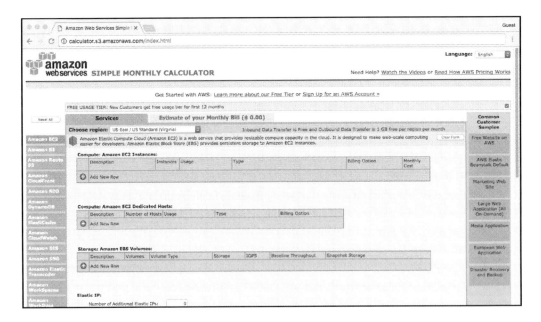

2. Select/deselect the free usage tier option as relevant for your account—if the account is less than 12 months old, you are eligible for the free usage tier.

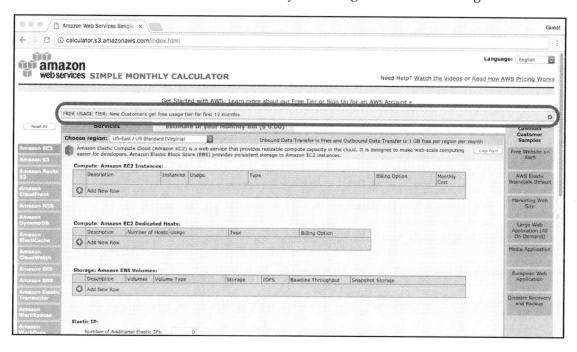

3. Make sure you have the correct region selected before adding resources, as they can differ in price from region to region:

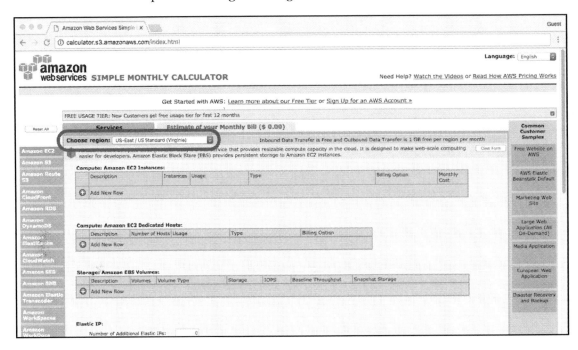

4. Add your resources by selecting the relevant service from the left-hand menu, and filling in your details:

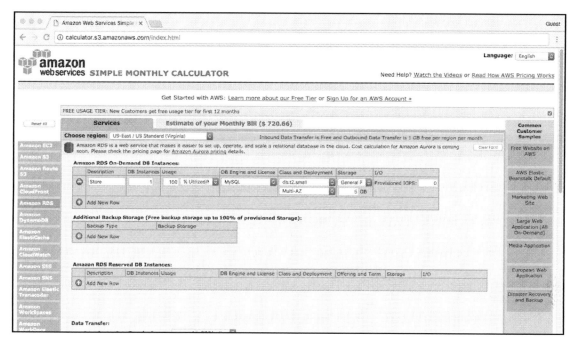

5. Continue to add resources as necessary:

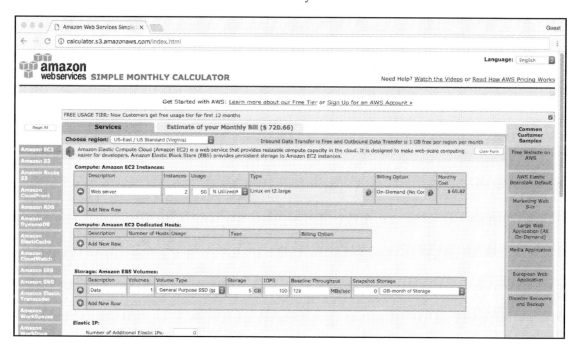

6. Once you've added all your resources, view the estimated monthly bill on the tab:

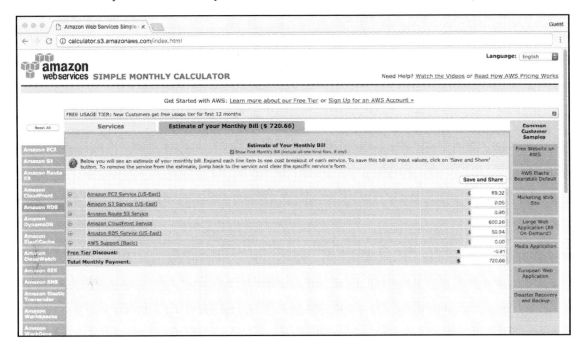

7. After confirming the estimate's detail, click on the **Save** and **Share** button to add some additional metadata about your report. All the fields are optional:

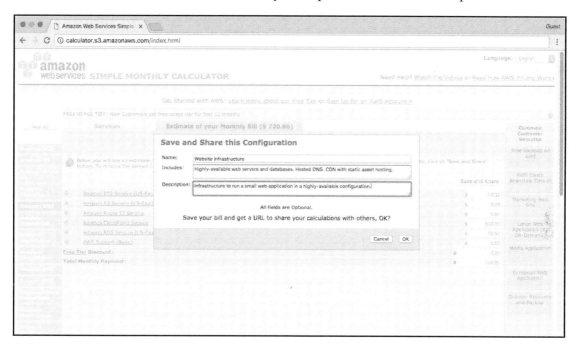

8. A specific, one-time URL will be generated for your report that you can then share with others:

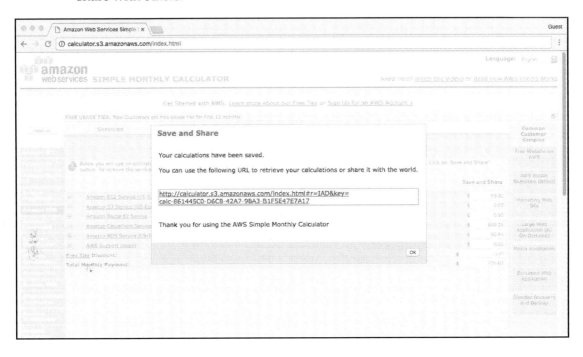

How it works...

The accuracy of the calculator is completely dependent on your ability to forecast your requirements and usage—not an easy thing to do when you first start using AWS!

Unfortunately, not all AWS services are present in the calculator (a notable exception is AWS Lambda). For those services, you will have to do your own calculations based on the service-specific pricing pages.

The cost of services and resources can vary from region to region. In general, the us-east-1 region is the cheapest, and also has the most services (not all services are available in all regions), so use that if you want to know the lowest-cost option. Other regions' prices vary due to supply and demand, cost of operations, and undoubtedly many other reasons that AWS doesn't go in to.

Some services (for example, DynamoDB, Lambda, and so on) have a free tier that applies even if your account does not qualify for the *standard* free tier (that is, the account is more than 12 months old). These services will have a note on their specific calculator page detailing the inclusions:

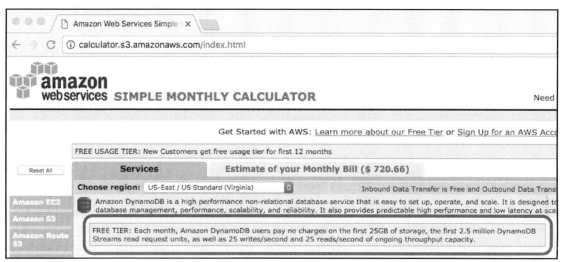

Once completed, you can generate a specific URL for your estimation report that you can share with anyone. There's no authentication to access this URL, so don't put any sensitive information in your reports. The only protection is that the URL is unlikely to be guessed (given it's just the calculator site with a GUID parameter).

See also

- The *Estimating CloudFormation template costs* recipe

Estimating CloudFormation template costs

Most of the recipes in this book have been managed and launched using CloudFormation, the AWS Infrastructure as Code service.

Getting ready

For this recipe, you will need an existing CloudFormation template. The template does not need to be deployed as a stack;, just the file is required.

In this example, we will use the template from Chapter 4, *Using AWS Compute*, to securely access private instances: `06-create-database-with-automatic-failover.yaml`.

How to do it...

1. Run the command to generate the report:

```
aws cloudformation estimate-template-cost \
  --template-body \
  file://06-create-database-with-automatic-failover.yaml \
  --parameters ParameterKey=VPCId,ParameterValue=test \
  ParameterKey=SubnetIds,ParameterValue=\"test,test\" \
  ParameterKey=DBUsername,ParameterValue=test \
  ParameterKey=DBPassword,ParameterValue=test \
  --query Url \
  --output text
```

2. Click or copy and paste the URL into a browser to see the report:

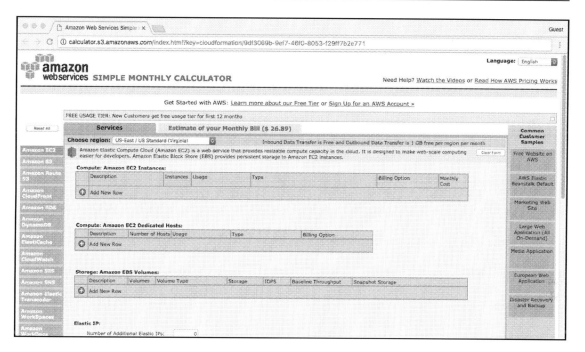

3. Click on **Amazon RDS** in the left-hand menu to see the individual service page details:

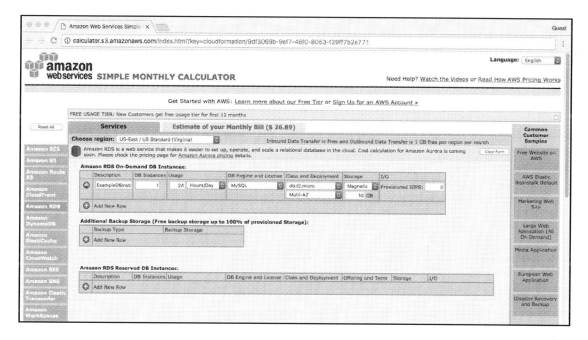

4. Click on **Estimate of your Monthly Bill** to see a total summary of the template resources:

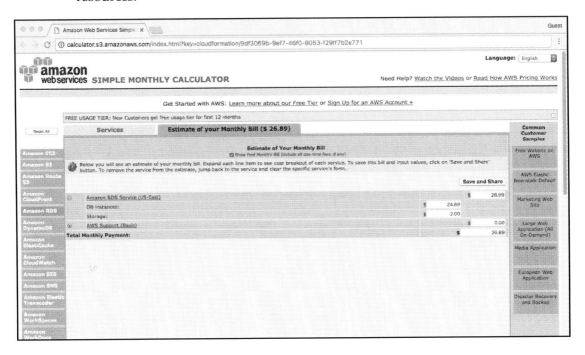

How it works...

The `estimate-template-cost` command requires all the parameters of your template. As you can see in the first step, the actual values aren't important because the template won't actually be launched. You simply need to make sure the type of value you give matches the required type for that parameter (for example, the `SubnetIds` value must be a list of values in this template).

> The region you specify is important! Some services (but not all) can cost different amounts depending on the region they are in. Generally, the `us-east-1` region is the cheapest.

At the end of the command, we limit the output to just the report URL via the `--query` argument.

You can share the URL generated with others, but you will not be able to retrieve earlier reports unless you keep track of the URL yourself.

On the calculator website, the template's resources will be pre-populated, even if you can't immediately see them. The report always defaults to the Amazon EC2 service page, so you will have to go to the relevant service page via the left-hand menu (in this case, Amazon RDS).

Finally, you can see a complete report of your template's monthly cost on the **Estimate of your Monthly Bill** tab. If your template contains many different types of resources/services, you will see them summarized here.

See also

- The *Create a database with automatic failover* recipe in `Chapter 6`, *Database Services*
- The *Calculating costs* recipe

Purchasing reserved instances

Reserved instances can be the cause of some confusion and are often misunderstood. Here are a few pointers to get you going down the right path:

- Reserved instances have no distinguishing technical features compared to regular on-demand instances.
- Reserved instances are not a specific type or class of instance.
- Put simply, purchasing a reserved instance entitles you to a discounted hourly rate on an on-demand instance that matches the properties of the reserved instance.
- The discounted hourly rate will be of a varying size depending on how much you pay upfront. As a general rule, the more you pay upfront, the higher the discount.

When you purchase a reserved instance, you're required to specify the following properties:

- **Platform (Linux/Windows)**
- **Scope (Region** or **Availability Zone)**
- **Instance Type** (for example, **m3.large**)
- **Tenancy** (shared or dedicated)
- **Offering Class** (standard or convertible)
- **Term** (1-12 months or 1-3 years)
- **Payment Option** (no upfront, partial upfront, all upfront)

We'll explore the ins and outs a little more later in this section. For now, let's dive in and see how to make a purchase.

Getting ready

You'll need an AWS account and some idea of which instance types you wish to reserve and for how long. Refer to the reserved instance properties mentioned previously for the exact information you'll need to proceed.

The **Payment Option** you choose will dramatically affect the price you pay when purchasing the reservation:

- **No Upfront**: This means you pay nothing now but you will be charged the discounted hourly rate for the entire term whether or not you have an instance that matches the reservation. Also note that choosing this option limits you to 1 year for standard reservations and 3 years for convertible reservations (we'll discuss these later in this section).
- **Partial Upfront**: These reservations mean that you pay a smaller upfront fee and then you are charged a discounted hourly rate only for the instance hours you use.
- **All Upfront**: As the name suggests, you'll be required to pay the full cost of the instance for the entire term. An effective 100% discount is applied to the hourly rate of your matching instances for that term.

Once you know all the properties of the instance reservation, you can go ahead and make a purchase.

How to do it...

1. Go to the EC2 web console, select **Reserved Instances**, then **Purchase Reserved Instances**:

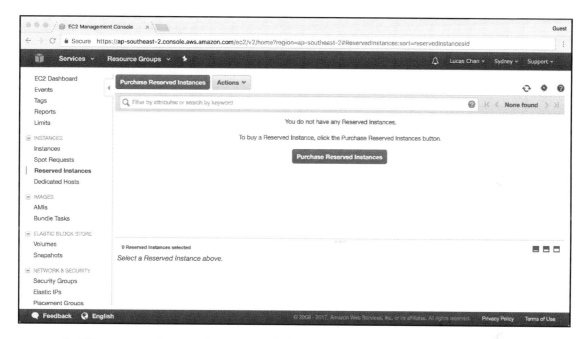

2. We now need to perform a search for the instance type you wish to purchase. In this example, we're going to choose the following:

- **Platform: Linux/UNIX**
- **Tenancy: Default**
- **Offering Class: Standard**
- **Instance Type: t2.micro**
- **Term: 1 months-12 months**
- **Payment Option: All Upfront**

3. Obviously, choose the options that best match your workload. You almost certainly want to choose **Default** as **Tenancy** here. Dedicated tenancy/instances are run on hardware that will be occupied by only one customer (you) and are a lot more expensive:

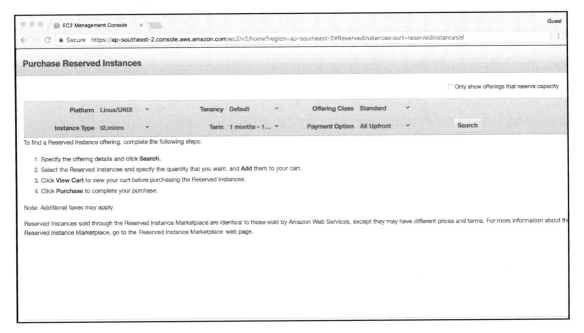

4. The console will return a price for the instance reservation. Note that because we didn't select **Only show offerings that reserve capacity**, what we are seeing is a single result, that is a reservation which applies to the region we're currently viewing in the console. Think of this as a *region level* reservation:

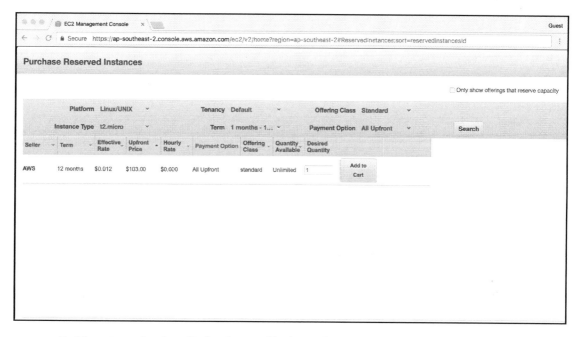

5. Now try selecting **Only show offerings that reserve capacity** and notice that all Availability Zones are showing for the current region. You can think of these as *AZ level* reservations. Choosing one of these options obviously locks you in to a specific **Availability Zone**; however, you also get a *capacity reservation* (discussed next):

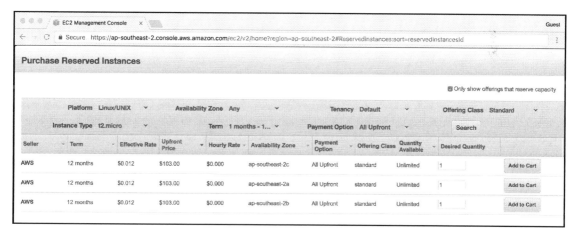

6. Choose the reservation that looks right for you, and then click **Add to Cart** and then **View Cart**.

7. The next page shows a summary of your imminent purchase. Click **Purchase** to proceed. Note that this is the point of no return. Reserved instances can't be canceled. Choose wisely!

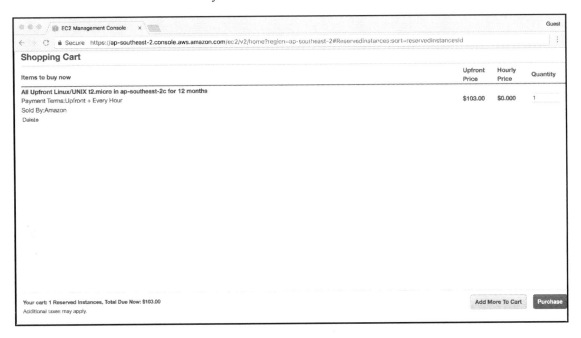

How it works...

After you've completed your purchase, your reservation will be marked as **Payment Pending** and then soon after **Active** (there's a third possible status, which is **Retired**).

Once your reservation is **Active**, the discount will automatically apply to matching instances. AWS refers to this hourly discount as a *billing benefit*.

Choosing a **Convertible** reservation class immediately rules out anything but a 3 year term. In return, you get a little more flexibility than the **Standard** reservations because if you decide the reservation no longer meets your needs, you can *convert* it to a reservation that is of equal or higher value, paying the difference of course.

If you made a reservation for a specific Availability Zone, AWS also provides you with a *capacity reservation*, which will give you some guarantees around the availability of instances in that zone. This is something you might want to consider if your workload needs to maintain a certain amount of capacity in the event of an entire Availability Zone outage, for example. An event such as this tends to cause a rush of new instance requests in the unaffected zones; however, customers without a capacity reservation may find their new instance requests can't be fulfilled because of a lack of capacity (this is not unheard of), causing them to miss out or forcing them to issue new instance requests for a different zone and/or instance type while at the same time crossing their fingers.

> Unlike the *billing benefit* (hourly discount), which is applied immediately after purchase, a capacity reservation is used by the first instance you launch in the zone matching the properties of your reservation.

There's more...

- Services that launch instances on your behalf (auto scaling, Elastic Beanstalk, and so on) are also eligible to have hourly discounts applied to them.
- **Standard** reservations can be made for either 1 or 3 years. As mentioned before, **Convertible** reservations are fixed at 3 years.
- Under a consolidated billing model, reserved instances discounts are applied across all your sub accounts. For example, if you purchase a reserved instance intended for account A but there is no server matching its properties, the reservation will automatically apply to matching instances in account B. This only applies to the billing benefit and not the capacity benefit.
- Reserved instances can be sold in the AWS marketplace. This is useful if the reservation no longer suits your needs. Note that you will need a US bank account for this.
- If reserved instances don't seem to match your type of workload, you might consider a scheduled instance instead.

Estimating total cost of ownership

The AWS TCO Calculator is designed to provide you with a ballpark view of how much it will cost you to run equivalent infrastructure on AWS in comparison to your co-located or on-premise data center.

The calculator has been audited by an independent third-party, but you should of course check its output against your own calculations before you make any purchasing decisions.

Getting ready

In this example, we're going to describe a typical three tier Rails image processing application running with a modest amount of hardware. You can use our example configuration or follow along with your own hardware requirements.

How to do it...

1. Navigate to `https://awstcocalculator.com/`.
2. Choose your currency, location, AWS region, and workload type. In our case we're going to choose the following:

   - **Australian dollar**
   - **Colocation**
   - **Asia Pacific (Sydney)**
   - **General**

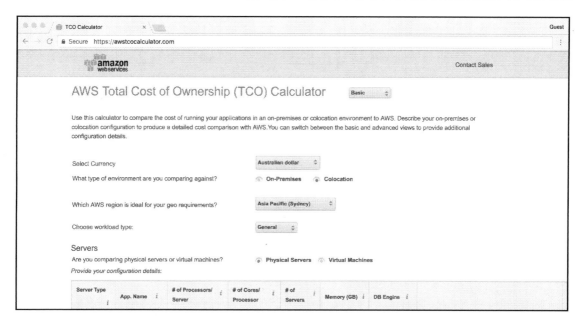

TCO Calculator—workload

3. Now we need to describe our server requirements. We're going to specify that our app is running on physical servers with tiers that look like this:

- **App Name**: nginx
  - **Server Type: Non DB**
  - **# of Processors/Server: 2**
  - **# of Cores/Processor: 2**
  - **# of Servers**: 2
  - **Memory (GB)**: 16
- **App Name**: rails
  - **Server Type: Non DB**
  - **# of Processors/Server: 2**
  - **# of Cores/Processor: 4**
  - **# of Servers**: 4
  - **Memory (GB)**: 32

- **App Name**: `mysql`
  - **Server Type: DB**
  - **# of Processors/Server: 2**
  - **# of Cores/Processor: 8**
  - **# of Servers**: 2
  - **Memory (GB)**: 64
  - **DB Engine**: `MySQL`

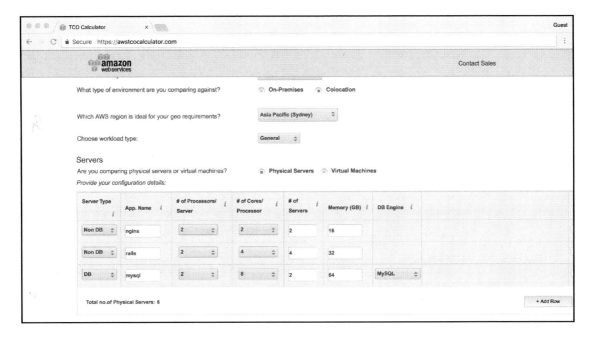

TCO Calculator—servers

4. Lastly, we need to input our storage requirements. For our example, the `rails` application, we need the following:

- **Storage Type: Object**
- **Raw Storage Capacity**: 2**TB**
- **% Accessed Infrequently**: 90

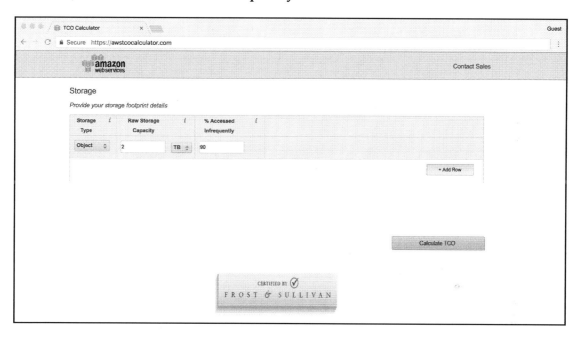

TCO Calculator—storage

5. Go ahead and click **Calculate TCO**.

6. The 3 year cost breakdown graphs provide a high-level view of your potential cost savings. You can see that, in our example, AWS estimates we'll save 68% on our infrastructure costs over the next 3 years. That's pretty impressive!

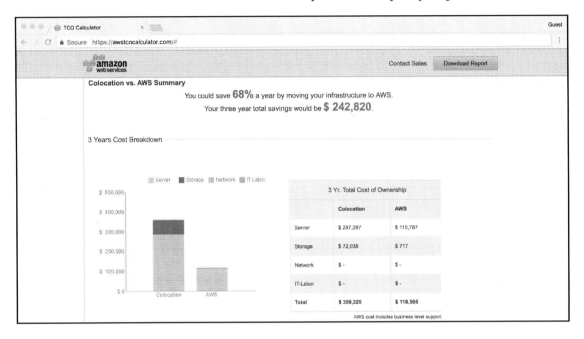

TCO Calculator—summary

7. Scroll further through the report to see cost breakdowns categorized by resource type:

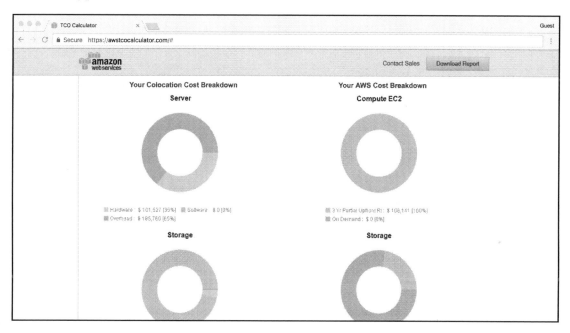

TCO Calculator—graphs

How it works...

The calculator will take your server requirements and map them to EC2 instances of an appropriate size. Since we've been specific that we need an object store for our storage, it will calculate our storage costs based on the price for S3 storage in our region.

There's more...

Let's take a look under the hood and see how we're able to save so much money on AWS:

- The prices for our EC2 instances are based on a 3 year reserved instance price with a partial upfront payment. Is this a fair comparison? Yes and no. You would probably be locked in to a fixed hardware contract with your on-premise or co-located solution, so it makes sense to apply similar contract terms to your AWS pricing model. In reality, you'd probably want to think about purchasing reserved instances *after* you've moved to AWS and performed some fine tuning around which instance types to use. On the flip side, the AWS costs could be reduced even further if your servers ran under **All Upfront** instance reservations.

- The comparison of object storage systems may or may not be fair depending on the feature set of your on-premise or co-located solution. For example, S3 has the ability to apply an *infrequently accessed* storage class on stored objects, which reduces their cost but also (theoretically) slightly reduces their availability. You'd probably not have this feature in your on-premise or co-located storage.

- The 3 year cost for storage in our on-premise/co-located facility is AU $69,660, of which a whopping 97% of that is the *monthly cost to operate a rack*. This includes rental of space, cooling, power, and so on.

- While the cost calculator is taking a purely infrastructure view, it also does factor in support costs. If you are new to AWS, you will probably be leaning on AWS support a little bit to get up and running.

- You'll also want to factor in some costs around training and potentially hiring staff who are skilled in deploying and migrating systems to AWS. Your developers are also going to start thinking differently about how to build and deploy their applications. Make sure to factor this in too.

- If you aren't totally happy with the on-premise or co-location estimates, you can go ahead and change the figures used in the calculation. Scroll to the top of the page and click **Modify Assumptions** to input your own hardware prices:

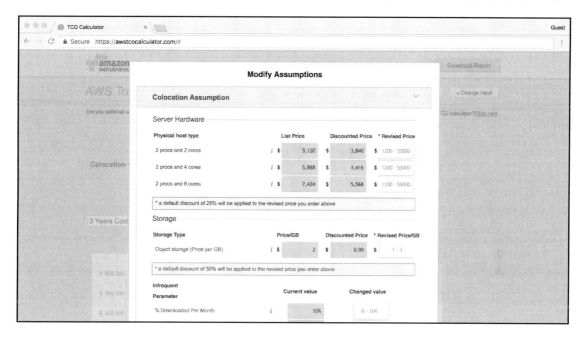

TCO Calculator—modify assumptions

See also

- The *Purchasing reserved instances* recipe

Index

75723345R00219

Made in the USA
San Bernardino, CA
03 May 2018